Management and Organization

Mcgraw-HILL SERIES IN MANAGEMENT

Keith Davis, *Consulting Editor*

MANAGEMENT AND ORGANIZATION

Louis A. Allen

President, Louis A. Allen Associates

McGRAW-HILL BOOK COMPANY

Auckland Bogotá Guatemala Hamburg Lisbon
London Madrid Mexico New Delhi Panama Paris San Juan
São Paulo Singapore Sydney Tokyo

MANAGEMENT AND ORGANIZATION
INTERNATIONAL EDITION

Exclusive rights by McGraw-Hill International Book Co — Singapore for manufacture and export. This book cannot be re-exported from the country to which it is consigned by McGraw-Hill.

Library of Congress Catalog Card Number: 57-13329

When ordering this title use ISBN 0-07-Y85012-7

PRINTED AND BOUND BY B & JO ENTERPRISE PTE LTD, SINGAPOF

Preface

Far-reaching changes have been taking place in the economy over the past twenty years. Growth and diversification mark the long-term character of the business climate. Technological improvements have been occurring with startling rapidity. New materials, new products and processes present a host of challenging opportunities to the individuals and the firms ready to exploit them. At the same time, however, shortages in skilled manpower are prevalent, the costs of doing business have increased sharply, and there is keen competition in every aspect of enterprise.

To succeed in this expansive and demanding economic climate, businessmen of every classification have been forced to look not only at the adequacy of their facilities and equipment and methods of operation, but also at the tools they use in managing and operating their business.

It is here that the greatest change is occurring. Leadership of the successful company today must be *management leadership*. From president to first-line supervisor, mastery of the skills and techniques of the emerging profession of management has become a matter of vital concern. Not only practicing managers but also students of business and aspirants for business leadership have found that they cannot prepare themselves adequately unless they are thoroughly familiar with these fundamental changes in thinking about the manager and the work he performs.

New and dynamic concepts of management and organization are evolving which are a measure of the span and the challenge of the business of tomorrow. These concepts are predicated upon the assumption that management is an identifiable, measurable, and transferable activity and that it can be mastered as can any other skill. Many of the older concepts of management and organization have been put to question and abandoned or replaced. Much of this new thinking has taken place so quietly and unobtrusively, even secretly, that it has not generally been reported. The fact is that some companies consider their methods of management and organization as much a competitive factor as marketing methods, applied research, or new production processes. And often they guard such information as carefully as other classified data about their businesses.

The concepts presented in this book are based on firsthand study and investigation of 230 leading companies. They are the result of the analysis and interpretation of key factors in the growth and development of these companies and the methods of management and organization that enabled them to assume a commanding position in business today. Many small businesses, as well as large, are included, and most of the large companies have been studied from their first early growth stages, when they also were small. The author has had opportunity to present this information in one- to three-day seminar sessions to over 2,200 executives, including 312 presidents and board chairmen, and to discuss it with 40 of the leading organization specialists in the United States. Their reactions have amply confirmed the validity and accuracy of the author's conclusions.

Acknowledgment is due individuals too numerous to mention who have contributed to the development of the data. The interest and cooperation of executives in each of the companies cited is particularly and gratefully acknowledged. They have given freely of their time and attention in making the data available, and in reviewing them for accuracy and completeness.

The primary source of authority for this volume is the operating data secured from the leading companies selected for study. Every statement referring to individual companies in the text has been carefully checked and confirmed by the companies named. Where reference sources for company quotations or referrals are not given, in each case the basic data have been secured from authenticated official documents or statements of the company itself. Since a wide variety of firsthand material has been freely used, a final disclaimer is made to the effect that the interpretations and conclusions in the volume are the author's own.

Louis A. Allen
Palo Alto, Calif.

To Ruth

Contents

company interpretations. Definitions of staff advice
and service. Variations in advice and service. Service,
auxiliary, and functional departments. Role of corporate and division staffs. Developing sound line-staff
relationships. A basic line-staff relationship.

Stockholders and board. Chief executive. What kind
of organization? Chief executive alone. Chief executive–chief operating officer. Chief executive–chief operating officer–chief staff officer. Executive group.

PART THREE: DYNAMICS OF ORGANIZATION

Staffing for organization change. Steps in organization
change. Develop objectives and other plans. Analyze
the existing organization. Information required. Responsibility analysis. Authority analysis. Organization
charting. Preparation of position guides. The organization manual. Organization analysis as basis for
change.

Prepare an ideal plan. Try out the plan. Prepare
phase plans. Establish uniform nomenclature. Develop
corollary personnel programs. Overcome resistance to
change. The future of organization change.

PART ONE

The Profession of Management

CHAPTER 1 *The Nature of Management*

The manager is one of the great unknowns in business. Although perhaps the most common word in the corporate lexicon, the term "manager" meets with little agreement as to nature, meaning, or scope. This is all the more surprising when we consider the vital importance of precise understanding of this expression to most enterprises. Most company organization charts are studded with dozens of boxes entitled manager of one kind or another. Each such position, presumably, has been assigned management responsibility and authority. In most cases, the performance of the person holding this position is being appraised as a manager and his potential for advancement is gauged against what is assumed to be a management yardstick.

Consider, further, that hundreds of millions of dollars are being spent every year in business and industry to develop management talent. Endless time and effort are devoted to training people in management skills. Many and complicated, also, are the salary administration programs designed to pay managers for performing management work and to award bonuses for managerial accomplishment. Finally, organization is, essentially, organization *for* management and the structure of the business itself cannot be designed successfully unless we know the purpose of that which we build.

WHAT IS MANAGEMENT?

It is obvious that if we are to consider management a profession, a key problem is to decide what a manager is. Only if we know what we are talking about can we deduce principles that will apply to the act of management wherever it occurs. It is true that, because of the varying nature of business enterprise, we can expect any definition to have many interpretations. And because few of the elements of business are fixed or constant, management will probably always be more art than science. However, this does not minimize the importance of first defining our terms. We shall begin by examining some of the reasons why agreement has not yet been reached on a definition of management. We shall then establish certain criteria that should apply to any definition we develop.

Difficulties in Definition

Study of a representative sample of companies reveals that "management" is many things. One assumption is that management is what a manager does. This seems to make sense, until you observe the variations in the kind of work done by many managers. The president of one large chemical company, for example, personally approves $2 weekly salary increases for clerical positions. The president of another, somewhat smaller, company reviews increases only on salaries of $10,000 or more a year.

The president of a $250 million company with headquarters in New Jersey opens and routes his own mail. The personnel manager of a large Chicago bank reprimands elevator operators and office boys because the office manager doesn't like to do it. A general foreman in a tool manufacturing plant in Pennsylvania spends a good deal of his time running a fork lift truck because, as he says, he "gets a kick out of it."

The sales manager of a pharmaceutical house is pointed out as one of the firm's outstanding executives. Asked the secret of his management ability, he says, "I believe in getting right down in harness with the boys. I'm the best salesman I've got. If a man wants to keep up with me, he's got to hustle every minute. If he can't keep up, he doesn't belong on my team." In another company, also dealing primarily in pharmaceuticals, the marketing manager does no direct selling himself and does not encourage his field sales manager to make sales contacts. "I pay him to manage, not sell," the market manager says. All this is confusing. At the very least, it makes it obvious that some managers are managers in spite of the work they do, not because of it.

There are other interpretations of management. Attempts have been made to identify the nature of management by selecting a representative sample of managers and administering to them batteries of psychological tests. The data thus derived indicate whether managers tend to be introverted or extroverted, high verbal or high analytical, whether they have the interests typical of the social service, accounting, teaching, or medical professions. However, after this information is collected and analyzed, it tells us only a little about the mental and personality characteristics of some people who are classified as managers. This can be valuable in indicating what kind of person will make the best manager, but since we have not determined specifically what work we expect of the manager, it is difficult to decide what kind of person we require.

Criteria for Sound Definition

What is management? Definitions and interpretations vary widely. Some see management as a complex of personal and administrative skills. Others view it as a technique of leadership. Still others define it as a means of coordination or cooperation. These are part of the picture, but they are inadequate to our needs. For our purpose, we must be able to identify management as a body of systematized knowledge, based on general principles which are verifiable in terms of business practice. We should be able to demonstrate that management is a distinct activity. Our concept should allow for the fact that a manager may manage with good or bad judgment, with great or little experience, with exemplary or undesirable character traits, that management may be practiced in similar terms by all kinds of people, in all kinds of companies. Our concept of management should provide for the identification of transferable skills and these skills should be susceptible of measurement.

Our first step in determining the nature of management is to identify the manager as a leader and to differentiate between two kinds of leadership exercised in the direction of business undertakings.

LEADERSHIP AND MANAGEMENT

A leader is one who guides and directs other people. Because he has others subordinate to him and subject to his command, the leader must give their efforts direction and purpose. How does the leader provide direction? Here we must establish two points. First, *leadership is a kind of work*. It is not the exudation of a special psychic quality or the exercise of a unique combination of personality traits. All kinds of people can be leaders just as all kinds can be led. The second point is that *all work performed by leaders is not management work*. This helps explain why, although a good manager must be an effective leader, many outstanding leaders have, in fact, been exceedingly poor managers. We can clarify the difference by distinguishing between personal leadership and management leadership.

Personal Leadership

The first and natural mode is personal leadership. A leader almost invariably begins his career in leadership in terms of his own personality and his own strongest aptitudes. A person is *born* with the talent for personal leadership; he must *learn* management leadership. Individuals tend to pass through successive stages from personal to management leadership; so do companies.

The founder of a business enterprise invariably operates in terms of personal leadership. Consider, for example, George Eastman, who established a great enterprise, the Eastman Kodak Company. He not only did much of the work of developing early commercial film and simple apparatus for its use but also helped design the machinery, conducted his own chemical experiments, did much of the selling, and supervised the operation of the plant.

Another, Harvey S. Firestone, was not only chief salesman and production head for the Firestone Tire and Rubber Company in its early days but also chief stock clerk, machine designer, and financier.

Examples are endless. Herbert H. Dow first established a place for the infant Dow Chemical Company in a rudimentary industry by inventing a new way of extracting bromine from brine and by introducing a whole series of products new to the markets of his time. Dow not only developed his own processes; he also supervised construction of his own plant, raised capital, and conducted much of his own research. Henry Ford is another outstanding example. Here we have a mechanical genius who developed a means of putting together standardized parts for an automobile more quickly and economically than had ever been done before. Every Model T and Model A that came off the production line bore his personal imprint. His personal leadership made the early Ford Motor Company.

Characteristics of Personal Leadership. Personal leadership has identifiable characteristics. First, authority is highly centralized. This means that the leader personally decides most of the issues, wherever they may arise. No matter how large the enterprise becomes, he allows subordinate leaders little freedom in making decisions related to the work they do. To check up on how things are going, he relies on personal inspection and audit of completed work. As we shall see later, the personal leader almost always finds it easiest to operate within a functional form of organization. The most significant characteristic of personal leadership is that *the leader does much work which the people he leads can do, or could be trained to do, as well or better themselves.*

Evaluation of Personal Leadership. There are many advantages to personal leadership, particularly if the leader is an outstanding individual or has a special talent. To the extent that the work of the leader excels, the results accomplished will be outstanding. Because personal leadership is centralized, it can mean fast, aggressive action and great flexibility.

The weaknesses of this type of leadership are, essentially, the weaknesses of the leader himself. If his judgment is poor, if he does not recognize or understand the importance of some vital aspect of the work, if he vacillates, this will be reflected down the line. As we shall see later, personal leadership, because it almost invariably *is* centralized, discourages independent thinking, precludes the development of broad-gauge subordinate leaders, and restricts the size and diversity of the enterprise to the personal scope of the leader himself. This scope may be great or small, but it *is* restricted and so limits the potential for accomplishment of the undertaking.

Management Leadership

In managing, the leader restricts himself, as largely as possible, to the performance of that work which only he, because of his organizational position, can perform effectively. Here is a significant distinction. The leader as manager still exercises personal attributes, but he does so in terms of work different from that of the people he leads. Because he so limits himself, he can spread his efforts effectively over a much larger undertaking. He can establish subordinate management positions which also will be devoted largely to performance of management work, and hence he can spread his leadership, by delegation, through an enterprise of great size.

Our question now is: What kind of work can only the leader, as a manager, perform effectively? To find the answer we must examine his organizational position.

Organizational Basis. Organizationally, every leader is removed from the immediate responsibilities of those he supervises. As a result, only the leader can weigh and assess the individual needs of his subordinates with objectivity, perspective, and balance. Only he can perform certain work which cannot be done effectively either by those he leads or those who lead him. *To the extent that the leader performs this kind of work, he is managing.*

Figure 1-1. Manager and Subordinates

Let us now examine the position of the leader with relation to his subordinates. In the situation charted in Figure 1-1, the manager cannot permit any of his three subordinates to determine the over-all goals for the group because each subordinate would inevitably color his decision in terms of his own interests and those of *his* group.

The manager himself thus must make all those decisions which directly affect any two or more of the subordinates who report to him. He can permit subordinate *A* to decide what kind or organization subordinate group *A* will have, but he cannot permit this subordinate to make this decision with respect to the total organization or, in fact, with respect to any part of the subordinate group *A* organization that directly affects or depends upon the organization of any of the other subordinate groups.

Again, if subordinate *C* has a grievance, he can expect an unbiased and objective hearing only from the manager himself. None of the subordinates can make final decision as to how well his own work or that of other subordinates is being performed with relation to the overall needs and goals of the group as a whole. This, uniquely, is the work of the manager himself.

Dual Role of the Manager. In organizations made up of more than one management level, the manager of each group is also a member of the next higher echelon, and hence he assumes a dual role. We can show this graphically as in Figure 1–2.

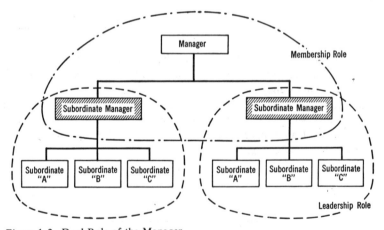

Figure 1–2. Dual Role of the Manager

Since he is a member of the group next above and at the same time the leader of the group reporting to him, the manager himself is best placed to bring to his group interpretation of the goals, decisions, attitudes, and actions of the higher group. The manager thus becomes the interlocking tie between higher and lower levels of the organization and the natural and most effective channel for communication.

Only the manager, as member of both groups, can weigh and assess the needs of his own group, together with the decisions of higher management, and arrive at a decision that reflects the needs of the total organization.

We can conclude that a leader manages to the extent that he fulfills his dual role adequately, that is, to the extent that he performs work that neither his superiors can do for him, nor members of his group can do, or can be trained to do, as well or better themselves. We can now come to focus upon the nature of the work a manager performs in managing by tracing the historical evolution of management.

HISTORICAL EVOLUTION OF MANAGEMENT

Leadership has been practiced as long as we have record of human activities. As we have noted, this has almost always initially taken the form of personal leadership. However, in various civilizations and at various times, circumstances have arisen which have forced leaders to restrict themselves to performing work different from that of their followers. These pressures have resulted from the increasing complexity of the task of the leader, as a result of the size of the groups being led, their physical dispersion, or the complexity and diversity of the work they performed. In these historical precedents we find the first development of what we can classify as management skills. Our examples range from ancient Mesopotamia to China and Rome.

Ancient Mesopotamia

In ancient Mesopotamian cities, dating far back to the beginnings of recorded history, we find record of what is, essentially, evolution from personal to management leadership in a business situation. In pre-Semitic times in the lower Euphrates valley, groups of nomadic peoples banded together and formed villages on the fertile plains of Sumer and Erech. Their first purpose in settling together was to facilitate production of food for their own use. Later, craft groups developed that specialized in copper work, carpentry, textiles, pottery, and sculpture. The leaders of these craft groups were the outstanding artisans; they exercised leadership because of their superior artistic and technical skills.

Gradually output exceeded the needs of the villages and a flourishing trade was established with other cities and countries. This expansion was successful largely because a type of management was evolved. Its origins are curious, arising as it did as the result of the growing power and scope of a corporation of priests. These priests directed and governed by virtue of their authority as representatives of the gods whom the people worshiped. Speaking for the deity, the priests represented all the mysterious and fearful powers of the divine will.

The corporation of priests performed management work. They planned trade routes and organized the work of laborers, artisans, soldiers, and traders. Because they could demand and receive rich offerings in food and valuables to propitiate the deities, they were able to amass reserves of capital to finance their undertakings. Thus the priests "invested" the offerings made to the gods to build great temples, subsidize the development of crafts, and organize trade expeditions to the cities of the Mediterranean and the Orient.

To facilitate their management work and keep account of their stewardship, the priests found it necessary to invent means of notation and of writing. Eventually, "staff" groups of scribes arose who kept records and prepared reports.

China

Some fifteen hundred and more years ago there flourished in China a diverse and complex civilization in which business and enterprise and the art of government had been developed to a high degree. Lao-tzū, the Keeper of the Imperial Archives, and a philosopher whose wisdom gave rise to the religion of Taoism, offered advice on the management of human institutions which anticipated our modern thinking in striking detail.

Lao-tzū prescribed a definite sequence of activities if men would manage their affairs properly. First, he taught, the proper climate and ways of thinking must prevail; therefore, men should attempt to know and understand the Divine Will and practice humanity and justice.

Once the proper philosophy was in effect, managers of affairs were to divide the tasks to be performed and differentiate between ranks and duties of the people who would be appointed to carry out the different kinds of work. Next a system of terminology was to be established to describe duties and positions. Quite accurately this is the approach a manager would follow today in organizing the work to be done.

Only after the organization was established were people to be appointed to fill the various positions. This staffing step also parallels our modern thinking on management. Lao-tzū's system next provided for review and appraisal of the records of the people who were doing the work. As a final step, the good and bad features of performance were to be determined and punishments and promotions meted out accordingly.

Rome

In ancient Rome, craft and trading groups developed early in the Latian villages of the Seven Hills. These groups operated under the personal leadership of strong or skilled individual leaders. As Rome be-

I

came a city and spread by growth and conquest, her industries became large and numerous, ranging from the making of armor through dressmaking and the pickling of olives to mining of metals and salt. Personal leadership persisted as the general pattern, even to organization of guilds of craftsmen and traders. The Roman guild was a social grouping, not economic, and devoted itself largely to group entertainment and the provision of burial services. The work done by members of the guild was carried on in small shops and factories, again under personal leadership.

Gradually there emerged in Rome a group of leaders that we can classify as managers. These managers developed largely as a result of the method employed by the Roman government to accomplish much of its work. When public edifices were to be built, the endless Roman roads laid, supplies carried to the outposts of Gaul and Britain, or taxes collected, the work was put up to contract to the highest bidder. Since great amounts of capital were required to win these contracts and carry them out, the citizens of Rome, both wealthy and near-wealthy, began to pool their resources to form business enterprises or companies. This gave rise to a significant development.

To conduct the affairs of the company, the shareowners employed or appointed directors, who, in turn, selected capable men to manage the affairs of the undertaking in Rome and the provinces. These managers employed staff assistance, such as accountants and scribes, bought slaves, and developed organizations to accomplish the missions of the owners. Here were arising a class of leaders that we can properly call managers in that their work pertained to the management of affairs and was not simply an extension of the work being managed.

MODERN CONCEPTS OF MANAGEMENT

The industrial revolution brought great impetus to the growth and diversification of business enterprises. Replacement of human and animal power by machines, new inventions, increased demand led to the expansion of commercial undertakings and the establishment of holdings in colonies abroad and in foreign countries. With it came an increase in the nature and variety of problems that had to be solved by business leaders and the need to consolidate and simplify the tasks performed by leaders so that they could make a maximum contribution to issues of primary importance and leave other affairs to subordinates. Not until the early 1900s do we find attempts at formal identification of the work of managers by individuals such as Taylor and Fayol and parallel activity in the Du Pont Company. In more recent years, we find similar effort in companies such as Lever Brothers, Radio Corporation of

America, General Foods, AMI, Incorporated, General Electric, Standard Oil of California, Atlantic Refining, and others.

Taylor's Contribution

Working in the steel industry during the early 1900s, Frederick W. Taylor saw the need for a systematic and scientific approach to industrial management. Taylor recognized that the methods of leadership and work performance then prevalent were haphazard and inefficient. He saw that the managers of his time secured results largely through personal leadership and for motivation depended upon special inducements, such as piece work, premium pay, and bonus plans.

Taylor proposed that managers bring order and system to their work in the form of "scientific management." He suggested that managers "take over all work for which they are better fitted than the workmen," and that these "new types of work done by the management" would make "scientific management so much more efficient than the old plan." [1]

Taylor suggested that instead of relying upon workers to learn their skills by watching others and developing their abilities in any fashion that struck them, managers should condense the great mass of traditional knowledge to a science by "classifying, tabulating, and reducing this knowledge to rules, laws and formulae." [2] Managers would train workmen to use these standardized methods, instead of permitting each to choose his own way of doing the work.

Taylor recommended that managers plan the work of the people reporting to them and devise means of coordination and control. As he put it, "The work of every workman is fully planned out by the management at least one day in advance, and each man receives in most cases complete written instructions, describing in detail the task which he is to accomplish, as well as the means to be used in doing the work. . . . This task specifies not only what is to be done, but how it is to be done and the exact time allowed for doing it." [3]

Taylor's plan called for managers to motivate their people, not by standing to one side and giving orders, but by selecting, teaching, and developing the workmen and "heartily cooperating with them."

Validity of Taylor's Principles. Frederick W. Taylor provided a base upon which much of current thinking about management is firmly established. He saw the need to systematize management, to analyze the work to be done, to measure it, and to assign portions to the people best placed in the organization to perform it.

---

[1] Frederick Winslow Taylor, *The Principles of Scientific Management* (copyright, 1911, by F. W. Taylor), Harper & Brothers, New York, 1942. See especially pp. 36–40 for a description of Taylor's basic concept.

[2] *Ibid.*, p. 36.

[3] *Ibid.*, p. 39.

Taylor recognized that the person planning work was often ill-equipped to carry it out. His initial assumption was based on the observation that a pig-iron handler lacked the requisite education and would be underpaid if he were put to the task of planning his work, while the supervisor who did the planning would be belittling his own abilities and would be overpaid if he were put to pig-iron handling.

Managers, Taylor believed, should concern themselves primarily with such work as setting and enforcing standards, improving methods and cooperation. This was something that could not be entrusted to the people being managed. The manager also had responsibility for developing his people and rewarding them for outstanding work. Taylor's conclusions seem rather commonplace today. However, they had almost an explosive impact on industrial productivity following their introduction and general acceptance; in fact, they were sometimes carried to undesirable extremes. While Taylor did not provide the whole answer to "What is a manager?" he helped us take a long stride forward.

Fayol's Conclusions

From his long and successful career as a manager in the French coal industry, Henri Fayol gained a keen insight into the factors that make for business success. He evolved a concept of administration, or management, during the early years of the century that considerably augments Taylor's principles.

Fayol analyzed the process of management as he had observed it first-hand. His conclusion was that all the work done in business enterprises can be divided into six groups.

1. Technical activities (production, manufacture, adaptation)
2. Commercial activities (buying, selling, exchange)
3. Financial activities (search for and optimum use of capital)
4. Security activities (protection and property of persons)
5. Accounting activities (stocktaking, balance sheet, costs, statistics)
6. Managerial (administrative) activities (planning, organization, command, coordination and control) [4]

Fayol believed that if any kind of business was to operate successfully, these six functions had to be performed. If any one was neglected, the enterprise would suffer accordingly.[5] While he recognized the importance of the five technical activities he identified, Fayol saw, at the same time, that the ability to manage was paramount for upper levels of managers.

[4] Henri Fayol, *General and Industrial Management* (first published in 1916, in French, by S. R. L. Dunod, Publishers, 92 Rue Bonaparte (VI) Paris). Published in English translation by Sir Isaac Pitman & Sons, Ltd., London, 1949. See pp. 3 *et seq.*

[5] A perceptive discussion and analysis of Fayol's work will be found in L. Urwick, *The Elements of Administration*, Harper & Brothers, 1943.

Fayol finally adopted this definition and explanation of the management function:

To manage is to forecast and plan, to organize, to command, to co-ordinate and to control. To foresee (prévoyance) and provide means examining the future and drawing up the plan of action. To organize means building up the dual structure, material and human, of the undertaking. To command means maintaining activity among the personnel. To co-ordinate means binding together, unifying and harmonizing all activity and effort. To control means seeing that everything occurs in conformity with established rule and expressed command.[6]

Applicability of Fayol's Principles. Does Fayol's classification describe management as it is currently practiced? There can be no question that he established the pattern upon which our concepts are built. It is significant that those companies which have analyzed the work done by managers in their organizations have largely arrived at groupings which approximate Fayol's.

In addition to his over-all concept of management, Fayol singled out and described with clarity and understanding principles of the unity of command and direction. He emphasized, as we are now beginning to learn to emphasize, the importance of nonfinancial incentives. He identified the key problem in decentralization and spelled out lessons which many companies are still groping for today.

There are two modifications to be made in Fayol's concept. Fayol saw management (administration) as one of six basic activities; that is, there are technical, commercial, financial, security, accounting, *and* managerial activities. However, our concept of management should be modified to say, in Fayol's terms, that management is the planning, organizing, command, coordination, and control *of* technical, financial, security, and accounting activities. A second modification is necessary. In terms of our understanding of what makes people work at maximum productivity, we should substitute *motivation* for *command*. It is true that a manager must direct, command, and order to get things done. But he also encourages, communicates, develops, and stimulates. He knows enough of the mainsprings of the motives of men to be able to motivate them to highest endeavor.

CURRENT MANAGEMENT PHILOSOPHY

The first application of a consistent *management* philosophy to the operation of a company is perhaps seen in E. I. du Pont de Nemours & Company. Here we find further material for our analysis.

---

[6] *Op. cit.*, pp. 5–6.

The Du Pont Company

In the summer of 1802, the Du Pont Company had its beginnings as a small powder mill on Brandywine Creek, near Wilmington, Delaware. During its first hundred years, Du Pont was a partnership, operated under a succession of highly capable leaders from the Du Pont family. Its product was explosives and its leaders were "black powder men," who spent day and night with the operating problems of the business and built the company to eminence in its field.

Typical of this pattern of personal leadership is General Henry du Pont who, for some thirty-nine years, closely supervised every detail of the operations of the company. He made most of the decisions, wrote the checks, opened the mail, and answered it, operating with the aid of four clerks and without even a secretary. When an engineer applied for a job, General Henry turned him down because he didn't think the company needed one. As he wrote, "We draw our own plans; make our own patterns; and have never employed anyone to design or construct our mills or machinery, dams or races, roads or anything else; being our own engineers and superintendents of all work done at our mills both here and in Pennsylvania." [7] Because Henry du Pont was operating the company, his limitations became its limitations. His conservatism, exemplified by his unwillingness to accept the typewriter, the railroad, and electricity and a general reluctance to consider new methods and products, inevitably marked a limit to the possible growth of the company under his leadership. The pattern is shown by a statement he made in 1889, "We make our own powder, and we make our own prices at which it shall be sold. . . . We do not allow anybody to dictate to us what prices, terms and conditions we shall dictate. . . . Our mode (of selling) today is the same as it has been since our firm was established nearly a hundred years ago and we expect to continue a hundred years in the same way." [8]

When General Henry du Pont died, Eugene du Pont ran the company for eleven years. He, too, attempted to exercise personal leadership, but the task proved too great and he killed himself with overwork. Following Eugene du Pont's death, no adequate leadership appeared, and sale of the company to a competitor, the Laflin and Rand Powder Company, appeared inevitable. However, a family group, Thomas Coleman du Pont, Alfred Irenee du Pont, and Pierre Samuel du Pont, finally bought the company for $12 million and instituted the concepts of management

---

[7] John K. Winkler, *The Du Pont Dynasty*, Reynal & Hitchcock, Inc., New York, 1935, p. 124.

[8] B. G. du Pont, *E. I. du Pont de Nemours and Company: A History*, Houghton Mifflin Company, Boston, 1920, pp. 129–130.

which enabled Du Pont to multiply its assets seventy times in less than 38 years and to attain a leading rank in the chemical industry of the world. Interestingly enough, within a few years Du Pont was able to buy out the Laflin and Rand Powder Company.

The pattern of management that developed in Du Pont has had a far-reaching influence on modern business enterprise. The importance of this thinking becomes apparent when we recognize that shortly after World War I, Du Pont had established basic management principles that even today appear new and progressive. Four such principles related directly to concepts of planning, organization, and control.

1. *Management Requires Skill in Application of Business Principles.* The Du Pont Company early recognized the difference between management and nonmanagement work. It emphasized skill in planning, organization, and control, rather than technical excellence, for general management performance.

2. *Constructive Advances in Business Must Be Planned.* During the early 1900s, Du Pont began to look beyond explosives and to plan for diversification. With capital of $60 million, authorized in 1915, the company began a systematic investigation of product possibilities that led into paints, organic chemicals, plastics, synthetic viscose rayon yarn, and a great many other fields. Planning extended into all aspects of the business. Young men were brought along systematically and made accountable for large projects at an early age. Du Pont consistently followed a policy of planned investment, enabling it to enter many areas of endeavor that proved highly profitable to the company.

3. *Organizational Provision Must Be Made For Sound Growth.* Du Pont endeavored to develop an organization that would enable each unit to contribute with maximum effectiveness to the over-all effort, and yet permit maximum freedom and initiative on the part of individuals. The demands of the market, and not merely similarity of work, were recognized as the primary basis for grouping the company's activities. Du Pont considered flexibility a first requirement in organization, and adopted the viewpoint that there may be many correct solutions to similar management problems, depending upon the circumstances in which they arise. The company stressed the importance of placing accountability for results in one individual, and giving that person the authority he needed to perform his work as a complete package. At the same time, it established the need for clearly defined superior-subordinate relationships if sound teamwork was to be achieved. Du Pont early used specialized staff groups to provide common services and to counsel managers in specialized areas of the business. These became a source of skilled professional help available to the organization at large.

4. *Control Should Be in Terms of Profitable Operation.* Du Pont
was perhaps the first to establish the concept of profit center decentralization that is only coming into general prominence today. The company consistently decentralized a great deal of authority to operating
managers. It evaluated the performance of individual units of the
company in terms of the rate of return it was able to earn on the investment applied to it. The company also developed a comprehensive
system for measuring and reporting operating and financial results that
still is an outstanding example of effective controls.

By the early 1900s, the groundwork had been laid for a concept of
professional management. The writings of Taylor and Fayol stimulated
further investigations into the theory of management and its application
to business. The example of Du Pont, a consistent leader in vigor,
growth, and profitability, provided a pattern that was followed with
noticeable success by many other companies. Typical of more recent
attempts to identify and formalize management is the work of such
companies as Lever Brothers, RCA, General Foods, and AMI, Incorporated.

Lever Brothers and Unilever Limited

The history of Unilever is the story of a world-wide enterprise built
under the dynamic leadership of a commercial genius and, outgrowing
even his broad scope, evolving to management leadership as a basis for
stable and profitable growth and continuity.

Some seventy-five years ago, in England, a bright and enterprising
young man with outstanding talent in salesmanship, William Lever, took
over the family business. He brought a flair for novelty and brilliant
marketing to the humdrum business of soap making. Literally running
the business by himself, he was able to convert tallow, oil, and resin into
an adjunct to health, comfort, and beauty and to make such trade names
as Lifebuoy and Lux household words in half the countries of the globe.

William Lever built a world-wide commercial empire under his personal leadership. Until his death in 1925, it was his energy, imagination,
and ambition that drove the company. His leadership was both highly
centralized and dictatorial.

Today, Unilever Limited is one of the great international manufacturing and marketing organizations, with operating units and factories in most of the countries of Europe and in some twenty-four other
countries throughout the world. This vast complex is governed by two
holding companies, one English, the other Dutch. Both have identical
membership. The holding companies exercise centralized command
largely through use of annual operating plans, which provide an estimate
of the obligations and commitments of the subsidiaries in terms of

the yearly sales and costs, and thus profit and loss. There is also a capital expenditure budget, which sets estimates of the money that will be spent for capital commitments. Finally, the top management group reserves for itself responsibility and authority for the selection of top management of each of the operating units throughout the world and the fixing of their remuneration.

Typical of the Unilever philosophy is the concept of management established by Lever Brothers Company, the United States subsidiary. This ascribes to the manager the work of planning, organizing, staffing, administering, coordinating, and controlling.

Planning involves the definition of objectives and planning of operations in terms of policies, plans, and budgets which will establish the most advantageous course for the company. Planning also requires that managers keep currently informed on all matters which will contribute to improved planning and performance in the position.

Organizing in Lever Brothers includes the delegation of responsibility and authority in accordance with approved position specifications and a continuing appraisal of the plan of organization with a view toward performing the needed functions at minimum cost.

Staffing encompasses the selection, training, and supervision of the activities of an efficient staff, with qualified understudies able to assume supervisory positions at all levels in case of promotions or absences. It also includes the work of the manager in maintaining a high level of individual and group morale through the consistent application of company personnel policies and effective leadership.

Administering is the process the manager follows in making decisions within the scope of approved policies in his area of responsibility and embodying them in specific orders and instructions. It includes carrying out all policies and plans when and as decided upon and recommending improvements in policies, plans, and procedures.

Coordinating involves the work of the manager in cooperating with all other organization units as required for the most effective operation of the business. It also covers the reporting of results of his organizational unit to his supervisor and drawing attention to problems or obstacles he has encountered or anticipates encountering.

Controlling embodies the measuring of performance against predetermined objectives, including the gathering and analysis of relevant facts and adjustment of plans as required. The manager in Lever Brothers controls his operations to achieve maximum effectiveness, holding costs down to a minimum and not in excess of approved budgets. He maintains complete and easily available records and files of future reference value, disposing of them after they have ceased to be of value. He develops performance standards when required.

Radio Corporation of America

Radio Corporation has identified seven elements of basic management work. These are listed without grouping. In general they follow the pattern of major responsibilities already identified.

Prepare as appropriate, and submit for approval, long- and short-range objectives, policies, and plans for programs and organization arrangements aimed at producing the most profitable results attainable from his assigned area.

Interpret approved policies and plans to his organization and direct its day-to-day operations so as to attain established objectives in accordance therewith.

Submit budgets realistically reflecting the anticipated income and/or expenditures of his activity and conduct his activity within approved budgets.

Staff his organization with capable people, train subordinates in the competent performance of their duties, develop suitable replacements at all levels and provide a successor for himself.

Require and appraise performance and report results fully to his senior; detect the need for and propose such modifications in plans and departures from established ways of doing things as are necessary to produce satisfactory results.

Keep abreast of developments of all kinds affecting his products, service or area of specialization and make such use of them as may properly be turned to RCA's benefit.

Cooperate actively with his associates, both line and staff, for the attainment of RCA's over-all objectives.

General Foods

General Foods identifies three major management activities:

1. *Planning* is the determination of the course or objectives of a business, division, or department to achieve maximum profit or effectiveness, the establishment of policies, and the continuous seeking and finding of new and better ways to do things. General Foods also includes here the determination of the steps required to accomplish the goals, once they have been established.

Planning activities in General Foods include
   Setting objectives
   Determining policies
   Planning organization
   Analyzing methods

2. *Execution* applies to the "doing" phases. After plans have been prepared, personnel must be selected and assigned to their jobs; they must be trained and motivated to perform properly. Activities must be implemented in terms of the plans initially developed; subordinates must

be supervised and directed and the efforts of groups doing different kinds of work must be coordinated.

This may include

Selecting personnel
Training personnel
Motivating personnel
Delegation
Direction
Coordination

3. *Controlling* refers to the evaluation of the performance of those who are responsible for executing the plans agreed upon.

This may include

Controlling adherence to plans
Appraising performance

The General Foods concept includes the primary activities of management that we have already cited. Organization is made a planning activity, while motivation and coordination are included with "execution." The General Foods analysis demonstrates that management work may be grouped on different bases with logic and ample justification. However, it is significant that this grouping does not include new elements, nor does it omit any that we have already identified.

AMI, Incorporated

An unusually comprehensive analysis is that by AMI, Incorporated, manufacturer of automatic musical instruments. This is divided into the categories of planning, organizing, coordinating, motivating, and controlling.

Planning

1. Make long-range plans for the activities under his jurisdiction. To accomplish this, he should:
   a. Keep informed of all phases of the corporation's plans that will affect the work for which he is accountable.
   b. Establish objectives and detailed plans for activities under his jurisdiction which will integrate with over-all corporation planning.
2. Recommend to appropriate higher authority policies for all activities under his jurisdiction and administer approved corporation policies. To accomplish this he should:
   a. Continuously appraise the adequacy and soundness of existing policies.
   b. Receive recommended revisions in corporation policy from associates and subordinates.
   c. Recommend appropriate policy changes to proper executives.

   d. Interpret corporation policies to subordinates and see that they are understood as well as carried out.

3. Ensure that adequate programs, procedures, methods, and techniques are established so that the work for which he is responsible is performed with maximum effectiveness and at minimum cost. To accomplish this, he should:

   a. Where appropriate, arrange for the preparation of written guides for use by personnel.

   b. Plan for adequate facilities including work space, equipment, supplies, and materials for economical operation.

   c. Schedule major assignments or operations in adequate detail and sufficiently in advance for subordinates to plan and schedule their own work properly.

Organization

1. Organize the activities under his jurisdiction. To accomplish this he should:

   a. Make certain that all necessary functions are provided for.

   b. Assign duties and define responsibilities and authorities of subordinates.

   c. Interpret to subordinates the plan of organization, as well as the subordinates' responsibilities.

   d. Be alert to opportunities to modify the plan of organization to increase its effectiveness or adjust to changing conditions in line with the approved over-all master plan of organization.

   e. Establish sound organizational relationships.

Motivation

1. Build and maintain an effective work force or staff to carry out activities required. To accomplish this, he should:

   a. Select or approve the selection of personnel with proper qualifications to fill subordinate positions for which he is responsible.

   b. Train and coach subordinates to do their own work well; analyze their strengths and weaknesses and help them to develop themselves accordingly.

   c. Counsel with subordinates to increase their productivity and raise their morale.

   d. Develop an understudy for each position, including his own, so that the removal of any individual from any job will not seriously disrupt operations.

   e. Communicate with subordinates, verbally and in writing, to keep informed on activities under his jurisdiction, as well as to help subordinates to understand their work in relation to the corporation's activities.

   f. Encourage participation and creative effort by maintaining a constructive attitude toward suggestions and by giving full credit to subordinates for their contributions.

g. Give attention to interests of employees so as to assure them of proper opportunities for advancement and recognition.
h. Adjust grievances thoroughly and promptly.
i. See that employees under his jurisdiction receive fair and equitable compensation.
j. Assign work to subordinates in clear terms and in reasonable quantity.
k. Supervise operations by personal observation and analysis of records so that work is performed at minimum cost and with proper standards of quality, quantity, and speed.
l. Make decisions promptly on all questions raised by subordinates, associates, or superiors.

Coordination

1. Ensure that his organizational work unit cooperates with and is of maximum assistance to other work segments of the corporation as a whole.
2. Clear important matters with his line superior and/or others having functional or administrative control, whose concurrence is advisable or required before taking action. Except in emergencies, notify interested parties in advance of contemplated action.

Control

1. Assist in the preparation of controls for the activities under his jurisdiction, and control the number of employees, costs, and expenses within limits of optimum economy. To accomplish this, he should:
   a. Establish performance standards based on objectives, policies, programs, and budgets.
   b. Arrange for maintenance of adequate records and statistics on operations under his jurisdiction so that he will be aware of direct and indirect expenses.
   c. Periodically use these and other data to form sound conclusions on expenditure, necessity, and profit opportunity.
   d. Justify operating costs and requests for expenditures on the basis of factual evidence.
2. Check compliance with established methods, procedures, and techniques.
3. Establish controls to provide adequate quantities of tools and equipment, materials, and supplies for uninterrupted production or work schedule maintenance.
4. Keep his superior fully informed on progress of activities under his jurisdiction and especially apprise him of new or major developments and important problems. To accomplish this, he should:
   a. Transmit regular statistical control reports demonstrating accomplishments of the activities under his jurisdiction.
   b. Arrange periodic meetings with his superior for the discussion of problems or reports of work status.

5. Make regular inspections or reasonably proper controls to ensure a high level of quality, quantity, and finished products.
6. Provide for safeguards to persons and properties and for the protection and maintenance of facilities.

SUMMARY

Determination of the kind of work a manager does in managing is a necessary preliminary to effective discussion of management. Definition requires distinction between personal and management leadership. All leaders begin their careers by exercising personal leadership, that is, by doing much the same kind of work as the people being led and by making most of the decisions concerning that work. Management leadership requires that the leader perform only that work which cannot be carried out effectively by those he leads.

Learning to manage is an evolutionary process for individuals, groups, and companies. This evolution can be traced back to ancient Mesopotamia, China, and Rome. A systematic and consistent analysis of management work was first made by Frederick Winslow Taylor in the United States, Henri Fayol in France, and the Du Pont Company. The findings of these pioneer thinkers are corroborated by the work of a number of modern companies.

CHAPTER 2 *A Unified Concept of Management*

As a working tool, the manager needs an integrated concept of management which will give him a detailed statement of the sequence of work he must undertake to manage effectively. Logically, this should include all those activities which only the manager, because of his organizational position, can perform effectively, and it should systematically exclude all others. Such a unified concept of management is presented below.

THE ELEMENTS OF MANAGEMENT

The manager performs the following work in guiding and directing the efforts of others:

1. *Planning*
   a. Forecasting
   b. Objectives
   c. Policies
   d. Programs
   e. Schedules
   f. Procedures
   g. Budgets
2. *Organizing*
   a. Identification and grouping of work
   b. Definition and delegation of responsibility and authority
   c. Establishment of relationships
3. *Coordinating*
   a. Balancing
   b. Timing
   c. Integrating
4. *Motivating*
   a. Selection
   b. Communication

   c. Participation
   d. Appraisal
   e. Counseling
   f. Coaching
   g. Training
   h. Compensation
   i. Direction
   j. Dismissal
5. *Controlling*
   a. Performance standards
   b. Measurement
   c. Interpretation
   d. Corrective action

PLANNING

Planning is the determination of a course of action to achieve a desired result. Planning involves thinking through the general form and detail of work so that it can be accomplished with greatest certainty and economy. Since planning is an anticipation of something yet to happen, it is at best a prognostication. The human intellect has a limited ability to foresee the future, even with the aid of mechanical computing and analyzing devices; consequently, the accuracy of plans decreases inversely with time elapsed. As Fayol points out, "The plan of action is, at one and the same time, the result envisaged, the line of action to be followed, the stages to go through, and methods to use. It is a kind of future picture wherein proximate events are outlined with some distinctness, whilst remote events appear progressively less distinct. . . ." [1]

Planning is largely mental. It can be characterized as the process of *thinking* before *doing.* International Harvester Company defines planning as thinking work through before it is performed. Pullman Standard Car Manufacturing Company looks upon planning as the thinking that precedes the actual performance of work. General Foods finds that planning primarily involves the use of intellectual faculties and thought processes. It requires imagination, foresight, and sound judgment and embraces such activities as the identification and evaluation of business opportunities and hazards, the determination of the course or objectives of a business, division, or department to achieve maximum profit or effectiveness, the establishment of policies, and the continuous seeking and finding of new and better ways of doing things. General Foods also includes under planning the determination of the steps required to accomplish the goals, once they have been established.

[1] Henri Fayol, *General and Industrial Management,* Sir Isaac Pitman & Sons, Ltd., London, 1949, p. 43.

Management planning involves the development of forecasts, objectives, policies, programs, procedures, schedules, and budgets. These various elements of planning are isolated and discussed separately in the following pages. It should be noted that, in practice, it is often both necessary and desirable to combine statements of forecasts and objectives with policies, programs, procedures, schedules, and budgets.

However, sound planning calls for separation, at least mentally, of the determination of goals, and of policy statements that govern the conditions under which the goals are to be reached, decision as to what sequence of activities must be followed to accomplish the goals, the preparation of time schedules, decision as to *how* standardized work is to be performed, and estimates of the units of money, time, materials, and so forth that will be required to reach the goals.

FORECASTING

Forecasting is a systematic attempt to probe the future by inference from known facts. The purpose is to provide management with information on which it can base planning decisions. While yet far from a science, forecasting is rapidly winning acceptance because managers are finding they can plan more successfully on the basis of forecasts than they can without.

A number of different techniques, essentially mathematical in character, are used in forecasting. In general, these first attempt to predict the frame of reference in which the activity for which the forecast is being made will operate. If the planning is being done for the company as a whole, the fate of the national or world economy for a decade ahead may be of concern; if for a department, the probable future course of the company, again in its larger context, is the basis for the forecast. Once the larger framework is blocked out, the probable trends in the activity being forecast are then predicted.

Skill in forecasting is a competitive tool that can have far-reaching effects on the profit and loss statement. Immediately after World War II, for example, the Dow Chemical Company studied the probable demand for organic chemical derivatives made from benzene. The forecasts showed that coke, the existing source of supply, would fall far short of the future demand. Alerted to this probable market opportunity, Dow took several positive steps. First it put its research gears into motion and developed a process to make methylstyrene, a substitute material made from toluene instead of benzene. It then built a plant for volume production. Further, the company developed a means of recovering benzene from an ethylene plant by-product and lined up sources for importing benzene from Europe. As demand climbed past existing coking capacity, Dow was able to tap its new sources and earn a good return on its forecasting ability.

OBJECTIVES

Objectives are goals established to guide the efforts of the company and each of its components. Effective management is always management by objectives. An organization can grow and change in an orderly and progressive manner only if well-defined goals have been established to guide its progress. Not only must there be an objective for the total organization, but, since each component can accomplish only limited work, there should be spelled out division and departmental goals which serve as specific guides for subordinate units. These enable individual managers to operate with maximum freedom but always within the framework of over-all company objectives. Unless such goals are established, there is likely to be haphazard activity, uneconomical commitment of capital funds, poor utilization of people, and mediocre operating results over the long term.

Well-managed companies establish objectives for the company as a whole and for all levels of management. Cleveland Electric Illuminating Company, for example, defines objectives down to the smallest organization unit. At upper levels, the objectives are general, applying to the company as a whole; at successively lower levels, they become more specific and detailed. The organization plan and position descriptions for individuals are related to these statements of objectives, as are the monthly performance reports for individual managers. Thus the statement of objectives in Cleveland Electric Illuminating becomes not only a guide to action but also a yardstick to measure work after it is done.

In Jones and Laughlin Steel Company, basic over-all objectives are established for the company as a whole. Each department is then required to define its own objectives consonant with the company objectives.

Objectives may be divided into two categories, economic and social. Economic objectives are goals with respect to the market place. Social objectives refer to the company's intentions toward its employees, shareholders, and the public at large.

Economic Objectives

Determination of economic objectives involves decision as to what kind of business the company is in and what it intends to accomplish in that business. Surprisingly, a great many companies have never stopped to think through this basic step. Consider, for example, the case of a manufacturer of highly specialized electronic components.

During and immediately after World War II, this company accumulated a healthy cash reserve. With a dwindling military market for its product in sight, the president decided that diversification was in order. He and his staff looked around for likely acquisitions. First they found a healthy, profitable small chain store operation which made candies and chocolates. The owner had recently died, the heirs wanted to sell. The electronics company bought their interests.

Air conditioning was getting considerable attention at this time. The electronics company found a small plastics company engaged in producing framing members, cabinets, and base plates for window air-conditioning units. Effective command of this enterprise was secured. Next a company manufacturing radiator grills and decorative trim for automobiles was acquired.

By now, the available funds were exhausted, so the company set about digesting and integrating its acquisitions. The task proved impossible. At the end of five years, each of the subsidiaries, once profitable in its own right, had lost both in market position and profitability. Finally the company disposed of all three. At this point, the president sat down with his board of directors to decide what kind of business the company was in. They decided their facilities and skills were best suited to the rapidly expanding civilian electronic market. With its course now firmly set, the company invested the funds it had salvaged in finding new markets in designing, manufacturing, and marketing electronic components for television, computer, data recording, and other allied fields. Its latest annual report shows a healthy profit and a promising future.

Most successful companies carefully think through their economic objectives. For example, Union Carbide Corporation has the resources to enter almost any field of activity. However, it has determined that its primary business is that of developing and processing raw materials for industry. It has concentrated on developing a technology, marketing approach, and people oriented in this direction. Its capital is invested consistently to further this aim. Thus every advance is built on a foundation already solidly established. The company has progressively carried some of its products to a stage where they can be sold directly to the consumer. However, it has seldom shown the inclination to plunge off into fields entirely unrelated to its basic technology, raw material position, and marketing skills. A 220 per cent increase in its sales volume in ten years is some indication of the soundness of its objectives.

Atlantic Refining Company Economic Objectives. A great many companies establish objectives which limit them to types of activity that will ensure maximum utilization of their assets. A clear and concise statement of what kind of business the company is in and what it intends to accomplish is found in the following objectives of the Atlantic Refining Company:

The basic objective of the Atlantic Refining Company is to engage, as an integrated company, in the various phases of the petroleum business, striving for such balance between these phases as may achieve a reasonable profit for the Company. In carrying out its basic objective, the Company will make the most effective use of capital, people, and other resources and will:

1. Explore for and develop sources of crude oil, natural gas or other petroleum product raw materials (in those areas where these materials can be made economically available) and produce in maximum quantities consistent with economy and sound conservation.

2. Manufacture petroleum products and by-products at the lowest cost consistent with quality that will assure public acceptance.

3. Market, with the maximum economy of distribution, petroleum products and by-products and related merchandise; provide associated services.

4. Operate, or secure the use of, all facilities necessary to meet Company transportation requirements; utilize to the best advantage any excess of such facilities.

Alan Wood Steel Company. As another example, Alan Wood Steel Company operates in terms of this basic objective: "To furnish at a profit steel and related products of maximum value to our customers, present and future. The Company will expand and diversify its activities where necessary to fulfill a need for steel and related products, to be of greater service to its customers, to produce a better quality product, or to obtain more economical production."

Economic Objectives as a Guide to Operations

When properly itemized, economic objectives can provide a consistent guide to channel the operations of the company into most productive channels on a day-to-day basis. For this purpose, the general objectives are spelled out in terms of sales volume, share of market, dollar profits and profit margins, return on invested capital, and other pertinent factors. For example, a cereal company has as its over-all objectives: "To purchase grains and cereals at favorable prices and to manufacture and sell at a profit cereals, cereal products and cereal derivatives."

To serve as operating guides, the company has spelled out the following corollary objectives: "To increase our share of the breakfast cereal market from 3% to 8% in five years. To reduce general administrative expense from 19% to 16% in three years."

In another instance, an electrical company has established these objectives:

1. To develop, manufacture and market a line of high reliability specialized electrical products.

2. To grow 20% annually for the next six years by expansion and extension of the present and related product lines. This will involve an $18 million increase in sales and $6 million in net worth.

3. To earn a minimum of 12% net profit on sales before taxes and 24% on capital investment.

Illinois Tool Works Objectives. Illinois Tool Works, a divisionalized company which manufactures metal cutting tools, inspection equipment, and metal and plastic precision fastenings, details its objectives in the following areas:

1. Five-year sales goals, established by product lines, expressed in units and dollars.

2. Five-year sales goals for new product lines currently in the engineering stage, the pilot-plant stage, or early commercialization.

3. Gross and net profit margins by product lines. Return on investment, computed by years, for each product division.

4. Capital availability, estimated after dividends and taxes for working capital and fixed capital additions.

5. Machinery and equipment expenditures, estimated in detail by product division for three years, and in total for the fourth and fifth years. These estimates may vary, because under the company's equipment replacement policy, requests for equipment replacement are refused unless economically justified.

Changing Economic Objectives

In some cases, companies find it desirable to change economic objectives, even to the extent of leaving one major field of endeavor and establishing a place in another. Declining markets, poor profit potential, or other reasons may provide the impetus. The change-over may be accomplished from within; however, often it is accomplished by buying a company in the new field or by merging with a company already strongly established.

ACF–Brill Motors Company and its predecessor companies, for instance, manufactured vehicles such as horsecars, and later, buses and automotive and aircraft parts for over eighty years. However, the company began to lose ground steadily in this industry after World War II and finally decided to sell out and go into the food business. Using the $7 million in cash it had retained from sale of its plants, the company bought Wrigley Stores, Inc., a supermarket chain, in 1955, and entered the food field. Later it bought other supermarkets to add to its chain and solidly established itself as ACF-Wrigley Stores, Inc.

U.S. Industries, formerly Pressed Steel Car Company, is another example. For more than fifty years, Pressed Steel Car suffered with the wide fluctuations of the freight-car market. The company finally concluded that it could invest its money and its energies more profitably elsewhere. Accordingly, it closed out its car plants and left the railway equipment business. Now, U.S. Industries has undertaken a planned diversification and has shown a sound and profitable growth.

In all these examples, we see careful consideration of the proper sphere of the company's activities in terms of its resources, manpower, and future intentions. These goals focus the total energies of company management upon consistent ends and minimize the divergence of interests which result in the company becoming a "Jack-of-all-trades and master of none." Over the long term, such consistency is the best guarantee of maximum utilization of corporate assets and profitable return on the investment of stockholders.

Social Objectives

What are the goals of the company with respect to its employees, policyholders, and the general public? Answers to this question provide a statement of social objectives.

Social objectives encompass all aspects of the business which do not refer to the market place. For example, Alan Wood Steel Company has these fundamental social objectives:

To provide our employees with good working conditions, to pay wages and salaries in line with those prevailing in the steel industry for similar work requiring like responsibility, experience, and skill, and to provide employment as secure and steady as possible, commensurate with the risks inherent in the steel business.

To be a good neighbor in the communities in which we are located and to foster and promote civic activities directed toward the fundamental improvement of these communities.

H. P. Hood & Sons states its basic social objectives as follows:

To establish wages, working conditions, benefits, job security, opportunity, and personal recognition which, combined, will make our company the best in our industry in which to work.

To demonstrate that H. P. Hood & Sons is a good neighbor and citizen by our active support of good government, education, health programs, and other good work which benefits the entire community in which we operate.

Subordinate Company Objectives

Managers at the top level formulate objectives for the company as a whole. At lower levels, managers break down these over-all goals into specific targets for their divisions, departments, and units. For example, if the company wishes to increase its market penetration, targets must be set for marketing, for production, and for other functions, to ensure that each will move at the proper speed and in harmony to the common goal. It is part of the management work of the chief executive to formulate and enunciate these objectives for the company, with the participation and cooperation of all subordinate managers who will be held accountable for their share of the total. He must explain and interpret these goals to each of his immediate subordinate managers and hold him accountable for setting subsidiary goals for his own unit and its components.

POLICIES

Policy is a term which is frequently used but not often described concretely enough to be applied to specific management work. Policies are characterized as "principles" and as "rules for action." They are confused with objectives. They are made immutable, unchanging, and eternal, or as changeable as the whims of the manager who sets them. This confusion is unfortunate, because the work of establishing and interpreting policies is a vital element of the process of management.

What do we mean by "policy"? A policy refers to a continuing decision which applies to repetitive situations. It is a standing answer to a recurring question. A policy decision is *continuing* because it is relatively permanent and continues in force until it is specifically repealed. A policy decision for the company as a whole is made by the chief executive and the board of directors and applies throughout the organization. Each manager is accountable for securing participation in policy making and for interpreting and explaining company policies to all who report to him.

McKesson & Robbins, Incorporated, in its organization manual, defines policies as "guides which chart the course of an organization and govern its activities toward the achievement of the purpose for which it was set up." Holden, Fish, and Smith [2] define policies as "the guiding principles established by the company to govern actions, usually under repetitive conditions." For example, they point out, "a decision by top management to reward an employee for some special act does not constitute a policy; but an announcement that each such case under similar circumstances is to receive such an award may be called a policy."

Policies serve several purposes. First, if the manager can anticipate repetitive situations which will be referred each time to him for decision, he can make one blanket decision to guide action wherever it occurs

[2] Paul E. Holden, Lounsbury S. Fish, and Hubert L. Smith, *Top-Management Organization and Control,* McGraw-Hill Book Company, Inc., New York, 1951, p. 79.

through the establishment of a policy. For example, the company may have an objective to maintain high standards of quality, novelty, and freshness in its merchandise. To effect this, it may be desirable for it to clean out its stocks of perishable or timely merchandise at least once a year. Instead of leaving this to the option—and the individual proclivities—of sales and warehouse managers, the president can ensure uniform and consistent action by establishing a policy such as "Stock on hand will be disposed of and warehouse inventories exhausted by March each year."

With this inflexible decision as a guide, sales managers can make plans for clearance sales, production control managers can adjust their schedules, and executives can be held to account for other actions necessary to implement this over-all decision.

As McKesson & Robbins observes, "In an organization in which policies are stable, understood and observed, the department head knows that he is operating as he should operate; he knows what his boss would do about a problem and he does not have to run to the boss and ask; he can do jobs and solve problems in a definite manner that is in line with top management's thinking."

Policies should be positive declarations. They are commands to the organization at large. Confusion between objectives and policies often occurs because the policy is stated as an expectation, not as a command. For example, the policy statement "to emphasize company brand names in advertising" should properly be stated, "Company brand names will be emphasized in advertising."

Green Giant Company Policies

The Green Giant Company, which processes and markets food products, has an over-all financial objective "to maintain adequate capital in liquid form for: (*a*) working capital and (*b*) expansion and modernization of production facilities." To accomplish this objective, the company has decided that it will enforce the following policies:

1. *Maintenance of working capital at 20% of sales.* In order to buy crops for canning, finance current operations, and support short-term borrowings, it is extremely important for a food processing company such as Green Giant to maintain adequate working capital. The company finds that a 20 per cent ratio to sales covers its liquid capital needs.

2. *A conservative dividend policy.* Green Giant retains a substantial portion of its net earnings in the business to provide funds for expansion, maintain regular dividend payments, and help assure continuous operation. Company dividends average about 25 per cent of net earnings. About half of the net income is used to increase working capital and to build a contingency reserve, and one-quarter is allotted to finance

capital expenditure. Dividends have averaged approximately 25 per cent of net earnings over a long period.

3. *Limiting the cost of replacement of existing facilities to an amount which is not in excess of the depreciation charged off.* The company charges off enough depreciation against operations each year to provide replacements as necessary due to wear and tear on buildings and equipment.

4. *Liquidation of each year's pack that year.* The company believes that a pack carry-over is speculation on what the conditions of cost and market will be in the succeeding year. Consequently, it literally paints the warehouse floors between packs. Green Giant finds that it can better liquidate short-term indebtedness, assure available funds for current requirements, and maintain liquidity of assets by following this policy in its operations.

5. *Financing short-term requirements by short-term borrowing.* The peaks for expenditures and income alternate in the canning business. Expenditures build up most heavily in the summer canning season, which is also the lightest in sales; conversely, sales income is heaviest in the nonproducing winter months. Instead of tying up enough working capital to finance the entire cost of a pack over twelve months, by following this policy the company is able to make short-term loans from banks on an unsecured basis at minimum interest.

6. *Financing long-term requirements by a combination of long-term debt and capital stock.* Green Giant finds that there are advantages and disadvantages in both long-term debt and capital stock. Common stock requires no fixed dividend and no redemption. Long-term debt is the cheapest way to raise money because it normally commands a lower rate than corporate stock, and interest is deductible for income tax purposes. However, long-term debt has a mandatory fixed interest payment and redemption factor. Currently, the company finds that it can serve its needs best by holding long-term debt to about 40 per cent of the capital stock and surplus together.

PROGRAMS

A program is a sequence of activities designed to implement policies and accomplish objectives. A program gives a step-by-step approach to guide the action necessary to reach a predetermined goal. Each manager develops programs for accomplishment of the objectives for which he is accountable. To ensure practicality and acceptance of his programs, the manager provides for full participation by all subordinates who will help carry them out.

Programs must be closely integrated with objectives. They may be combined with budgets; for example, some companies call their total process of programing and budgeting the "Company Program." Schedules are often combined with programs to provide a chronological sequence of activities.

Development of programs by individual managers should be preceded by the establishment of over-all company objectives and objectives for each major division and department. These goals provide the data on which to base the program. Programs may be prepared in narrative or tabular form. When the narrative form is used, it should fully describe the projects or activities which are to be carried out, preferably with an accompanying schedule to indicate dates for initiation and completion. It is desirable to coordinate the program with the budget, for the one is the basis for the other.

Manufacturing Company Personnel Programs

Excerpts from both long- and short-range narrative programs as prepared in one multiplant manufacturing company for the implementation of *newly inaugurated* personnel activities in the selection area are reproduced below. Note that a schedule is built into the program.

PERSONNEL PROGRAM
1958–1969

GENERAL

The objectives of the personnel department are to provide such services or assistance as may be requested by the line divisions and staff departments in making maximum utilization of the human resources of their units.

SELECTION

1. Each year the standards for recruiting and employment practices will be raised to assure that the most promising candidates are employed for both hourly and salary jobs.

2. Each year cadet recruitment and selection standards will be improved. By December, 1959, close working arrangements with designated colleges and universities will be established to aid in the employment of the desired types of college graduates.

3. Standardization of personnel forms will be undertaken on a continuous and long-range basis. Where practical, basic personnel forms used throughout the company will be made uniform by December, 1959, and most paper work involving personnel activities will be standardized by December, 1960.

4. Psychological tests will be introduced and installed on a long-range basis. Types of tests best adapted to company needs will be selected, company norms will be established, and the selection and training of test administrators will be completed by December, 1963.

A statement of the annual program for 1958 follows:

PERSONNEL PROGRAM
1958

GENERAL

The 1958 Personnel Program is geared to the attainment of basic personnel objectives of the company. In addition to providing advice and services on personnel matters to the line divisions and staff departments, as may be requested, the program includes specific projects for advancement or completion during the year.

SELECTION

1. By January 10, the numbers and qualifications of new college graduates will be determined, by division and department. Recruiting schedules will then be established. Recruiting trips will be made on a scheduled basis until 'the company's requirements have been filled.

2. Work will continue on the standardization of personnel forms throughout the year. Where practical, all basic forms will be reduced to uniformity by December 31.

3. By June 15, psychological test batteries will be developed, preparation of company norms will be initiated, and testing of clerical personnel throughout the company will be begun. By December 31, psychological testing for all potential sales personnel will be introduced in the Eastern Region on a pilot basis.

4. The operating divisions hiring new college graduates will be encouraged to administer the company psychological testing battery for college graduates to all candidates for positions in the division. . . .

Carborundum Company Programs

Carborundum Company has a comprehensive system of programing that includes all its organizational units. Programs in this company are based on the general objectives of the company and its "Concept of the Future." This is a forecast which contains an estimate of all internal variables affecting the success of the business and those external variables which, while beyond company control, influence its success. Once prepared, the program is used to measure the performance of the company as a whole and each of its component elements.

Carborundum programs are prepared on a five-year basis. Annual revisions are made, with an additional year's programing added at the time of each revision to maintain the five-year continuity. The first-year program of the period is developed with great care and with as much detail and accuracy as possible. Programs for succeeding years are prepared with successively less detail.

These programs are systematic and directed efforts of the company to command its own future. In Carborundum, the program is based not only on past and current experience but also on a systematic evaluation of the probabilities of the future. The company plans for growth and expansion by building into each program an improvement factor. This is not simply wishful thinking; it is documented by programed introduction or use of new equipment techniques, processes, and plans. Evidence in support of this anticipated improvement is built up throughout the year, as a basis for further programing. Thus the planning work of the manager is continuous. There is constant feedback, through the reporting system, of accomplishment against the program. This is in terms of dollars and ratios and of actual work accomplished.

SCHEDULES

Scheduling is the process of establishing a time sequence for the work to be done. Usually it is an integral part of programing. A schedule followed in installation of a compensation program for salesmen in a merchandising chain is reproduced below:

Schedule for Installation, Salesmen's Compensation Program

Division	Start job eval.	Complete job. eval.	Start merit rating	Complete merit rating
Eastern	Feb. 17	Sept. 30	Oct. 1	Dec. 1
North Central	Mar. 3	June 30	July 1	Aug. 1
Central	Feb. 17	Dec. 1	Dec. 2	Dec. 30
Western	July 1	Oct. 1	Oct. 1	Nov. 1
Southwestern	Jan. 15	May 15	May 15	July 30
Southeastern	Apr. 15	Oct. 15	Oct. 16	Dec. 30

PROCEDURES

Procedures prescribe the manner or method by which work is to be performed. If the manager wishes all work of a specified type to be carried out in a standard or uniform manner, he sees to it that a procedure is prepared detailing how it is to be done. Where the program tells *what* is to be done, the procedure tells *how*.

Written procedures have many advantages. The process of preparing a procedure statement encourages analysis and study of the work being described. This often results in work simplification and elimination of overlap and duplication.

Once the procedure is established, it ensures a uniformly high level of performance. At the same time, it provides a standard for appraising work completed and thus serves as an effective control agency. If properly prepared, the procedure constitutes a useful outline for developing people. It helps to reduce the time and expense of job training and minimizes errors resulting from lack of information or the wrong information. Since the procedure establishes a uniform method of doing work, applicable to all departments, it can help eliminate friction and disagreements between departments.

Procedures are an effective means of reducing the burden of decision making. In effect, the procedure is a decision as to how work is to be done. As such it provides a standing answer to many operating problems. This not only helps improve efficiency but also ensures close coordination.

The manager must see to it that suitable procedures are prepared or are available to establish consistent action for routine work. This will help the manager to free himself from the need for handling detail and permit him to devote his time to the more important aspects of his job.

Procedures have one real disadvantage. To the extent they prescribe how work must be performed, they discourage initiative and innovation and the development of new and more effective ways of doing the work. Best precaution here is to review procedures constantly and to make managers accountable for evaluation and improvement of the procedures they establish.

Many companies maintain a comprehensive set of administrative procedures, which apply uniformly to repetitive work, wherever it is performed in the company. Koppers Company maintains such a manual, which is constantly revised and kept up to date. Koppers finds that these administrative procedures act as an approved set of rules for carrying out work which, when observed by all units, help to ensure that maximum use is being made of the resources and efforts of the company. A typical procedure from this manual is reproduced in Figure 2–1, page 39.

BUDGETS

A budget is an estimate for use. In its most common form, it is an appraisal of expected expense projected against anticipated income for a future period. Budgets may be stated in time, money, materials, or other units required to perform work and accomplish specified results. Since most values are ultimately convertible to monetary units, money budgets are commonly used.

Budgets may cover any and all aspects of the business. Budgeting for the company as a whole must start with projection of both long- and short-term goals by the president. Such objectives can be set realistically

A Unified Concept of Management 39

PROCEDURE

ORIGINATED BY: RESEARCH DEPARTMENT
Patent Section
SUBJECT: Copyrights

NO. 6-A-10
DATE March 31, 195
PAGE NO. 1 OF 1

GENERAL:

There are numerous company publications, including technical bulletins, brochures, prints and labels, whose contents warrant copyright protection. Company employees in charge of such publications should proceed as follows:

PROCEDURE:

1. In case of doubt as to whether copyright protection is desirable or effective, consult the Patent Section before printing.

2. Instruct the printer to print the copyright notice, consisting of word "Copyright" or abbreviation "Copr." together with the year of publication and "Koppers Company, Inc.", on the title page or the page immediately following. In certain cases © may be used but this should be done only on advice of the Patent Section. The printer is not to file the application for registration.

3. Three copies of the printed publication should be forwarded to the Manager, Research Department, accompanied by authorization for filing an application for copyright registration, and by information as to author's name, address, citizenship and date of birth (also date of death, if deceased), as well as date of publication, name and address of printer and of binder.

4. Reproduction of a copyrighted work must bear the copyright notice, giving the same date as in the original notice.

Figure 2–1. Copyright Procedure, Koppers Company, Inc.

only with the full participation of managers at all levels. Over-all company goals set the pattern for the contributory efforts of subordinate elements of the business. Programs and budgets developed by the subordinate elements to reach these goals, when integrated and combined, provide the over-all programs and budgets which will guide the operations of the company and each of its component parts.

Budget preparation within this framework is part of the work of every manager. The most significant aspect of this process is the activity that precedes compilation of the figures representing anticipated needs. Before a manager can develop a budget, he must think through the objectives he is trying to achieve and the program he will follow. This consideration is practical and realistic, for it can be meaningful only if it is based on such data as wage rates, personnel needs, material costs, machine rates, space requirements, and so forth.

Since his accomplishment of these goals is in part dependent upon the adequacy of the objectives, programs, and budgets of other managers, the accountable manager must coordinate his own plans to ensure that the other members of the team will be implementing programs that will reinforce and support his own activities and that he, in turn, will be performing a similar service for others.

The goal-setting and programing preliminary to budget preparation helps resolve differing viewpoints. In this preparatory activity the manager anticipates road blocks and makes specific plans, with dollar labels attached, to overcome them. This provides a realistic, consistent approach which, once translated into budget terms, can be applied as a universal yardstick to every component of the business.

Budgeting in Armstrong Cork Company

Armstrong Cork Company follows a comprehensive system of budgeting for planning sales, production, personnel, administrative, and financial operations for each year. Armstrong Cork department managers use budgets to help in supervising and controlling individual operations and administering the business as a whole. They are a tool for appraising operating results and serve as a guide in establishing financial control policies, including capital expenditures, inventory investment, and cash position.

Budgets in Armstrong Cork anticipate that if managers operate efficiently, definite levels of income can be expected and corollary expenditures will have to be made. The budgets are prepared on the basis of careful study and evaluation of the probable requirements of the business and the conditions which are expected to prevail for the budget period.

To help pin-point accountability, the budgeted income and expenditures are classified, organized, and assigned so that they can easily be related to the managers who have responsibility for carrying out specific activities. Thus each department manager is charged for all expense incurred by his people for items ranging from stationery to the maintenance of equipment. Actual performance is compared regularly with the budget standards and exceptions are noted and reported.

Armstrong Cork holds managers accountable only for those expenditures which they command. Special allowances are made to cover costs which result from policy decisions which are beyond the command of the accountable manager. The company also uses flexible budgeting techniques, so that budget allowances can be adjusted readily to varying volumes of production.

To ensure acceptance and cooperation at all levels in the use of budgets, the company requires managers who approve budgets to provide, at the same time, for full participation in their preparation and approval by those who will be held accountable for their use. Portions of budget forms used in Armstrong Cork Company are shown in Figure 2–2, page 42. The Statement of Operations is a summary operating statement prepared for commodity line, divisions, and plants. Plant costs are reported against budget in the Plant Cost Summaries. The Expense Budget Summary reports performance against budget to foremen and plant and division managers.

ORGANIZATION

A manager, in managing, must develop an organization capable of accomplishing his objectives. Organization here refers to the structure which results from identifying and grouping work, defining and delegating responsibility and authority, and establishing relationships. The organization activity will be discussed in the chapter following.

COORDINATION

A manager, in managing, must coordinate the work for which he is accountable by balancing, timing, and integrating it. *Balancing* means that enough of one thing is provided to support or counterbalance another. For example, balancing of line and staff involves provision of adequate staff support to the line. *Timing* requires that different activities, proceeding under their own schedules, are brought into phase so that both advance in such a manner as to reinforce one another. *Integration* refers to the unification of all the unrelated or diverse interests which must be brought together if purposeful work is to be accomplished effectively.

Coordination, in terms of timing, balancing, and integrating, is as necessary at the foreman level as at that of the president. The foreman must see to it that production schedules are prepared by production control on time, that materials are available when he needs them, that he has enough people with the proper skills to do the work of his unit, and accomplish his objectives.

The president must perform an intricate job of coordination to ensure that the product his company sells is meeting standards of quality

STATEMENT OF OPERATIONS

Year 19 _____

	Month of				January Through			
	Actual (000)	%	Forecast (000)	%	Actual (000)	%	Forecast (000)	%
Gross Sales Price - Trade								
Units - Trade								
Units - Intra- Company								
Net Sales $ - Trade								
Net Sales $ - Intra-Company								
Net Sales $ - Total								

PLANT COST SUMMARY

Glass and Closure Division

Month _____ 19 ____

CURRENT MONTH				YEAR TO DATE		
Actual	Allowance	Forecast	Description	Actual	Allowance	Forecast
			STD. DIR. COST OF PROD.			
			VARIANCES - GAIN (LOSS)			
			Material Util.			
			Direct Labor - Eff.			
			Scrap			
			Direct Expense			
			Reconditioning			

EXPLANATION:
This report shows actual expenses and deviations from the budget. When actual expense is higher than budgeted, the deviation is an overrun and is indicated as such by the symbol ov. When actual expense is lower than budgeted, the deviation is an underrun and is indicated as such by the absence of a symbol.

ARMSTRONG CORK COMPANY
EXPENSE BUDGET REPORT

CPD   OPER

Control	Source	Class	Description	CURRENT MONTH		YEAR TO DATE	
				Actual	Deviation from budget	Actual	Deviation from budget

Figure 2–2. Budget Forms, Armstrong Cork Company

which are not too high and not too low. He must see to it that the sales department carries its full weight in determining what standard of quality will satisfy the customer and in imparting the information to the engineering department so that it can be built into the product. He must see to it that engineering coordinates its designs with manufacturing; otherwise the quality specified may be impractical to manufacture. On the other hand, the design must be coordinated with sales, or the cost of the quality built into the product may result in pricing it out of the market.

Most of this coordination will be accomplished automatically if sound objectives, policies, procedures, and organization are established. At the same time, however, the manager must mediate and decide when differences of opinion or judgment are apparent, and he must be prepared to initiate other means of reconciliation when his personal intervention is not desirable or possible. It is up to the manager to decide when coordination best can be secured by establishment of new objectives, policies, or procedures, by the delegation of new responsibility or authority, or by the withdrawal of authority and centralization of command of the activity to secure effective coordination.

MOTIVATION

A manager, in managing, must motivate to highest productivity the people who work for him. People are the unique element in every company. Outstanding people can make even a poor organization operate successfully. Poorly motivated people can nullify the soundest organization.

In motivating, the manager must *select* the people he wants on his team. He must know what kind of people are needed to fill the positions to which he intends to delegate. He must make sure that the people who join his organization are compatible both with himself and with those with whom they will work.

To inspire and impel his people to highest endeavor, the manager provides for *communication* and *participation*. He sees to it that his people have an opportunity to be heard on matters that affect them and that they participate in the preliminary discussion and analysis of decisions that directly involve them.

The safety engineer on the central manufacturing staff of a multiplant metal products company illustrated the common oversight of this most elementary need. "Here is my annual budget, signed, sealed, and delivered," he said, holding up a sheet of paper. "The manufacturing vice president got together with the controller and made it up without a word to me about it. Now he presents it to me and expects me to live by it."[1]

His further remarks aptly illustrated his feelings of hurt pride and frustration.

Motivation includes other skills. It requires that the manager know how to keep his people informed, that he take the time and make the effort necessary to secure suggestions and recommendations from his people on matters of general interest.

When queried about his means of communication, one finance manager said, "I keep everybody up to date at our monthly staff meeting. Besides, my door is always open." The truth of the matter came out when several section heads in his department were interviewed. "Working in this place is like working in a well," one said. "If you want to know what's going on, you have to ask the secretaries or the elevator operator." It so happened that the assistant manager had quit and was being replaced. Confirmation of his successor came out through the typing pool. At the same time, plans were being laid for moving the finance department to larger quarters. The elevator operators knew the details of the move and broadcast them before the employees were informed. In each case, the finance manager was waiting for the monthly staff meeting to make formal announcement.

In motivating, the accountable manager *appraises, counsels,* and *coaches* the subordinates who report directly to him. He makes himself available to arbitrate disagreements, to reconcile opposition, to receive and handle grievances and complaints. Only the manager is organizationally placed to do these things effectively. He may secure the help of personnel staff in preparing himself, but he cannot divorce himself from the final performance of this work without abdicating his responsibility as a manager.

Finally in motivation, the manager must develop the skills of command. He must know how to direct others without arousing offense or resentment and he must be able to secure obedience without destroying initiative and creativity.

CONTROL

A manager, in managing, controls the work for which he is accountable. Work must be carried out in terms of the performance standards which the manager establishes. Most commonly, these performance standards are the objectives, policies, programs, procedures, and budgets initially established to guide the work.

The term "control" is frequently misunderstood and misapplied. This is largely because of imprecise definition. Control means to guide something in the direction it is intended to go. This is not the same as simple command—the giving of orders—with which control is often confused. Control involves determining where you want to go, observing to see that you keep on course and schedule, and giving orders when necessary to correct any variances.

The work of the manager in controlling involves four specific activities:

1. *Establishing Standards of Accountability.* He sees to it that there are valid, understandable, and acceptable yardsticks for measurement of work as it goes forward. These standards are based on the plans established to initiate the work.

2. *Measuring Work in Progress.* Record must be kept of work as it progresses so that performance can be compared to the applicable yardstick. Measurement may be in terms of dollars spent, units expended, customers contacted, activities completed, and so forth. Effective measurement also requires accurate *reporting* of the work accomplished.

3. *Interpreting Results.* The results accomplished must be evaluated in terms of the standards by which work is being judged. Interpretation involves not only comparison of actual against standard but also identification of discrepancies or variations and analysis of why these variances have occurred. After the manager approves the initial plans and standards of performance, he may delegate to his line subordinates or staff units much of the work of measurement and interpretation. However, there is a last step in control which must remain the prerogative of the manager himself.

4. *Taking Corrective Action.* When variations from plan occur, it is necessary to bring the work going on back to the desired course. The manager himself must decide what is required to attain the results he expects. Only he can give the orders which lead to effective corrective action.

MANAGERS MUST MANAGE

We can conclude that only *when he is planning, organizing, coordinating, motivating, and controlling the work of other people is a manager managing.* We are justified in naming as managers only those people who are mostly concerned with doing these things. This is the kind of work for which we should pay managers. These are the activities which we should train and develop managers to perform. It is on this basis only that we can organize and control the work of managers.

Should a manager himself do *all* the work involved in planning, organizing, coordinating, motivating, and controlling? Obviously he cannot, or he will be eternally mired in details. As we shall see in our discussion of delegation, the manager should concern himself as largely as possible with *initiating* these activities and with *making final decision* concerning them. He *initiates* by making sure that plans, organization, coordination, motivation, and controls are provided and effectively used by those who report to him. And he makes the *final decisions* that will dictate the importance these activities will assume and the characteristics they will exhibit in his unit.

Operating Work Performed by Managers

At every level, managers perform some work which involves "execution" or "doing." It is this "doing" or "operating" work which completes the administrative process.

The manager is accountable for *operating,* just as he is for managing. Frequently he must perform operating work himself. For example, the manager of research might be particularly expert in some phase of physical chemistry. He might have to take a research problem at a certain point and work it through personally or it cannot be done. The company president may be on particularly good terms with a major customer. His personal intervention may be required to throw a large order to his firm. This is not management work. But it may be part of the job of a manager. If such activities take up a large part of the manager's time, his job should be analyzed to help him delegate more effectively or to reclassify his position to reflect more accurately the work he is doing.

ADMINISTRATION AND MANAGEMENT

We have defined terms which identify the management and non-management components of a manager's job. We need a term which we can apply to the total work done by managers. We use "administration" in this sense. Administration is the total of planning, organizing, coordinating, motivating, controlling, *and* operating work.

It should be noted that each of the elements included in administration is interdependent and, in fact, a reciprocal of each of the other elements. Plans must be developed, not only for operations but also for organizing, coordinating, motivating, and controlling. The organization must provide for and encompass planning, coordinating, controlling, and operating work. Coordination must proceed with respect to plans, organization, motivation, controls, and operations. Motivation is the energizing force behind all other activities of management. Controls must be established for plans, organization, coordination, motivation, and operations.

There is an operating phase to each of the management activities described. Plans must not only be established but also carried out. Organization must be implemented. Coordination, motivation, and controls also have their operating aspects.

HOW TO USE THE UNIFIED CONCEPT

Our ability to characterize specific kinds of work as *management* work has several desirable results. First, it provides a logical basis for holding managers accountable for performance of management work and delegation of nonmanagement work. It enables us to analyze the job of any manager and determine to what extent he is *managing* and to what extent he is doing work that could be done by his subordinates.

If we identify management work, we are at the same time deciding what work can be decentralized and what must be centralized for effective performance. If we wish to determine what staff assistance and advice managers require, we can best do so in terms of what legitimate need the manager has for help in work he *should* be performing and to what extent assistance encourages him to withhold responsibility and authority from his subordinates. Identification of management work gives us a rational basis for determining how much money we should pay a manager for the work he is asked to do. It is much more logical to pay a manager for his work in the development of programs, the maintenance of a sound plan of organization, and the appraisal and counseling of subordinates than it is in terms of the "responsibility for confidential data," "working conditions," "mental-visual demand" of his job, and similar criteria that are often used as factors in salary plans for managers.

Finally, if we know what management work is, we can appraise, counsel, and coach managers to *manage*. It is more meaningful, for example, to evaluate a manager's accomplishment in preparing budgets for his group than it is to appraise his ability to "exercise sound judgment in the expenditure of funds."

The unified concept enables us to divide each major activity into separate tasks and projects, which can be shown to have a definite beginning and end. This work requires time, manpower, materials, and money for its accomplishment, all of which can be measured. The presence or absence of, and the adherence to, goals, policies, and procedures can be observed and evaluated. The effectiveness of organization charts and position guides, the accuracy of cost estimates, the availability of promotable subordinates can be determined in specific terms.

The unified concept identifies transferable management skills. A person proficient in managing one kind of work can transfer his skill to managing other work with relative ease. The *management* of a family, a company, church, or country may differ in complexity and difficulty, but they involve the same basic skills.

The transferability of management skills enables us to explain why outstanding managers of military affairs can assume high governmental and business posts without lengthy apprenticeships. It accounts for the capacity of business managers to transfer readily to management of public and governmental agencies. It also explains the success of many accomplished managers in transferring from manufacturing to service industries, from steel to chemicals. As Charles Schwab is reputed to have said, "It takes the same kind of know-how to manage the United States Steel Corporation as it does to manage a peanut stand."

SUMMARY

A unified, integrated concept of management is presented which outlines the work a manager must accomplish in managing.

1. Planning is the means whereby the manager forecasts and develops objectives or goals to guide the over-all flow of work. He anticipates repetitive problems and situations and provides answers to them by establishing policies. He develops a definite program of work to be undertaken, and he places time limits by use of schedules. Procedures are developed to specify uniform methods by which work is to be accomplished. Budgets provide estimates of the units of money, time, materials, and people that will be required to complete the work.

2. Management organization is treated separately in Chapter 3.

3. Motivation encompasses the selection and placement of the people the manager wants on his team, provision for communication and participation, appraisal, counseling, coaching, and training. It involves compensation, direction, and, if necessary, dismissal.

4. Coordination is accomplished through the balancing, timing, and integration of the work to be performed.

5. Control is the entire process of appraising work. It includes the preparation of performance standards, measurement of work through recording and reporting systems, evaluation of actual performance, and, finally, the taking of appropriate management action.

PART TWO

Organization for Management

CHAPTER 3 *What Is Organization?*

Almost any business manager will affirm that sound organization is highly important to business success. Many will characterize organization as the foundation upon which the whole structure of management is built. Unfortunately, there are many differences of opinion as to the precise nature of organization, as of other aspects of management; and there is even less concurrence on what specific work must be accomplished in organizing.

Does organization consist of the design or mechanism within which people operate? Or does it also include the finding, placing, and developing of people within this structure? Does it encompass the formulation of the goals toward which the organization will progress? Or is it primarily concerned with procedural aspects which will guide everyday actions? Until we agree upon what work our concept of organization includes, we can hardly hold a manager accountable for establishing a sound and workable organization, nor can we train, develop, or compensate managers for the work of organizing.

Consider the predicament of one company president who suspected that his organization was inadequate to the needs of a projected expansion program. "I don't know whether my organization is good, bad or indifferent because I don't know with what to compare it," he said. He had investigated an "organization planning" program in one company which was devoted exclusively to employee counseling and coaching and the interpretation of color-coded organization charts for management inventory purposes. In another company, he had found the "organization planning" staff department primarily concerned with wage and salary matters; in still another, as he put it, they were "keepers of the organization charts." In a fourth instance, the function reported to the auditor and was responsible for procedures.

51

UNIVERSALS

Organization is a mechanism or structure that enables living things to work effectively together. The evolution of all forms of life and of human society demonstrates the need for organization. In their primitive forms, living creatures have minimum need for integrated group effort. Simple, functional organizations are generally adequate. As life evolves, however, organizational forms must be developed to facilitate the formation of increasingly complex group action and relationships.

In his beginnings, man lived off the earth and its bounty. He ate roots and berries and whatever animals he could trap or kill, clothed himself in skins, and lived in caves or rude shelters. At this stage, the family as an organizational unit was sufficient to his needs. The family unit provided adequate roles for women as the mothers, berrypickers, and weavers and for men as the fighters, hunters, and arrowmakers.

As the centuries passed, men learned they could fight, work, worship, and produce the wherewithal to live more satisfactorily by forming larger and more intricate organizational units. Groups of hunters, fighters, and artisans, by combining their individual skills, could better satisfy the needs of a group of families than could one person provide for his family alone. As these groups developed, they prospered to the extent their individual members learned to specialize, on the one hand, and to pool their specialties for the common good on the other.

The ability to organize his efforts has become increasingly important to man as the groups in which he lives have become larger and more complex. It is organization that has enabled men in groups to apply their brain and muscle power to the available natural resources for the production of material goods. And in modern times, organization has enabled men to increase their riches far beyond the dreams of the wealthiest potentates of old by making effective use of a potent multiplier—machine power and mechanized tools.

Throughout history, the evolution of organization has been mostly a process of trial and error. Improvement has resulted because successful and productive forms have persisted and have been refined in use. Until very recently, there have been few principles to follow in the evaluation of an existing organization or the design of an improved structure.

As a preliminary to identifying such principles, we must first determine what we mean by organization. We shall begin by describing three kinds of work that must be performed whenever organization takes place. These three universals are the division of labor, identification of the source of authority, and the establishment of relationships.

1. *Division of Labor.* If the group is to pool its efforts effectively, there must be a division of the total effort so that all do necessary, purposeful work which contributes to the attainment of the objectives and so that the work of one member of the group does not duplicate or overlap the work being done by others.

2. *Source of Authority.* There must be some means of securing compliance of individual members of the group in contributing their efforts to the common goal. Whether this power or authority arises from instinct, culture, the consent of the governed, superior physical strength, intelligence, cunning, or some other influence, it must exist. Unless there is a directing authority, each individual will do what he wants, when he wants, and integrated effort and consistent attainment will be impossible. The result will be a rabble, not a purposeful, organized group.

3. *Relationships.* How are individuals to work together in the organized group? If two individuals not in an authority relationship to one another are working together and a critical decision must be made, who makes it? Does the individual with authority owe greater loyalty to those he directs or to the one in authority over him? If individuals in different units, at different authority levels, must establish contact and work together, what channels do they follow? To answer questions such as these, it is necessary to establish standing answers in the form of relationships between individuals and groups working together within the organization. These relationships are, in reality, rules for teamwork. They are often overlooked in considering organizational problems, but they are an integral and important part of the activity.

ORGANIZATION OF THE HUMAN BODY

The human body is the most complex and infinitely varied of any organization we know. It is highly stable, yet unbelievably adaptive. Nature is the master organizer. In the body we find an arrangement perfectly adapted to the consistent yet constantly varying ends to which man sets himself, an organization that is capable of infinite adaptation to the vagaries of climate, of effort, of personality, and of growth. Study of the organization of the human body will exemplify certain profound yet obvious principles. We find that the body has evolved into progressively more complex forms of structure, and that in this evolution it has developed organizational forms which are perfectly adapted to its needs.

The body is capable of great differentiation. It has organs and appendages, each of which does a highly specialized kind of work. These organs and appendages are capable of independent action in themselves, yet exist for the purposes of the body as a whole. We find a central authority which establishes policy, which can make decisions affecting the over-all operation and welfare of the body, yet which is restrained from concerning itself directly with the local operation of some of its parts. This organization may exist for purposes peculiarly selfish to its own ends, yet may also exist for purposes greater than itself. The structure is so soundly constructed and stable that the cells which make it up may die and change hundreds of times during the lifetime of the body itself, yet with no sensible alteration of the organization as a whole. Here we find an organization suited to endless variations in personality and temperament, adjustable to extremes of environment, adequate whether governed by an idiot or a genius.

If we can observe and analyze it properly, the work of the Great, Organizer can provide us with principles applicable to management organization.

Authority in the Human Body

The mainspring and integrating force of the body's organization is the brain and nervous system. The brain is the seat of command and direction. It tells the body as a whole what to do and also directs the individual organs. The brain operates at two levels, the conscious and the autonomic or subconscious. The conscious brain makes decisions which actuate purposeful movements of the body. The information which stimulates and gives form to these decisions is gathered and relayed to the brain by an intricate system of nerves.

It is notable that the body has a relatively high degree of decentralization. Thus if the foot is placed near a fire and becomes too hot, a short-circuiting nervous pathway will cause a reflex withdrawal of the foot to safety. A slower volley of communications is integrated at the conscious level to recognize the pain and its source and determine conscious action, that is, treatment of pain or extinguishing of the fire, the source of pain.

Most of the vital organs of the body operate with a good deal of independence of the conscious direction of the brain. If a breakdown occurs in the blood vessels of the leg, for example, a compensatory collateral circulation develops, all without intervention from the conscious brain. Because practically all such detail and routine are handled locally on a decentralized basis by the tissues involved, the conscious level is left free for independent and creative thought; it can devote itself to the needs and interests of the body as a whole. It becomes concerned with and devotes thought to an individual organ only when that organ is in an abnormal state—when it sends messages of pain or danger that call upon the resources of the whole body and hence of the central intelligence.

The body can operate in this decentralized fashion effectively because it makes two kinds of decisions. First are those decisions made by the conscious brain. These usually refer to nonroutine situations and problems (nonroutine with reference to the internal organization of the body) which require the coordinated effort of two or more organs or parts of the body. The movement of the body toward food and ingestion of that food require the coordinated effort of many organs, choice as to the food eaten, interpretation of a great many signals which may involve the taste organs, smell, and so forth. The conscious brain initiates this movement and gives those commands necessary to place the body in a position where there is minimum need of conscious choice and direction.

At this point the second kind of decision is made by the autonomic brain. These are subconscious decisions which apply to routine, repetitive situations and are guided by established relationships. For example, once food is swallowed, the process of digestion and absorption is largely decentralized, in that practically all decisions with respect to digestion take place where the work is being done.

The conscious brain never completely divorces itself from accountability for what is going on. In effect, it establishes a set of policy decisions which are exercised through the subconscious brain and apply in all routine, repetitive matters. In setting this accountability, however, the body in effect establishes standards of performance. It sets tolerances of pain for heat, distention, cold, and so forth. If the stomach has difficulty digesting its food, it sends its first signal to the autonomic nervous system, which will, automatically and without conscious intervention, pour in more gastric juices and take other local steps. However, if the difficulty continues, the standards or tolerances of pain or discomfort are exceeded and the need for overt action is flashed to the conscious level, which sets the body looking for bicarbonate or the doctor.

Differentiation and Specialization

As the human embryo grows and becomes capable of greater scope and movement, it shows increasing differentiation and specialization of its parts. Each organ and appendage assumes a particular function, that is, it limits itself to a particular kind of work. The stomach and intestines are the digestive organs, the heart circulates the blood, the legs provide locomotion, and so forth. The economy and efficiency with which the differentiation and specialization occur are remarkable. The vascular system specializes in conveying the blood. However, lymph, not blood, fills the interstitial spaces. This lymph must also be circulated. The heart, which is the specialized pumping organ, pumps not only blood and lymph but also oxygen and other nutrients and materials throughout the body. Since the digestive apparatus is too gross to absorb and diffuse oxygen as well as food, the lungs serve as specialized organs for this task. The skin is not only a protective covering, it also excretes moisture and acts as a temperature regulator. This specialization makes possible a vastly complex and intricate organization.

Cooperative Relationships

The greater the differentiation and specialization of individual organs, the greater the need for coordinating the activities of each organ with those of others. When the legs move, the heart must pump more blood and the lungs must respire more quickly. If the eyes open, the iris must expand and contract to accommodate varying amounts of light. When food is swallowed, the epiglottis must close, the stomach must begin its churning motion, and dozens of glands must pour in their secretions. This cooperation and coordination depend upon the establishment of relationships among the various parts and organs of the body.

These relationships are made up of the connections and the arrangements for cooperative effort provided by the organization. The stimulus of fear causes the suprarenal glands to pour out adrenalin, which, in turn, stimulates the appropriate muscles to violent exertion. There is a definite relationship between the stimulus and the physiological reactions that occur. This relationship is not developed anew each time; it is provided as a part of the organization of the body itself.

It is remarkable, for example, that the conscious brain cannot intervene in many situations in which the autonomic nervous system has authority. It cannot knowingly decrease the flow of perspiration or affect the rate of coagulation of blood in a wound. The organizational relationship between these two authority centers is maintained even in the face of acute discomfort or danger. If the conscious brain wishes to influence such activities, it must do so by indirect or supportive means.

MANAGEMENT ORGANIZATION

Organization, wherever it takes place, occurs in terms of the three basic elements we have described. To identify the specific work that must be done by the manager in organizing, we describe each aspect as follows:

Identification and Grouping of Work

In organizing, the manager must first identify the work that must be done to reach his objectives. This work must be divided into parcels that can be performed by single individuals. Each such parcel will be made up of closely related work that fits the established patterns of education, training, and experience of individuals who will staff the positions. Just as he tries to unify the work done by individuals, the manager will make up teams of individuals, each doing the same kind of work, or closely related work.

Definition and Delegation of Responsibility and Authority

The manager will see to it that each individual knows exactly what work he is to do and what rights and powers he may exercise in doing it. Can the person doing the work use unlimited materials or only specified materials? Can he spend $10 or $1,000? Can he hire people to help him? Can he fire them? Definition of responsibility and authority, preferably in writing, will provide answers to such questions. In *delegating,* the manager will decide what part of this work he will perform himself and what he will entrust to his subordinates and will make his assignments so as to ensure effective performance.

Establishment of Relationships

The manager sets up certain rules for teamwork to enable his people to work harmoniously together under all possible circumstances. These relationships can be allowed to develop fortuitously, in which event they will be as various and changeable as the personalities involved. Or they can be established on a permanent and continuing basis, so that they will form a pattern to which people can be trained and developed.

Definition of Organization

We can define organization as *the process of identifying and grouping the work to be performed, defining and delegating responsibility and authority, and establishing relationships for the purpose of enabling people to work most effectively together in accomplishing objectives.*

This concept closely approaches that of many authorities and companies. Alvin Brown, Vice President, Johns-Manville Corporation, in his carefully defined analysis of organization, states, "Organization defines the part which each member of an enterprise is expected to perform and the relations between such members, to the end that their concerted endeavor shall be most effective for the purpose of the enterprise." [1]

Mooney and Reiley describe organization as ". . . the form of every human association for the attainment of a common purpose." They

[1] Alvin Brown, *Organization, a Formulation of Principle*, Hibbert Printing Company, New York, 1945, p. 6.

visualize it as the process of "relating specific duties or functions in a coordinated whole." In their treatment, they emphasize the "interrelation of duties as well as duties in themselves." [2]

In its organization manual, General Foods defines organization as "the plan by which a group of people pools its efforts toward designated objectives through definition and division of activities, responsibilities and authority."

PEOPLE OR STRUCTURE?

Is organization simply a structure, or does it also include the people of the company? This question arises continually to harass organization specialists. The only tenable answer is that organization is not people, any more than coordination and control are people. However, just as management planning, coordination, and control are always done for, and with respect to, the work of people, so with organization.

People have about the same relationship to the organization as the driver and passengers in an automobile have to the automobile itself. If we want to improve the effectiveness of the automobile in reaching its objectives, that is, improve it as a means of rapid, safe, and comfortable transportation, we can do a number of things. We can improve the design of the automobile to better adapt it to the people who will probably use it. We can modify it to better conform to the characteristics of the roads it will travel. We can alter the furnishings of the automobile or adjust certain of its mechanical features to human needs. Such flexibility is inherent in good design. The design of the automobile must always be predicated upon the characteristics of the people who will use it and the environment in which it is to be used. The automobile is neither the people nor the environment, but it is inextricably linked with both.

Organization is developed *for* people. To assume otherwise would be as fallacious as to assume that an automobile can be designed apart from the people who will drive it. However, just as it would be unwise to design an automobile exactly to fit the dimensions, personality, and tastes of one individual, because it would then be unlikely to fit the needs of anybody else, in the same way, the organization should not be tailored to fit individual personalities.

People who build an organization around themselves shape it to their day-to-day actions. They fit the mold because the mold is themselves. But the fit is never good for the next occupant. This is not to say that the new incumbent will be a perfect fit for even a well-organized job.

[2] James D. Mooney and Alan C. Reiley, *The Principles of Organization*, Harper & Brothers, New York, 1939, pp. 1–4.

It does mean that the work to be done should be so grouped that any one of a large number of persons with appropriate training and experience can perform it effectively.

CHANGING CONCEPTS OF ORGANIZATION

The concept that organization is a mechanism that enables people to work most effectively together brings into juxtaposition the old and new concepts—the mechanistic and the humanistic. The two are not irreconcilable.

The conflict in ideas ensues because of failure to consider the evolutionary nature of group—and hence, of modern business—effort. The dominant thinking in organization still tends to be that which prevailed during the formative years of the "scientific movement" in business, in terms of "scientific efficiency" and not "human efficiency." The two often are not parallel. Three concepts mark the evolution in thinking about human behavior:

The "Herd" Concept

Much of the early thinking underlying organization structure was based on the idea that people, especially those who performed manual labor, were an undifferentiated rabble that could be coaxed or coerced toward a definite goal only through the use of strict and authoritarian measures, such as rules and regulations, with accompanying punishments. This concept perhaps stems from military organization, with its regulations and disciplines, which prescribe the details of daily activity ranging from the manner in which belts must be worn to the recognition due a superior in the form of the hand salute. The herd concept places exclusive power to decide with the leader and enforces unquestioning obedience in his subordinates.

The Person-to-person Concept

Industrial organization has evolved from the herd concept. However, because of obvious inadequacies, the industrial model has varied in emphasis. Instead of viewing the supervisor as the leader of six or twelve or twenty faceless automatons, business organization tends to see each subordinate functioning in terms of a direct relationship with his superior. This relationship exists because of the direct and personal delegation of authority and responsibility from superior to subordinate.

The Group Concept

The modern theory of organization tends to carry this process one step farther. The person-to-person relationship of superior and subordinate is now seen to include the relationship of subordinate with subordinate, as well as with the superior. This has led to a natural and evolutionary development in thinking about organization of groups. In some instances, these new findings on group interaction and its effect on motivation and productivity have been taken as evidence that the older concepts of organization are not only outmoded but ineffective and that the best recourse is to discard the old concepts and to start afresh. The danger here, of course, is that the baby will be thrown out with the bath water. The business enterprise has need of some elements of all three conceptual approaches to organization.

FORMAL AND INFORMAL ORGANIZATION

We can further clarify the distinction between "humanistic" and "mechanistic" concepts by establishing that there is both a formal and an informal organization structure.

The Formal Organization

The formal organization is a system of well-defined jobs, each bearing a definite measure of authority, responsibility, and accountability, the whole consciously designed to enable the people of the enterprise to work most effectively together in accomplishing their objectives. The formal organization is characterized by being well-defined, bound by delegation, and relatively stable.

The formal organization is a more or less arbitrary structure to which the individual must adjust. It tells him to do certain things in a specified manner, to obey orders from designated individuals, and to work cooperatively with others.

The formal organization facilitates the determination of objectives and policies. A relatively fixed and predictable form of organization is necessary if the company is to forecast its probable future accomplishment. If there is not a constant organizational base, prognostication becomes no more reliable than soothsaying.

It is true that the capacities, attitudes, and character of the people within the organization will eventually determine the degree of success of these objectives; however, spontaneous predetermination of objectives is not likely to arise from the workings of the informal organization with enough consistency to warrant confidence in this means of initiating organizational goals.

Definite limits for the activities of people are set by the formal organization. Defined responsibilities and authority provide relatively fixed fences within which people can develop their own work areas to the maximum without encroaching on the work of others.

In the formal organization, the work that each individual does is part of a larger pattern. Except in the case of a few individuals at the top, no one person can see both the beginning and the end of the work he does. Because each person in the formal organization is, to an extent, working "blind," in terms of the over-all plans and objectives of the organization, he needs to have his part in the over-all activity spelled out for him; he cannot determine this for himself.

Coordination proceeds according to a prescribed pattern in the formal organization. People meet in committees to unify and time their joint activities. One person is required to check with another before proceeding. Word has to come from "upstairs" before a project can get under way.

Because of these arbitrary requirements, the formal organization tends to restrict and circumscribe the activities of individuals. It sets up boundaries, signposts, and pathways which must be followed.

The Informal Organization

The informal organization refers largely to what people do because they are human personalities—to their actions in terms of needs, emotions, and attitudes, not in terms of procedures and regulations. In the informal organization, people work together because of their personal likes and dislikes. In a large Middle Western bank, everybody goes to the executive vice president because he really "runs the company," while the president is only a figurehead. In a food chain with headquarters in New York, the boss's son is head of the marketing division, but subordinates go to the head of the sales administration department if they want a decision.

Informal groupings may extend to other groups, as well as existing *within* the organizational unit. For example, in a manufacturing company, the manager of sales promotion was assigned the responsibility of "promoting the development of new uses of the company's products." The sales promotion manager could perform certain parts of his job by himself, other portions he could delegate to two subordinates who were assigned to him. On occasion, he was able to get his boss to do some of his work for him. However, if the manager confined his efforts to these formal channels and relationships with other staff and line departments which were sanctioned by the formal organization, he would be able to do his job only slowly and in a cumbersome fashion.

To facilitate his work, he made use of informal organizational relationships as frequently as he needed them. When he wanted to discuss an idea with the engineering design section of the engineering department, the formal organization would require him first to go to his own boss, then to the head of engineering, and finally to the design engineer. Instead, he used the natural or spontaneous channel. Since the company economic analyst was concerned with his problem as well as the design engineer, he asked both to meet with him. It so happened that the design engineer had the strongest personality, the best grasp of the over-all problem, and the best insight into what people might or might not buy. When the meetings took place, even though the sales promotion manager had the problem, the design engineer took over active leadership of the discussion.

The effectiveness of this group depended upon informal relations: the recognition of a common goal and the desire to work together in accomplishing it. There are no principles of formal organization which apply to the formation or operation of such groups, but they are a commonplace and necessary part of the operation of every company. The formal organization which fails to recognize and provide for the effective operation of such groups loses its own effectiveness.

IMPORTANCE OF ORGANIZATION

Sound organization can contribute greatly to the continuity and success of the enterprise. This is often not apparent to the average businessman, who tends to equate sound organization with neatly drawn and symmetrical organization charts and to assign it to a subordinate who is not too busy with more important things. This attitude is understandable. But it overlooks the importance of organization to the long-term profitability of the company. As Lounsbury Fish points out,

> Organization is more than a chart—it is the mechanism through which management directs, coordinates and controls the business. It is, indeed, the foundation of management. If the organization plan is ill-designed, if it is merely a makeshift arrangement, then management is rendered difficult and ineffective. If, on the other hand, it is logical, clear-cut and streamlined to meet present-day requirements, then the first requisite of sound management has been achieved.[3]

Sound organization facilitates administration of the company and its parts, encourages growth and diversification, and helps improve the operation of the business as a whole.

Facilitates Administration

A properly designed and balanced organization facilitates both management and operation of the enterprise; inadequate organization may not only discourage but actually preclude effective administration.

[3] Lounsbury Fish, *Organization Planning*, American Management Association, General Management Series, no. 142, New York, 1948, p. 15. This also contains excellent suggestions for developing a sound organization.

Organizationally, the company may fail to provide for planning, organization, motivation, coordination, and control, and as a result these activities are not effectively accomplished. The assumption that managers will manage by instinct or common sense takes too much for granted. Management work takes place with certainty and continuity only if it is built into every management job and appropriate functional groups are provided to help managers to manage.

Many companies have analyzed the needs of their managers for management advice and service and have provided appropriate staff groupings to perform this work. Continental Oil Company, for example, is continually confronted with complex and extensive problems having to do with long-term planning of its operations and coordination of its widely separated exploration, production, manufacturing, transportation, and marketing operations. To provide assistance to both top and divisional management on these matters, the company organized a coordination and planning department which specializes in management assistance.

Lockheed Aircraft Corporation has exceedingly complex operating problems. The company must not only design, manufacture, test, and deliver aircraft and missile weapon systems but must also determine the specifications of components and subsystems and arrange for their development and delivery. To provide guidance for management decision and policy relating to good order and effective programing, particularly in the development of new products for the corporation, Lockheed has organized a Development Planning function which has primary responsibility for providing advice and service to corporate management on problems of long-range planning of its products and operations. This provides a valuable service to all managers concerned.

General Motors, as it increased in size and diversity, found a growing separation between its franchised dealers and the management of the company. It found that it could bridge the gap most effectively and provide for satisfactory coordination between top management, factory management, and dealers through organizational means, by creating a new function—the Executive Vice President in Charge of Dealer Relations.

The manner in which the total work is divided and grouped into organizational units may directly affect operating results. Important work may be subordinated, or it may be overlooked entirely. As a case in point, one chemical company which expanded rapidly during World War II concentrated heavily on production and marketing. Research was limited to development work on existing chemical products. The research and development department reported to the chief engineer who was an old-timer with the company, had a great deal of line experience in the company's largest plant, and was largely concerned with process development. Immediately after World War II, sales slumped badly because many of the company's products were being supplanted by entirely new chemical compounds. A management survey quickly identified the failure and led to the addition of a strong research department reporting directly to the chief executive.

Overload, which directly affects operating efficiencies, may stem from poor organization. In some cases, the work itself may be too unrelated for effective performance. In many plants, for example, such work as tool design, factory layout, tool stores, and plant engineering are scattered among many departments. Invariably the inclusion of an incompatible activity in a department creates unnecessary work. "I spend more time trying to find out what's going on in the tool room and why service is poor than I do with all the rest of my work put together," said the chief industrial engineer in one fabricating plant who should never have been assigned tool engineering.

Because of poor organization, the president may be so overwhelmed with decisions on routine matters and operating detail that he has neither the time nor the strength to do an adequate job of long-range planning. As a result, the company may lose its competitive position or turn in mediocre performance. In some cases the load on the top man is so heavy it proves fatal. In one manufacturing company, for example, two presidents died of heart failure within two years of one another. Asked to become the third incumbent of the top office, the executive vice president declined until a reorganization had been effected. He lived to retire after nine years in office.

Duplicate and waste motion due to poor organization are shown in the case of a large Middle Western food processing plant, where the responsibility for hiring employees had not been clearly assigned. The employment manager took it upon himself to hire and assign employees to jobs on requisition, without securing approval of the superintendent concerned. Since he was an old-timer in the plant, he was able to operate without opposition. However, a new superintendent with training in professional management was brought into the plant. He felt that he should have authority for hiring the people in his department and in some cases refused to go along with the employment manager on his choices. The silent struggle went on for almost a year. It was finally ended when the plant manager, who had occasion to pass in and out of the waiting room during the course of a prolonged union contract negotiation, noticed a man in a striking red shirt reading magazines. He became suspicious when the red shirt was still present on the third day and instituted an investigation. It turned out that the man was a new hand who had been hired by the employment manager but rejected by the superintendent because of his flamboyant taste in shirts. By the next morning, both the superintendent and the employment manager had permanently clarified their positions.

Poor organization often results in waste motion and expensive overlap in work. Investigation will usually reveal a surprising amount of duplicated effort in almost every company. This may range from the preparation of duplicate records and reports to the actual duplication of functions by managers and committees.

Clarification of work by organizational means is shown in Sylvania Electric Products, Inc. In analyzing the organization of a plant of 500 employees, Sylvania found 100 assigned to maintenance. Further investigation revealed that the Maintenance Department was actually performing the function of a Plant Engineering and Construction Department. This had come about because they had taken on the responsibility for renovating some areas previously used for storage and for installing production equipment in them. The procedure of setting up the production equipment included a "trial run" period. The original intention was that after this trial had been successfully completed, the new production facility would be turned over to the Production Department. However, this had not come about in several of the processes which required considerable mechanical skill. As a result of the analysis of the organization, a program for transferring such new activities to Production as soon as practicable was worked out. The Maintenance Department was reorganized and expanded into a Plant Engineering Department in line with the work it was actually performing in the organization.

Sound organization facilitates delegation. This is particularly true of managers who are so busily concerned with doing work that should be handled by subordinates that they have no time to perform their management responsibilities. The planned organization relieves this situation. By proper division of labor, consistent delegation, and clear job definition, the organization structure siphons off the routine duties and makes them the responsibility of lower rated positions. Ford Motor Company, for instance, finds that an organizational plan is in itself an orderly method for delegating responsibility. It frees executives so that they can devote most of their energies to planning and programing the work of their units and coordinating their efforts with other functions in the company.

Rockwell Manufacturing Company has used organization planning to reduce the number of operating responsibilities carried by executives. This frees them for policy formation and forward planning. It also enables them to delegate responsibility and authority for operating decisions closer to the operating levels.

Facilitates Growth and Diversification

The organization structure is the framework within which the company grows. Expansion and diversification can proceed no farther than the organization structure permits. Some types of organization are ideally suited to the small company in its early stages of growth; however, these same structures may prove inadequate as growth and diversification occur. The firm primarily concerned with day-to-day operations often grows beyond the scope of its existing organization and finds itself in a serious administrative crisis before it undertakes the necessary basic organization changes. On the other hand, the alert, *managed* enterprise anticipates the need for change to facilitate growth before it is hampered by shackles of its own making.

This is well borne out in the case of a large department store, which, faced with the challenge of suburban growth after World War II, began to build branch stores at strategically located centers of population. Three stores were opened during the first three years, but they failed to meet sales and profit expectations. Their volume was poor in relation to smaller, independent competition, and their profit ratios compared unfavorably with the main store.

After exhaustive study, the company found the reason: the suburban stores had simply been tacked on to the basic functional organization of the main store and were being treated as branches, with their major departments reporting to the functional heads in the main store. However, the suburban stores could not operate successfully as branches. Each had its own market characteristics; its customers had different demands and shopping habits; goods that sold well in the main store often did not do well in the suburbs. The conclusion was that each suburban store required its own individuality, to match its customer preferences, and hence also should have relatively independent command of some of its basic functions. The firm divisionalized on a geographic basis and decentralized. Within another three years, two of the stores had almost reached the sales volume of the main store and one had surpassed it.

General Mills has shown a successful pattern of anticipating and providing for organizational change to accommodate its growth and diversification. Formed by merger of a group of flour and feed companies in 1928, General Mills operated successfully under a basic functional, centralized organization for many years. However, by 1953, its flour, feed, and grocery business alone was 2½ times larger than the company as a whole in 1930, and the company had plans for further growth and diversification. From every indication, this growth promised to continue with vigor if properly encouraged.

Moving first to ensure continued successful growth of the core of its business, General Mills in 1953 divided the large Food Division into three products divisions: Grocery Products, Flour, and Feed. Anticipating a move toward further diversification, the company also broke out Chemical, Mechanical, Soybean, Institutional Products, Special Commodities, and the O-Cel-O Divisions. It thus organized for manufacture and sales of a broad line of products, which has contributed measurably, over the years, to the scope and profitability of the company.

Monsanto Chemical Company has also facilitated its continued growth and diversification by appropriate change in its organization. Monsanto was formed in 1901 in St. Louis by John F. Queeny, purchasing agent for a wholesale drug house. Known first as the Monsanto Chemical Works, the company manufactured saccharin, then added vanillin, caffeine, and other chemicals used in making pharmaceuticals and flavors.

Growth was highly successful under a functional, centralized organization. In 1939, realizing the need for organization change to accommodate its continued expansion, the company moved toward decentralization by establishing divisions, staff departments, and an Executive Committee of the Board. In the light of having doubled sales volume about every five years, Monsanto made further organization changes in 1954. It established a basic product division structure and further decentralized to the operating units. At the same time, in its Executive Offices of the President, it built up a strong, experienced management group to guide the forward progress of the company as a whole.

Provides for Optimum Use of Technological Improvements

New technological developments increasingly influence the need for more adequate organization structures and for understanding the proper forms of organization best designed to accommodate these new factors. A pertinent example is the increasing use of automatic controls and data processing. The high cost of installing, operating, and maintaining such equipment calls for concentration in one physical location. To some, this means centralization, with a reversal of any existing trend toward decentralization and the organizational forms that facilitate it.

However, this assumption fails to recognize that the use of equipment for automatic data recording and analysis may considerably strengthen the decentralized and divisionalized structure by helping to reinforce the efficiency and scope of the centralized *management* group. In fact, every company must be both centralized and decentralized, and placement of equipment to facilitate centralized decision making should, logically, be at a central location. This principle is of particular importance to the company initiating a long-term automated installation.

Encourages Human Use of Human Beings

The organization structure can profoundly affect the people of the company. As we have seen, organization has often been considered a problem of how to arrange work most efficiently, with subsequent adaptation of people to the work being done. This mechanistic concept stems from the early findings of scientific management, which demonstrated that startling improvements in productivity could be obtained through analysis and rearrangement of the work being performed and specialization of the people doing the work. Unwavering emphasis upon specialization, however, has given rise to problems almost as great as those which it helped overcome. On the assembly line, specialization has led to monotony, boredom, and frustration, with accompanying psychological unbalance and distress.

Countermeasures in the interests of human use of human beings have had significant results. One company reorganizes its production lines so that people can work in teams and not like robots. The improvement in morale and productivity is measurable and immediate. Another company changes its basic organization structure so that a large sales department is broken into small, cohesive groups. Product sales spurt immediately. In still another instance, a company reorganizes so that it can break up its mammoth drafting rooms, in which hundreds upon hundreds of draftsmen perform in maddening anonymity, into small units, each with its own identity and goals. The drop in turnover and increase in drawings per man-hour is perceptible at once.

The Upjohn Company during its long history has made use of organization to improve the morale and productivity of its employees. Upjohn was founded in 1883, in Kalamazoo, Michigan, by Dr. W. E. Upjohn. In those days, the pills in common use tended to harden into impenetrable masses, very difficult and uncertain of assimilation. Dr. Upjohn improved the process by inventing a method of rolling powder into "friable pills." With his three brothers, he built the early Upjohn Pill and Granule Company into a leading producer of pharmaceuticals, with operations throughout the United States and in foreign countries.

From its early days, when, as a Kalamazoo newspaper of 1886 put it, "notwithstanding the fact that most of the work is performed by machinery invented by a member of the firm, six or seven hands are kept constantly employed packing the finished product," Upjohn has been highly mechanized. However, in its growth from "six or seven" to more than 4,000 people, the company has continually stressed the importance of high morale and has made organizational provision for most effective employment of its people. For example, it has organized its production groups so that machine operators can rotate to different types of work at short intervals. As a result, it finds that interest and productivity tend to go up, errors and absenteeism to go down.

The organization structure may have a strong influence on the development of managers. In some cases, the organization tends to encourage a high degree of centralization and there is little delegation of authority. When this is the case, most decisions are made by some central group. As a result, supervisors and middle managers have little or no opportunity to exercise their administrative muscles; when needed, they may be found incapable of filling top executive positions.

There are other reasons related to organization which prevent managers from developing. The company may fail to create positions suitable for training purposes. Consequently, members of the management group do not have opportunity to move from job to job so that they can master the principles of administration as well as of a technical specialty.

If the boss has too many people reporting to him, he may not have time to carry out his responsibilities. If there are too many levels in the organization, a man may not encounter problems of more than local significance until he has risen so high that he is almost foredoomed to a narrow viewpoint.

Stimulates Creativity

Sound organization stimulates independent, creative thinking and initiative by providing well-defined areas of work with broad latitude for the development of new and improved ways of doing things. There is often a feeling that the very act of organization restricts and hampers the people involved. Poor, inept organization will do this. However, people are also handicapped when there is no systematic organization, with the result that work is divided by main force and aggressiveness and authority is exercised as indiscriminately as a whip.

Properly conceived, the organization structure will demand creative results from creative people and will drain routine and repetitive work to supporting positions. By establishing clear-cut accountability, it will provide recognition for the professional and the specialist in terms of their achievement.

SUMMARY

Organization is a mechanism or structure that enables living things to work effectively together. The basic elements of organization are division of labor, a source of authority, and relationships. This is true of all forms of living organizations.

Management organization, in these terms, means first identifying the work that must be accomplished to attain objectives, then grouping that work in logically related and balanced positions. Responsibility and authority are then defined and delegated. As a final step, relationships are established between positions and units to facilitate harmonious teamwork.

Changing concepts of organization require distinction between the formal, defined, and highly structured organization and the informal, personal organization. Both kinds exist and are necessary. The aim of the manager should be to develop a formal organization of such scope as to encompass the varying, highly personal needs of the informal organization. Organization, as described, is extremely important to the business enterprise. It facilitates administration, encourages sound, balanced growth and diversification, provides for best use of human beings, and stimulates creativity.

CHAPTER 4 *Designing the Company Organization Structure*

There is a common assumption that the design of the company organization structure is largely a matter of striking an acceptable balance among an assortment of rectangles on an organization chart. This is a fallacy. The organization depicts the structure that has been created. It is the last step in design, not the first. Even experienced practitioners find it difficult to describe the process they follow in designing the basic structure. Much of their work is intuitive. From long experience, they *know* that certain kinds of work belong together, that others are incompatible. There are few accepted principles of design and no step-by-step procedures which give detailed instructions for determining what kind of structure is needed and how it can be built.

There are good reasons for the nebulous state of the art. Few managements are ever confronted with the need to organize from scratch. The early growth of most businesses is haphazard and the first form of organization almost always occurs fortuitously. Since personal leadership prevails in the early years and success depends upon the talents of individual personalities, the structure tends to be built around the personal abilities and interests of the people available within the company. Many a treasurer has become purchasing agent because he was closest to the cash box. In more than one company, production control has been thrown in with industrial engineering because only the industrial engineer knew what was involved in scheduling, dispatching, and inventory control.

DETERMINING THE DESIGN

Organization design is almost invariably reorganization of the existing structure. The first problem is to decide what kind of structure the company needs. We must determine what kind of work must be performed in the organization and how we should arrange that work for most effective performance. We can arrive at the best answers first, by identifying the primary work of the organization in terms of its objectives; second, by arranging this work in properly grouped and balanced packages; and third, by arranging for a proper span of supervision for each management position.

Organize in Terms of Objectives

The organization as a whole exists for the purpose of accomplishing predetermined objectives. All work done in the organization should be dedicated to this end; if it does not contribute to objectives, the work is not necessary and should not be performed. This is true also for each element of the organization. Each section, department, and division should have clearly defined objectives which are part of the total objectives of the organization and consonant with them.

An Eastern food processing company provides an example of the need for determining objectives before organizing. This company set, as a ten-year objective, broadening of its canned fruits and vegetables line to include frozen products, prepared food specialties, and sauces and condiments. The company forecast a sales increase of over $10 million in five years, contrasted to its current rate of barely over $1 million yearly increase.

The company prepared for this growth and implemented it organizationally by making provision for several new kinds of work to be performed in the organization. It added product development and research and new sales and manufacturing units and broadened staff support. All this in turn led to reorganization of the basic structure of the company as a whole to accommodate the anticipated growth and diversification.

A sound statement of objectives will in itself identify the major kinds of work to be performed and hence the primary line activities of the company. For example, if the basic objective of the company is to develop, manufacture, and market a given line of products at a profit, we can quickly identify the basic activities of the organization as research and development, manufacturing, and sales.

These primary, or line functions, represent the end activity of the enterprise. The organization itself exists primarily to effectuate, improve, and expedite these functions. Organization as a management activity must be devoted to proper identification of this basic work and to provision of adequate management positions and grouping of advisory and service agencies to facilitate it. Conformance to this principle is a basic requirement of soundly organized management effort.

Organize From Bottom Up and Top Down

We must recognize the need for organizing from the bottom up, as well as from the top down. Conventional organization planning starts with the job of the manager of the organizational element, or of the president, if the company as a whole is being organized, and breaks this up in a series of delegations and redelegations until the zone of contact and performance is reached. This approach is necessary to explain and analyze the delegation of responsibility and authority and the establishment of accountability once the organization structure is established. However, if we are concerned with designing an organization for the marketing function, we do not start with the marketing vice president and divide and subdivide his job. Rather, we first discover what kinds of work the marketing function must perform to accomplish its end results. We organize the end activity first. We next decide what positions we need to manage this primary work. And, finally, we determine what management positions must be created to manage the managers. At this juncture also we separate line from staff, as will be described in a later chapter. Only in this way can we identify the important and necessary work that must be done in the organization.

Group Related Work Together

Grouping is the process of arranging work to form positions, functions, and other organizational elements. To provide for most effective performance, closely related work should be grouped together.

The problem in grouping is deciding what belongs with what. Should safety be placed with personnel or manufacturing? Does plant engineering more properly belong with engineering or production? Finding the proper solution to grouping problems can be of far-reaching importance to the company. For example, in one mining company, market research was placed in the finance department because it seemed mostly concerned with figures, income predictions, and statistical computations. Only after severe inroads had been made in the company's markets by new plastic, glass, resin, and compressed wood products did it awaken to the fact that market research should properly concern itself with the customer's needs and requirements and hence was a marketing, not a finance function.

Since grouping is the process of building balanced packages of work to accomplish objectives, the best method of deciding what work should be placed in a function is to evaluate its placement in terms of the purpose of that function. If we want to do a sound job of organizing the marketing function, for example, we first must decide specifically what we want the function to accomplish. If the purpose of marketing is to discover what demand exists for present and potential products of the company, to recommend manufacture of appropriate products, to sell the products, and to service customers to ensure continued satisfaction, we have a clear-cut indication as to the specific kinds of work that should be placed in marketing. Certainly this would include market development, field sales, sales promotion, advertising, and sales service. Do we want to know whether tool design belongs with production control or manufacturing engineering? If we decide that the purpose of production control is to provide advice and service in the movement and storage of materials from beginning to end of the production process, the proper placement of tool design becomes obvious.

Balance the Groupings

Sound grouping is balanced grouping. Each function should be given its proper emphasis with respect to its basic purpose in the organization. No primary function should be permitted to dominate. If the company is equally dependent upon marketing and manufacturing, both must have equal organizational status. The company that gives prominence to finance, for example, will tend to fall behind in sales, or manufacturing, or engineering; the sales-dominated company will lose out on product innovation, quality, or some other vital factor which has been given an organizational back seat.

Establish an Appropriate Span of Supervision

The span of supervision, or so-called "span of control," refers to the number of people one manager can supervise. The classic solution offers numerical limits for the span of supervision. The best known of these formulas [1] places a limit of five or six at the top and twenty at the bottom levels. Under this arrangement, with six levels it is possible theoretically to accommodate 62,500 workers and 3,905 executives.

Arbitrary designation of limits is misleading. In practice, the span of supervision may vary widely. For example, one large commercial organization has two major organizational components, one devoted to retail outlets, the other to assembly and packaging of the product. The retail side of the business is made up of store units of various sizes. The stores are highly standardized and operate under strong policy direction from central headquarters. Procedures are well developed and followed closely in all the stores. Because of the standardization achieved and the similarity in problems encountered in store operation, one

---

[1] See V. A. Graicunas, "Relationship in Organization," in Luther Gulick and L. Urwick (eds.), *Papers on the Science of Administration*, The Institute of Public Administration, New York, 1937, pp. 183–187.

manager can supervise twenty to thirty stores. There are only four levels from company president to first-line management. In the assembly and packaging side of the business the span of supervision runs from five to ten and there are from five to seven levels of management. This example illustrates some of the factors that determine the span of supervision.

The number of subordinates a manager can supervise will vary in terms of the type of management and organization in which he operates, the character of the work he supervises, the nature of the staff assistance available to him, and the capabilities of his line subordinates.

Influence of Type of Management and Organization. The number of subordinates a manager can supervise is limited, because human capacity is limited. A manager has only a specified amount of time during the working day during which he can supervise. What he does during that time determines the number of people whom he can contact and personally motivate. It is obvious that the manager who has to arrive at an individual decision for every problem that comes up will spend more time making decisions than the manager who anticipates repetitive problems and makes policy decisions to apply whenever the problem arises. For example, most company top managers spend a good deal of time deciding how to capitalize new plant additions and equipment. Can we afford this facility? Can we borrow money to install this improvement now, or should we wait until next year? One large company has eliminated the need for much of this by arriving at a policy decision: no money will be borrowed; all growth will be financed by reinvestment of profits.

Clear and comprehensive policy statements at all levels reduce the volume of personal decision making required of a manager and hence increase his span of supervision. This applies also to other administrative processes that predecide problems. Definitions of responsibility and authority decide what work is to be done, who is to do it, and what powers he has to perform. Performance standards predetermine the yardsticks by which a person's work is to be measured. Programs decide what schedule of activities is to be followed. Procedures dictate how work will be performed. Budgets provide a standing answer to the question, "How much money can I spend?" Predeterminations such as these decrease the number of decisions the manager has to make and increase his potential span of supervision.

Influence of Character of the Work Supervised. The nature of the work the manager directly supervises has an influence on his span of supervision. If the work is uniform and highly standardized, the manager has the greatest opportunity to establish relatively permanent policy and procedures because the problems that arise tend to follow a pattern.

For example, a district manager in one chain store organization can effectively supervise thirty candy store managers because his product is shipped to his stores from a central candy kitchen; store layout, display, and promotion are highly standardized by company headquarters; the marketing pattern is constant; and few emergency decisions have to be made.

But consider the case of a company that runs a chain of small discount stores in several cities. Here a district manager finds his capacity taxed by five or six stores. Competitive factors are more intense; the stores are harried by the unfriendly attitude of local merchants and the outright opposition of some manufacturers. There is little policy or procedure to guide him, so the store manager is forced constantly to refer to headquarters or to try to gather facts and decide himself on most operating and management problems.

Influence of Staff Assistance. The capacity of the manager to supervise is determined by the character and amount of work he reserves for his own performance. If he has assistance in performing his reserved responsibilities, he will obviously be able to bear a greater load. When specialized staff is organized with sufficient scope and coverage, accountable managers have available a full range of expert advice and service in the major technical and administrative areas of their jobs. If he can call upon internal consultants for this help, the manager can free himself for those parts of his job which only he can perform effectively—and this will include a maximum supervisory span.

Personal staff can also help the manager free himself of detail. However, since personal staff shares the work of the manager but cannot independently exercise any of his authority, effective use of assistants requires fairly close supervision on the part of the manager. The accountable manager, in supervising assistants, generally finds himself supervising the performance of routine and detail work. The time and energy he devotes to supervising an administrative assistant, for example, might be upgraded to supervision of an additional subordinate line manager. This increase in his span of supervision would be conditioned, of course, upon his ability to delegate to other agencies the work he would otherwise assign to his personal staff. It is at this point that provision of a full line of specialized staff services and effective delegation to line subordinates is most important.

The presence of specialized staff alone will not broaden the manager's span of supervision. Everything depends upon his ability to delegate fully and effectively to these agencies, so that they will be able to take over parts of his work and perform it for him. This requires not only capable staff but also the kind of working relationship that engenders mutual faith and confidence.

Influence of Line Subordinates. Closely allied to the availability of staff in determining the potential span of supervision is the capability of line subordinates. In most operating matters, the accountable manager should be able to delegate practically all detail and routine to his subordinate line managers. For example, the marketing manager should be able to delegate to his regional sales managers the work of actually selling the products, without personal supervision of their sales activities.

TYPES OF COMPANY ORGANIZATION STRUCTURE

Design of the company organization is ordinarily considered a matter of choice among a larger number of alternatives. If we shop around, we can discover that there are line, line-and-staff, and staff type organizations. There are also committee and decentralized types. However, if we study a large number of companies, we find that all are both line and staff, all have committees, and all are decentralized to some extent. Attempting to classify organizations in these terms is about as useful as trying to differentiate a Pacific type locomotive by saying it has wheels.

The manager concerned with selecting the type or organization best suited to the needs of his company has only two major alternatives—the functional and the divisionalized types of company organization structure. Since almost every company begins its existence with a functional type of structure, the decision in company organization design is *at what point should the company change from a functional to a divisionalized type of organization?* If divisionalization is indicated, choice must then be made between product and geographic groupings.

Once the decision as to type of organization is reached, a corollary decision can be made with respect to the extent to which authority is to be decentralized within this structure. However, it should be noted—and this will be emphasized later—that while the type of organization may facilitate decentralization, the process of decentralization itself may take place within either a functional or divisionalized structure.

FUNCTIONAL TYPE ORGANIZATION

As we have seen, most companies are founded by one or a few people, who are primarily concerned with creating a business to express and satisfy their own personal abilities and ambitions. The new enterprise, typically, is small; all work is closely supervised by the proprietor; its operations must be flexible and its decisions swift. The natural emphasis is on operations rather than management, because the immediate problem and the need to get things done seems more pertinent and immediate than planning for tomorrow. The best vehicle for this type of operation in the young, small business enterprise is a functional organization structure.

The development of S. C. Johnson & Son, Inc., illustrates this point. When S. C. Johnson founded the company in 1886, he *was* the company. For five days of the week he traveled through the country selling parquetry flooring. The sixth day he was in Racine arranging for the filling of his orders in a plant comprising two men and two boys.

As his sales increased, Mr. Johnson had to add more factory employees. To conserve the amount of time he needed to spend in supervision, he put one man in charge of the others at the factory. On the sales end, his customers continued to increase until he could not handle them alone. He employed a salesman, then another, until it took all his time just to direct them. His secretary became advertising manager. Troubles with new products created a need for a chemist and later led to establishment of a laboratory. Gradually, as the business grew, department heads were added until there was a fully developed organization with research, production, sales, advertising, and financial functions. Thus we see the business developing under personal leadership, with centralized authority, and in terms of a functional organization structure.

Characteristics of the Functional Organization

The functional structure is the building block of organization. It is the module from which other forms are built. It is formed by grouping all the work to be done into major functional departments or divisions; that is, all related work of one kind is placed in one organization com-

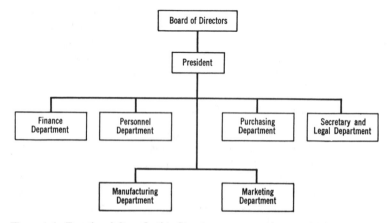

Figure 4–1. Functional Organization Structure

ponent under one coordinating head. Thus the manager of manufacturing is responsible and accountable for all manufacturing work done throughout the company, in all plants and for all product lines. The same would hold true for marketing, engineering, personnel, finance, and other major kinds of work.

In a company organized for the purpose of manufacturing metal and plastic products, a functional type structure appears as shown in Figure 4–1, page 78. Notice that each major function is coordinated at the top of the function. In this case, both metal and plastic products are manufactured in the same plant. Both lines are sold by a common sales force.

Typical also of the functional organization is that of the Atlantic Refining Company (Figure 4–2, page 80). Here the primary functional divisions are crude oil production, manufacturing, transportation, and marketing. The refining operations both in Texas and Pennsylvania report to the manufacturing head; crude oil exploration and production activities, both foreign and domestic, report to the crude oil production manager; marine, pipe line, and other forms of transportation report to the transportation general manager; and both domestic and foreign marketing are accountable to the marketing general manager.

The staff departments in Atlantic Refining are shown on the bottom level of the chart. Here, again, we find functional division, with accounting units reporting to the controller, personnel units reporting to the general manager of industrial relations, and so forth.

Key to understanding of the strengths and weaknesses of the functional organization is its method of growth. When the functional structure undertakes additional work, the addition is made to the existing functions. If a new product is manufactured or sold, if additional engineering is undertaken, the added positions and departments are made part of the existing functional structure (Figure 4–3, page 82). Each function grows by adding layers to the base of the pyramid and to the span of supervision and number of levels reporting to each manager within the functional pyramid. Thus growth becomes a process of horizontal and vertical elaboration.

Advantages of the Functional Structure

The functional type of structure has many assets if properly utilized. It facilitates specialization, economy of operation, economic flexibility, and helps make the abilities of a few outstanding individuals available to the enterprise as a whole.

Facilitates Specialization. When the organization is grouped in terms of the work to be done, emphasis upon specialization is built into the organization. Each manager below the chief executive is concerned with only one kind of work and can concentrate all his energies upon it, with minimum diversion.

The pattern of growth of the functional organization encourages the development of a hierarchy of skills, which roughly correspond to the various levels of the organization. The larger the group, the greater the variety of skills available and the more expert become people within the functional groupings. Thus a company which depends for success upon highly specialized skills can keep intact longest the skills it develops by retention of a functional organization.

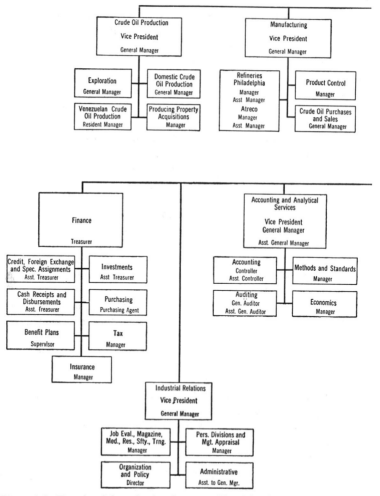

Figure 4–2. Functional Organization Structure, The Atlantic Refining Company

Specialization leads to competitive advantage. By throwing its limited resources into one specialized type of work or by emphasizing the engineering, manufacturing, and sales of one specialized product, even the small company can compete with the giant corporation on quantity, delivery, and price. A small plastics molder in New Jersey, using his

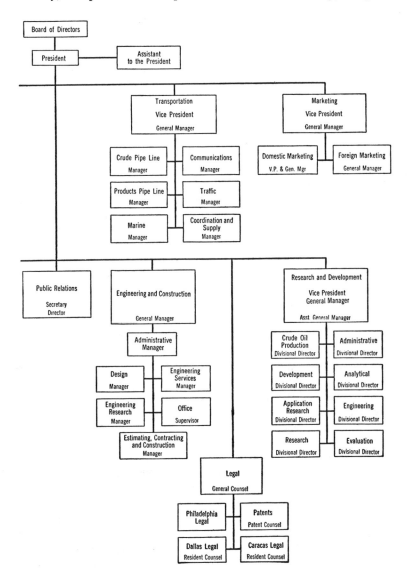

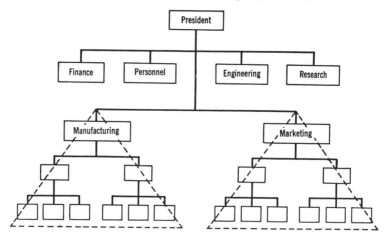

Figure 4–3. Pyramidal Growth of Functional Structure

garage as his plant, for example, regularly bests his larger competitors in local markets by providing highly speciaiized products and services which do not require large capital investment. A small food manufacturer marketing condiments in two boroughs of New York City outsells its larger competitor trying to sell fifty food lines including condiments.

The advantages of specialization are retained only so long as the company is able to keep its primary effort focused on one or a very few closely related products. When the company diversifies, it quickly becomes a "Jack-of-all-trades and master of none" if one functional group tries to handle all engineering, another all manufacturing, a third all sales, and so forth.

Texas Instruments, Inc., for example, found that the functional organization which had served it well as a highly specialized company making reflection seismograph surveys rapidly became inadequate as it diversified and began to compete with the industry giants in transistors, semiconductors, and electromechanical and optical instruments. National Distillers, once a specialist in distilled spirits, broadened into chemicals, titanium, and zirconium. Finding that its highly specialized skills in the liquor business, exercised through a functional organization, were inadequate to the new and varied demands of its diversified operations, it reorganized to meet the new challenge.

Facilitates Coordination within the Function. Because one man heads up all of one kind of work, coordination *within* functions is simplified in the functional structure. Contrast to this the problem in many divisionalized companies, where, for instance, individual production managers may develop new and useful devices and short cuts which could be of great value to other units of the company. Frequently these ideas are not circulated because of the difficulty of maintaining contact between the unrelated product groups.

In a functional organization, the functional head gives budget approval to build the new device; requests for technical or administrative assistance go to him; he clears the new procedure, method, or quality specification. This coordination automatically results in prompt application of the innovation to all other problems of similar nature.

This coordination also ensures uniformity of performance. If quality standards are high in one operation of a functional manufacturing department, they tend to be high in others. If one field sales crew is aggressive and forceful, there is likelihood that this will be true of the other sales crews. A unity of management and direction and the tendency for the standards and characteristics of the leader of the functional group to filter down through all levels usually gives rise to uniformly high—or low—performance. This may be a strength but, of course, it can also be a weakness.

Promotes Economy of Operation. The functional type structure is economical. Since all products are manufactured by one administrative unit, there is a tendency to make maximum use of the available machinery, equipment, and facilities. Functional organization, for example, encourages consolidation of the manufacturing of different products in the same plant location and facilitates common use of office space. This leads to more complete utilization of the available facilities, with accompanying economies. If each product is housed and administered separately, as is common in divisionalization, each requires a large enough plant to meet peak production requirements. However, if the total floor space is shared by several products, as is more often true in the functional organization, one expansion area can serve all.

Operation of the functional organization units minimizes staff and administrative expense. With production facilities combined, the costs of receiving, shipping, maintenance, plant protection, and, to some extent, engineering, can be pooled. Shipments can be consolidated. The same specialized personnel, purchasing, and accounting staff can serve all units.

Allows Economic Flexibility. Another advantage that derives from the pyramidal development of the organization structure is the ease of decreasing or expanding the size of the function without sacrificing its resources of skill and experience. Since the highest skills and greatest experience are concentrated in the higher levels of the pyramid, the function as a whole can be cut by eliminating positions at the lower levels without seriously affecting its total performance. Expansion can proceed in the same fashion, by adding lower skills to the bottom of the pyramid.

Projects Outstanding Skills. As we have already indicated, personal, centralized leadership enables one outstanding individual to embody his special skills in every activity of the company. We should note that this kind of leadership is best exercised through a functional organization structure. The reason for this is that, in the functional organization structure, only the president is so placed, organizationally, as to be able to coordinate problems and make decisions having to do with one or more of the major functions. As a result, the structure itself forces all such decisions to the top and ensures that the special abilities of the chief executive can be transmitted to the point of action in most of the important affairs of the company.

It was personal leadership, operating within a functional organization, for example, that enabled John F. Dryden to introduce a concept of industrial insurance, for the "little man," in the infant Prudential Friendly Society and to push it so energetically and persistently that it soon permeated the entire company.

Aluminum Company of America secured its ascendancy in aluminum through the outstanding abilities of three men operating in a functional type organization structure. Charles Martin Hall, who had invented an electrolytic process for separating aluminum, gave the company its technical foundation and built into it a continuing emphasis on "creative imagineering." Alfred E. Hunt, its first president, provided administrative leadership. Arthur Vining Davis, by tireless search for new markets for the infant metal and endless zeal in promoting its virtues, created demand first for novelties and cooking utensils, later for large-volume castings, forgings, sheet, and transmission lines.

The Goodyear Tire and Rubber Company owes its dynamic early growth to three outstanding personalities operating in a functional organization. Frank A. Seiberling, the aggressive and imaginative entrepreneur who headed the company during its early years, saw the potential in the infant automobile industry and coupled his company to it. P. W. Litchfield, as manufacturing head, established the engineering and manufacturing standards which gave the company a leading position in the industry. G. M. Stadelman, the first sales head, conceived and developed the company's pattern of nationwide distribution and later created demand for "new-fangled" balloon tires on the part of automobile owners.

WHEN TO CHANGE?

When the enterprise is small and operating under personal, centralized leadership, the advantages of the functional type organization heavily outweigh its disadvantages. However, as the company grows in size and diversity, the drawbacks tend to increase almost geometrically. Specialization and the tendency toward centralization of authority eventually result in a monolithic and inflexible structure. Many levels arise between the centralized authority who makes decisions and the people who carry out his directives. More and more people report to each supervisor. Communications slow down because of the long and cumbersome channels they must traverse. Precedent tends to become the law because of the vast amount of time and energy it takes to modify or question that which has already been approved.

There is no categorical answer as to the proper point at which to change. This is a matter for careful analysis and judgment. In some cases, change is indicated while the company is relatively small. Although the dangers of trying to compare companies in terms of dollar amounts of sales must be recognized,[2] as a rough figure, some companies should undertake change at a sales volume of $10 million or even less. In other instances, a functional structure may be best suited to the needs of the enterprise even after it reaches a volume of hundreds of millions of dollars.

General Motors operated well enough under a functional organization to stay at the top of its industry past $500 million sales volume, $605 million assets, and 81,000 employees, when it divisionalized in 1920. Boeing Airplane Company maintained a functional organization to the $853 million mark in sales, $256 million assets, and 65,000 employees. Nationwide Insurance retained a basic functional organization structure until 1951, with over $108 million assets and 4,431 employees.

These companies were characteristically highly specialized while functional, and each provided a single product or service or a narrow integrated range of products.

Many companies change from a functional to a divisionalized structure at a much smaller size. Characteristically, these smaller companies are more highly diversified or have plans for diversification. Aeroquip Corporation, manufacturer of flexible hose lines, couplings, straps, clamps, and fittings, changed in 1955, when it had a sales volume of $25 million, $14 million assets, and 1,400 employees. Manning, Maxwell & Moore, Inc., manufacturers of gauges, valves, industrial instruments, aircraft engine controls, cranes, and hoists, changed from a functional type of organization structure to a divisionalized, decentralized organization in late 1955, with $34 million net sales, $29 million assets, and 3,100 employees. The first year of the change, company sales shot up to $46 million and assets to $34 million. Much of this improvement the company attributes to the reorganization.

[2] It is obviously difficult to compare sales volume of companies with products varying as widely as a $2 casting, a $2,000 automobile, and a $2 million airplane. Dollar volume is used here only as a very approximate measure. Total assets and number of employees are also quoted, where applicable, as further indices.

As a rough approximation, we find that the transition point for the growing, *diversified* company seems to occur most commonly somewhere between $25 and $100 million in sales volume. This is often the danger zone in which the company outgrows the capacity of the men, the administrative techniques, and the organization which were adequate to carry it to its first success.

INDICATIONS FOR CHANGE

What warning signs alert us to need for change from a basic functional structure? First signs are usually excessive centralization, delays in decision making, difficulties in coordination between functions, managerial deficiencies, and difficulty in establishing controls.

Excessive Centralization

As we have noted, the functional organization tends to force *coordinating decisions,* that is, those which involve two or more different activities, to the top of the organizational pyramid. This tendency increases with the size of the company because, as the operating units become further separated from their coordinating heads, they also tend to become more remote from their opposite numbers in other functions. There is an increasing tendency to refer problems and decisions to the top because this is the only point at which sufficient information or a broad enough viewpoint is available for effective decision making.

Delays in Decision Making

A corollary handicap arises in that the more levels added to the functional organization, the more difficult it is for decisions to filter from top to bottom of the enterprise. This invariably results in slowing of action at the operating levels, decreased flexibility, and unwillingness of first-line supervisors to exercise initiative.

The Prudential Insurance Company of America, for example, found that its growing functional organization made it increasingly difficult to make prompt, effective decisions on such matters as local investments in California, Indiana, and Canada when the functional head in the Newark central office had to approve each transaction. The physical distances involved, the many layers of organization that had to be crossed, and the number of hands and minds that had to deal with the problem proved effective impediments to speedy and decisive action.

Overt signs of difficulty in decision making often appear. One is the multiplication of assistant and assistant to positions. As top executives become overloaded, they attempt to add more eyes and ears to themselves by appointing assistants of various kinds. This improvisation does not get at the real cause of the difficulty however, and usually serves only to forestall the inevitable.

The functional structure encourages narrowness of managerial viewpoint. Because he is concerned only with his own specialty, the functional specialist often fails to relate his performance or the cost of his function to the business as a whole. Characteristic of this attitude is the engineer in a heavy machinery plant in Philadelphia, who insisted on designing his own bolts and fasteners although adequate stock materials were available. Evident also are the "frills" which tend to develop in public relations, advertising, and personnel functions with little or no economic justification. These problems exist in every form of organization so far as the so-called "intangible" functions are concerned. However, it is easier to establish a criterion of profitability if the intangible function is not an end in itself but can be related directly to the manufacture and sale of a given product.

Difficulty in Exercising Control

It is more difficult to measure and evaluate results in a functional type of organization. A control is effective only to the extent that a yardstick or standard exists to measure performance. The functional organization provides few logical control points. Since the one manufacturing department manufactures all products and marketing sells the complete line, it is difficult to break out the costs of making and selling individual products in the line. "Common pot" accounting is encouraged and comparative cost analysis becomes unlikely. Chrysler Corporation, for example, encountered this difficulty with a functional structure. Chrysler found that it could not determine accurately how much it cost to make a Plymouth, a Dodge, or a De Soto, nor could it discover how much profit it was making—or losing—on each type of automobile. This is not peculiar to Chrysler. It is significant that both General Motors and Ford encountered the same problem when they operated with a functional organization and that both found the best solution in divisionalization.

Shortages in Management Talent

The functional organization structure does little to encourage development of managerial talent. Since there are few over-all coordinating positions and, in fact, only one which coordinates the total product interests, there are few opportunities for managers to learn to manage in terms of the entire range of functions that go to make up the enterprise. Hence there is, characteristically, a chronic shortage of people who have the broad training or experience necessary for top executive positions.

Difficulties in Coordination among Functions

Close coordination among functions is necessary for effective operation of the enterprise as a whole. However, in the functional type organization, the interests of each of the functional units is identified with one kind of work going into the product and not with the product itself. As a result, the functional unit tends to be insular, jealous of its prerogatives, and inherently difficult to coordinate.

The organizational group which is to achieve high production needs to develop strong internal loyalties and to present a united front to outsiders. This cohesion can be advantageous to a divisionalized organization, because it helps develop competition among divisions. It may be something of a liability in a functional organization because cooperation is mandatory and competition among functions is often detrimental to the product itself.

As is true with decision making, coordination tends to be forced to the top of the functional organization. This makes coordination laborious and often means that the people whose work is being coordinated have little or no say in the process.

One indication of difficulty in coordination is the creation of many committees and coordinating positions. Some companies use committees with great effectiveness. Theoretically, at least, the committee can simplify the problem of coordination by bringing together the coordinators in one place. Superimposed on a basically inadequate organization, however, the committee often proves to be inadequate both as a communication device and as a decision-making agency.

Coordinating positions are often created to establish links between intermediate levels of the organizational pyramids which go to make up the various functions. For example, an engineering coordinator may work with market research people, manufacturing engineering, and the design engineers. However, this type of coordination fails to bring together the decision-making managers; it merely facilitates exchange of information and viewpoints at the operating levels. While this is not without value, it fails of the necessary result.

Retention of a basic functional structure is indicated while the company is small, the product range is narrow, production facilities are concentrated in a few locations, there is a fairly consistent marketing pattern, and major competitors continue to operate with a functional structure. Sooner or later, consideration must be given to divisionalization in greater or lesser degree.

SUMMARY

The company wishing to develop the organization structure best suited to its needs can simplify its task by recognizing that there are only two basic forms of company organization structure—the functional, in which all work of the same kind is put into one organizational unit; and the divisionalized, in which all the different kinds of work necessary to accomplish a specific end result are put into one organizational unit. The different kinds of work required to make up a division may be grouped either on a product or a geographic basis.

The problem of organization is simplified by the fact that every company starts with a basic functional organization. The question for the company is: At what point should it start a move toward divisionalization? The functional organization is the structure of choice while the company is small, and has only one or a closely related group of products. Here the functional organization encourages specialization, facilitates coordination, is most economical, provides economic flexibility and ready projection of outstanding skills of one or a few top people to the primary activities of the company.

Change is indicated largely by factors which result from growth and diversification. Thus, centralization becomes excessive; there is increasing delay in decision making; it becomes difficult to exercise effective controls; coordination between functions diminishes; and shortages in management talent occur.

CHAPTER 5 *Divisionalization*

Divisionalization is a means of dividing the large and monolithic functional organization into smaller, flexible administrative units. This move enables the company to recapture some of the advantages of the small, functional organization, while minimizing the disadvantages that come with increasing size, diversity, and dispersion.

The divisionalized structure is formed by creation of a series of relatively small, autonomous units at the periphery of the organization. Divisionalization can proceed either in terms of product or geography. Product divisionalization places major emphasis upon the end results to be accomplished—the product or service being created and offered for sale. Geographic divisionalization focuses the major effort of the company upon the needs of the markets being served.

PRODUCT DIVISIONALIZATION

The product division structure involves establishing each product or group of closely related products as a relatively autonomous, integrated unit within the framework of the company as a whole. Such primary functions as manufacturing, sales, engineering, finance, and personnel are dedicated to the interests of the product itself. This brings a change of emphasis from the work being performed to the product or service being manufactured and sold. When a product division is broken out completely, it should be relatively self-sufficient. Within the grouping should be placed all the activities necessary to effective operation.

As a specific example, in a company organized for the purpose of manufacturing and selling metal and plastic products, a product division type of structure would appear as shown in outline form in Figure 5–1.

In this example, each division has its own manufacturing and sales, its own accounting and personnel specialized staff groups. Over-all coordination for each product takes place at the top of the product grouping, thus enabling the president to push down decision making one full level for complete segments of the business. The president retains his own centralized special staff group to assist him in over-all management of the enterprise. Note that the president has a manufacturing and marketing specialized staff group to provide him with advice and service in over-all management of these two activities, which are line in the product divisions.

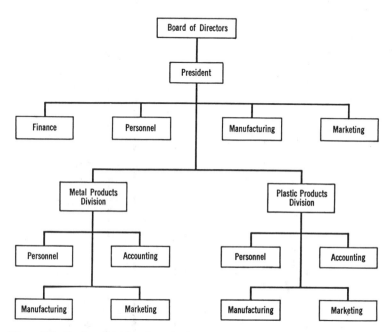

Figure 5-1. Product Division Organization

A detailed chart of Westinghouse Electric Corporation (Figure 5-2) shows a typical operating organization based on product divisionalization. On the chart, each indentation represents a level of management. The Apparatus Products Group, for instance, reports to the Group Vice President, Apparatus Products. The product divisions are grouped to form five major product groups: Apparatus, General, Consumer, Defense, and Atomic Power. The product divisions in turn are made up of product departments, each of which contains the functions essential to profit on a product line and thus constitutes a basic profit center. There are sixty-seven of these relatively self-sufficient profit centers within the framework of the product divisions and groups.

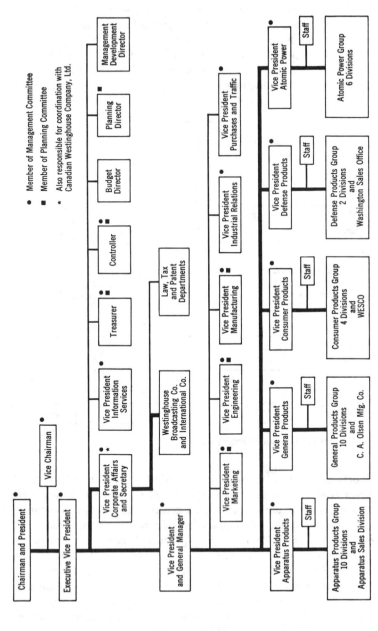

Figure 5–2. Product Division Organization, Westinghouse Electric Corporation

● Member of Management Committee

■ Member of Planning Committee

* Also responsible for coordination with Canadian Westinghouse Company, Ltd.

Chairman and President

Vice Chairman

Executive Vice President

Vice President Corporate Affairs and Secretary ● ■ *

Vice President Information Services ●

Westinghouse Broadcasting Co. and International Co.

Law, Tax and Patent Departments

Treasurer ● ■

Controller ● ■

Budget Director

Planning Director ■

Management Development Director

Vice President and General Manager ●

Vice President Marketing ● ■

Vice President Engineering ● ■

Vice President Manufacturing ● ■

Vice President Industrial Relations ●

Vice President Purchases and Traffic ●

Vice President Apparatus Products ●

Staff

Apparatus Products Group 10 Divisions and Apparatus Sales Division

Vice President General Products ●

Staff

General Products Group 10 Divisions and C. A. Olsen Mfg. Co.

Vice President Consumer Products ●

Staff

Consumer Products Group 4 Divisions and WESCO

Vice President Defense Products ●

Staff

Defense Products Group 2 Divisions and Washington Sales Office

Vice President Atomic Power ●

Staff

Atomic Power Group 6 Divisions

WHEN TO CHOOSE PRODUCT DIVISIONALIZATION

Once the decision has been made to divisionalize, choice must be made between product and geographic divisionalization as the basic pattern for reorganization. Product divisionalization is indicated when product expansion and diversification and the engineering, manufacturing, and marketing characteristics of the product are of primary concern.

Product Expansion and Diversification

There is a limit to the number of products that can be handled successfully by the functional organization. Where a variety of products of different types must be manufactured and sold by the same organization, some are certain to be slighted, while others will be overemphasized. This may be reflected in the salesman's preference for one product over others in the varied product line he offers, differences in advertising and promotion expense, research and engineering effort, and commitment of capital funds in favor of the product that promises to pay out quickest and best. This favoritism is natural and understandable. However, it may seriously handicap other products which require persistent promotion to win a place among competitors or to develop customer acceptance.

The Du Pont Company. Du Pont provides one of the earliest and best examples of divisionalization on a product basis to facilitate product expansion and diversification. In Du Pont, more than 60 per cent of the company's sales today result from products that were unknown, or in their commercial infancy, twenty years ago. Part of the company's success can certainly be attributed to its ability to improve existing products and develop new ones. However, during the early years of the century, innovation was not a strong feature of Du Pont's business. As a matter of fact, most research and development was carried out by works superintendents in plant laboratories or by company executives in their homes. Du Pont became outstanding in product development and innovation because it consciously built this function into its organization and gave it the emphasis it needed for top performance.

Du Pont decided, around the turn of the century, that expansion of its product line was necessary to the sound growth of the business. At this time, the company operated through a functional structure. All manufacturing throughout the company was handled by the manufacturing department and all sales by the sales department. In 1903, a Development Department was organized and added to the basic structure, with responsibility for studying ways in which the business could be expanded and diversified.

Du Pont added to its product line over the years in two ways. It bought companies with well-established products and added such lines as electrochemical products, paints, lacquers, varnishes, finishes, pigments, inorganic chemicals, nitrocellulose plastics, rubber-coated fabrics, and, in the early thirties, guns and ammunition. The company also acquired patent rights and processes of foreign companies—notably in France—and began to manufacture and sell in America intermediates and dyes, ammonia, rayon, and cellophane, in each case improving or transforming the product through Du Pont's own research work.

Growth by acquisition was successful and in that era of the company's development helped to provide a greater range and depth than the company could have accomplished solely by internal development of new products. Soon, however, Du Pont found that it had reached technological frontiers. If it wanted to expand and diversify further, it would have to invent more of its own products and processes. The company made further organizational changes which helped it to move toward this objective. That these changes were successful is witnessed by the fact that today practically all new products and processes originate in the company's own laboratories.

The organizational changes that helped Du Pont to become a prolific developer and introducer of new products emphasize the importance of the proper basic structure.

In 1911 a functional, centralized Chemical Department was established on a staff basis to provide research as a service to all the operating departments of the company. As the company grew, more competitors entered its markets. The dominant factor in the company's growth became that of introducing new products at the top of the barrel as fast as it drew old ones off the bottom because they had become less attractive due to technological obsolescence, competitive factors, or changes in customers' desires. In 1921 Du Pont reorganized again. The principal product lines were grouped and organized into product departments. Within each department, production, sales, and research were established as line divisions, with the directors of each of the three functions reporting on the same level to the general manager of the department.

The Chemical Department remained as a staff department with research as its only function and with emphasis on long-range or fundamental research for the company as a whole. A member of top management, a vice president, was given responsibility for acting as adviser on research to all departments conducting research programs. Such programs are conducted by all operating departments and two other staff departments—Engineering and Employee Relations, the program of the latter being chiefly in the field of industrial medicine.

This basic organization has served the company effectively for over thirty-five years. It has enabled Du Pont to pioneer boldly at the frontiers of chemistry, while keeping its existing product lines sound and vigorous in increasingly competitive markets.

The organization of the research effort in the Organic Chemicals Department is a good example of the Du Pont approach. The Organic Chemicals Department now manufactures over two thousand organic chemical compounds, ranging from dyes and intermediates to chemicals for the textile, paper, refrigeration, and other industries. In this department, for example, in order to perfect the production of dyes—starting almost from scratch—Du Pont risked an investment of $43 million; it was eighteen years before earnings from dyes and related chemicals were sufficient to offset accumulated operating losses. There were several reasons why the department was able to overcome this tremendous handicap and forge to the front as a leading money-maker among the operating departments of the company. Among these reasons some of the most important are closely linked to the product division type of organization structure.

First, the product type organization structure brought into better focus the problems of the Organic Chemicals Department, separating them from those of the other operating departments. The general manager of the department could concentrate on bringing his lagging horse from out of the ruck and up with the leaders. He was not trying to ride all the horses at once, as would have been true under Du Pont's old functional organization, in which one manager handled the manufacture of all products in the company.

Another important reason was the organization of the research function as a line activity, on the same level as production and sales. This identified research as a basic function of the operating departments and emphasized that the success of the company depended as much upon developing new products and processes and improving existing ones as upon manufacturing and sales. From a practical standpoint, this also gave research an equal voice with production and sales in operating decisions.

Organizing the manufacturing departments so that each had its internal research function also helped assure closest coordination and cooperation among research, production, and sales in working toward the success of the department as a whole.

Another reason was that the research function in the Organic Chemicals Department was primarily concerned with new products and processes that would be of benefit to that particular department; research of a longer range or broader significance to the company as a whole has become the primary concern of the central staff Chemical

Department, although all operating departments conduct their own programs of long-range or fundamental research. This staff department undertakes long-range research chiefly in the fields of chemistry, biochemistry, and physics, involving such varied fields as plant growth hormones and polymers for synthetic fibers, films, plastics, and coating compositions. Once it has uncovered a promising lead, the staff Chemical Department turns it over to one of the product departments. For example, the Chemical Department, as a part of its basic research, discovered that strong fibers, later named "nylon," could be spun from high molecular weight polyamides. The staff Chemical Department turned over responsibility for developing commercial processes for the production of nylon to the research divisions of the appropriate departments.

Carrier Corporation. Carrier provides an excellent example of the values of product divisionalization in expansion and diversification. Carrier operated under a functional type structure for many years. So long as sales volume was relatively small, Carrier found that a single engineering, manufacturing, and sales function could handle a variety of air-conditioning products ranging from heavy air-conditioning machinery for the Pentagon Building to ⅓ horsepower air conditioners. Immediately after World War II, however, the company faced a combination of growth factors. Room air conditioners had become a booming market; there was convincing argument to diversify into heating to complement the existing air-conditioning product line; the demand for air-conditioning equipment of all kinds mushroomed with the boom in house construction.

Carrier's manufacturing and sales setups lent themselves to separation. The manufacturing processes for different types of air-conditioning equipment vary markedly. Room air conditioners are designed and engineered for volume production and are assembled on a production line. Equipment suitable for installation in large buildings is "tailored" in a heavy machine plant.

Sales methods also vary. Room units are sold through distributors and dealers. Heavy units are sold, installed, and serviced by men who must have several years' mechanical engineering experience. As sales climbed past the $25 million mark, Carrier found that the diversity of problems presented by the different types even within this one major product line taxed the capacities of a single functional organization. Reorganization by product lines became necessary for the company to grow and expand its markets (see Fig. 14–2, page 314).

Other Examples. Many other examples illustrate that, to the company with goals of continued product diversification and expansion, a product division type of organization must be given careful consideration. American Radiator and Standard Sanitary Corporation manufactures and sells a widely varied product line of both home equipment and engineered products, including plumbing, heating, air conditioning, kitchens, electronic controls, heat exchangers, fluid drives, and atomic reactor components. It has been able to accomplish this diversification successfully by establishing ten product divisions, each accountable for one related line of products.

Product Characteristics

The manufacturing, engineering, and marketing characteristics of the product influence choice of product divisionalization. If separate administrative units are to be formed, each product or group of products should lend itself to separation from other products with reference to engineering, manufacturing, and sales.

For clean-cut product divisionalization, it should be possible to separate manufacturing so that each product or group of products can have its own facilities. At times, this may be a long-range goal, particularly if one plant is now manufacturing the complete line of products by use of pooled facilities and equipment. Engineering should also be separable so that each product division can design and develop the products it sells. The different products or product groups should be sold to different customers through different distribution channels. If the customer is essentially the same, as for example, in the sale of foods and liquors, the products should be capable of brand-name differentiation and sale through different sales forces.

Product divisionalization is generally to be preferred over geographic when the product is relatively complex and a great deal of capital is required for plants and facilities, when administrative costs for engineering and staff are high, and when it is difficult to build and maintain pools of skilled operators and supervisors. This is characteristic, for example, of automobiles, electrical equipment, farm machinery, radio, television, and electronics when the line becomes diversified and the volume large.

How Sylvania Made Its Choice. Sylvania Electric Products provides an excellent example of a company reorganizing from a functional to a product division structure. Sylvania has as its objective the manufacture and sale of a diversified line of electrical products ranging from radio and television, through lights and fixtures, tungsten and chemical products, to atomic energy equipment. These products are marketed in every state; practically every family and every company is a potential customer. Once the company had decided that divisionalization was necessary if it was to meet its growth and diversification objectives, it had to choose between product and geographic divisionalization.

The first step in this decision was easy enough. Each of the major product lines was manufactured in a separate plant which included the division headquarters for that product. One of the basic policies of the company was to carry on its manufacturing activities on a decentralized basis in relatively small plants geographically dispersed throughout the country. As plans for additional plants were made, a decision had to be reached as to whether these plants would be devoted to a single product or would manufacture a number of different product lines. This boiled down to a basic question of whether the company should adhere strictly to a product divisionalization or should mix or replace it with geographic divisionalization.

Sylvania's reasoning went something like this: To build plants primarily to serve market areas would mean an expensive and inefficient hodgepodge of facilities spotted across the country, because plants would have to be placed primarily with reference to markets and not in terms of availability of materials, most effective utilization of skills, and ease of coordination and standardization. What would be the cost and efficiency of manufacturing television sets in Texas, Oregon, Illinois, and New York, for example, with local managers accountable for design, engineering, and manufacturing, compared to the cost and efficiency of manufacturing at locations selected for product reasons and shipped to local markets?

Again, if geographic rather than product divisionalization were selected, each geographic division manager would, logically, be held accountable for profit and loss. He could be expected to manufacture as many different products as possible in each of the regional plants, to keep unit costs down on the relatively small volume he would manufacture. This would lead to all of the disadvantages of manufacturing a diversified product line in a functional type organization.

The reasoning on marketing followed similar lines. Obviously, salesmen must be located where the customers are, which means geographically. But if a geographic division manager is to be accountable for sales, he must be given responsibility and authority for sales of all products in his region. This again leads to the disadvantages of a functional marketing organization for a diversified line. Sylvania's decision for marketing organization was made in favor of product divisionalization, with breakdown of the product division sales forces to serve each local market. (See Figure 14–3, page 315.)

GEOGRAPHIC DIVISION ORGANIZATION

Geographic divisionalization involves grouping of the primary activities of the business in terms of the geographic region or area to be served. Carried to completion, the geographic division becomes a relatively complete administrative unit in itself, capable of catering to the needs of the region which constitutes its boundaries.

The building blocks of the geographic division are either subordinate functional or product groupings, or a combination of both. The geographic grouping draws a territorial fence around these basic components.

We can illustrate geographic divisionalization in the case of a company organized for the purpose of preparing and marketing a perishable food specialty on a nationwide basis. To enable it to cater to local tastes and to provide fast, efficient service, the company finds it advantageous to organize on a geographic division basis.

The Eastern and Western regions operate as relatively independent administrative groupings within the over-all framework of the company as a whole, processing the line of food specialties in the regional plant and providing fast service by truck to its outlets in all the cities and towns of the region. Each region has its own procurement, processing, and marketing functional units, together with the necessary

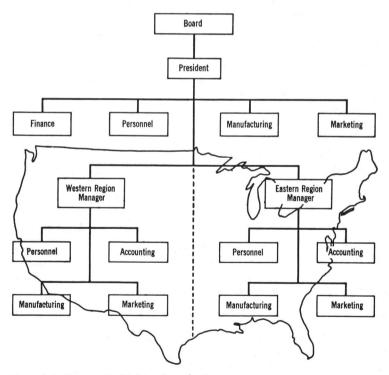

Figure 5-3. Geographic Division Organization

personnel, accounting, and engineering staff. The central headquarters, located in New York, manages the regions. Here are located the corporate personnel, finance, and technical (food processing and development) units, and the central procurement office. Since engineering is almost completely of regional concern, there is no central engineering specialized staff.

A simplified organization for a company divisionalized on a geographic basis is shown in Figure 5–3. Each region has its own manufacturing plants and sales force, together with personnel and accounting staff groups. The corporate headquarters has the necessary functional staff groups.

WHEN TO CHOOSE GEOGRAPHIC DIVISIONALIZATION

Change to a geographic division type of organization structure is indicated when customer needs or product characteristics can best be satisfied on a local basis and when the demands of the product itself are not so complex as to make the establishment of regional "businesses" too costly or impractical.

Market Characteristics

The characteristics of the market to be served are an important consideration. If the tastes, needs, or demands of customers vary so widely from one geographic area to another that they can be satisfied best by modification of the product or the sales methods to local requirements, geographic division should be considered.

The geographic division is capable of serving the local market with greatest effectiveness. The manager on the spot is more sensitive to local needs. He can spot variations in demand which spring from local conditions and capitalize on local situations more quickly than can a manager hundreds or thousands of miles distant. He can render better service because he is physically closer and since he is usually "home folks" either by adoption or by birth, he is more readily accepted than the "outsider" coming in to do business for a day or a week. The prevalence of "Buy West Coast" advertising on the West Coast or the conspicuous "Built in Texas by Texans" stickers found on Texas products are characteristic of the appeal to local pride.

Product Characteristics

The engineering, manufacturing, or other characteristics of the product may be important factors in the decision to change to a geographic division structure. Effective geographic divisionalization should admit of the eventual establishment of separate manufacturing, engineering, sales, or other primary functions in the geographic areas to be served. Since each such installation is the equivalent of financing a separate business, the capital and operating costs may be high. This is true with respect to machinery and equipment, plant and facilities, and the additional administrative costs for operating and staff personnel. The product best suited to geographic divisionalization is relatively simple to design, manufacture, and sell.

In some cases, the additional expense involved in geographic divisionalization is counterbalanced by advantages which can only be secured through use of facilities physically located in the area to be served. If bulky or extremely heavy material can be secured within the area, significant savings may be made in shipping costs. This is true, for example, in the preparation of sand and gravel, manufacture of cement, bottling of beverages, and processing of many food products. Where freshness of the product is a primary factor, as in dairy products, bakery goods, and candy, geographic divisionalization has obvious advantages. Excellent illustrations of the advantages of this type of divisionalization are found in the insurance, railroad, oil, and utility industries.

Insurance

The Prudential Insurance Company of America illustrates the advantages of geographic divisionalization as a basis for decentralization. Founded in Newark, New Jersey, in 1875, the Prudential operated successfully on a centralized, functional basis. Growth came rapidly, in both the United States and in Canada. As the volume of business grew in California, Texas, British Columbia, Ontario, and Hawaii, it became increasingly difficult to run the company from Newark. Premium notices, inquiries, and mail of all kinds had to travel too far. There were many delays in securing approval for local investments of company funds when the executives who made the decisions were strangers to the area and separated from it by thousands of miles.

Starting with a Western Home Office in Los Angeles in 1948, Prudential reorganized to form seven geographic divisions. The record for the Western geographic division is typical of the results accomplished. In one year after reorganization and decentralization, the Western Home Office reported an increase of over 18 per cent in sales of ordinary life insurance, while sales in this area by the rest of the life insurance industry showed no increase. Mortgage loans in force in the Western Home Office increased over 40 per cent in the same period, compared to an increase of 33 per cent for the rest of the life insurance industry. This improvement has continued.

Nationwide Insurance has divided its business into fifteen geographic regions, each of which operates as a small insurance business in itself.

Each issues insurance, collects premiums, pays claims, hires and fires, and services its policies.

Railroads

Railroad transportation lends itself logically to geographic divisionalization after the railroad has outgrown the functional form of organization. The New York Central Railroad Company is divided into four geographic districts. Each District Manager is responsible for the operating, freight sales and service, and passenger sales and service within his territory. The central specialized staff advises and serves the president and the key line and staff officers of the railroad.

Oil

An oil company derives all its products from the same basic crude, consequently it usually finds it best to divisionalize on a geographic rather than a product basis after it has outgrown a functional structure. Standard Oil Company of California, as a case in point, has its headquarters and primary marketing area in the states west of the Rocky Mountains. The company operated for many years under a functional

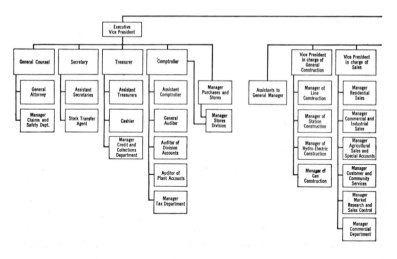

* The Comptroller exercises line control over stores accounting activities

Figure 5–4. Geographic Division Organization, Pacific Gas and Electric Company

form of organization structure. By 1948, however, it had reached over $1 billion in assets. The entire enterprise, including the West Coast operations and some one hundred subsidiary companies, was being administered by the same group of executives in San Francisco. The burden became so great for these men that the company decided divisionalization, on a geographic basis, was in order.

The division was made to place the western and world-wide organizations under separate administrative managements, but with a common superstructure. Within these geographical divisions, there are further functional and geographic subdivisions. For example, Standard of California Western Operations, Inc., the largest subsidiary, contains functional divisions devoted to exploration, production, manufacturing, supply, and transportation and has its own staff functions.

Some twenty-five operating geographic divisions or subsidiaries are

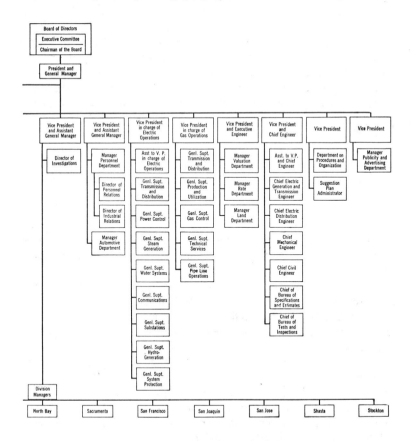

administered as relatively autonomous businesses within the framework of the over-all objectives, policies, and controls for the company as a whole. A typical geographic division has its own president, secretary and treasurer, controller and supply, refining, transportation, and marketing functions.

Continental Oil Company has divisionalized on a geographic basis. In Continental, company operations have been divided into six regions, each headed by a general manager who is responsible for all activities in his region. The regional department heads, in turn, are members of regional advisory committees, which act as coordinating and advisory groups. In Continental Oil, authority is delegated to regional general managers and is redelegated on down the line to the point of application as the nature of each problem permits.

The headquarters staff of this company retains primary responsibility for policies, plans, programs, establishing measurements and controls, and for counsel and advice to regional managements. The company finds that this method of grouping, coupled with decentralization, systematically funnels to each regional headquarters for solution and decision many field problems that formerly burdened top management. Since regional managers have the authority they need to handle problems at close range, they can make decisions with speed and economy.

Utilities

Utility companies which serve a large territory frequently find geographic divisionalization desirable. Pacific Gas and Electric Company, for example (Figure 5–4, page 102), is divided into thirteen geographic divisions. Each division manager directs and coordinates the electric, gas, water, or steam-heat operations of his division. P.G. and E. purchases gas from other sources and does not produce gas except for minor amounts for peak load requirements. A centralized control is maintained from San Francisco over the dispatching of electric power and natural gas for the entire integrated system of the company.

All division managers in P.G. and E. handle their own sales promotion, service to customers, and collection of accounts receivable. Handling of other primary activities varies, depending upon individual factors. Some divisions operate their own electric-generating and steam-heat plants and water-distribution systems. In some cases, the divisions are serviced by a central specialized staff group for such work as domestic, commercial, and small industrial customer billing; power accounting and billing of large industrial customers; and general accounting, including payroll, accounts payable, and major plant accounting. The company is establishing a computer system to centralize all customer billing and general accounting activities.

PREPARATION FOR DIVISIONALIZATION

Divisionalization is no panacea. It can be expensive, ineffective, and wasteful of both manpower and facilities. One company, confusing divisionalization of organization structure with decentralization of authority, established nine regional groupings but remained highly centralized. It lost several million dollars before it realized that a divisionalized structure can be even less efficient than a functional if appropriate decentralization does not also take place. Another company divisionalized and decentralized; however, only after it began to receive complaints from several of its major customers about the multiplicity of salesmen's calls did it realize that it had failed to take into account the needs of the most important element in the situation—the customer. In another case, a company divisionalized without establishing a central headquarters. As a result, the autonomous division heads disregarded the need for research and new product development, failed to coordinate their advertising and marketing, and overlooked possible major economies through central purchasing. Falling profits and loss of market position led to reassessment and organizational realignment to correct the deficiency.

Divisionalization is a radical procedure. It involves dismemberment of the existing organization structure, institution of far-reaching changes in the social groupings which have developed, and, frequently, physical separation of the component parts of the company. If it is to be accomplished successfully, it should be looked upon as major surgery, otherwise it may create more problems than it solves. Before reorganization takes place, divisionalization requires proper administrative preparation. This includes provision for decentralization, coordination, controls, management development, and time.

Decentralization

In many respects, divisionalization may be looked upon primarily at a vehicle for decentralization. The operating divisions of companies which divisionalize most successfully are highly decentralized. This is true of Du Pont, General Motors, Thompson Products, General Electric, Ford Motor Company, General Foods, Borg-Warner, Food Machinery and Chemical, and a great many others. Authority for making decisions having to do with the internal operation of the individual divisions should be delegated to the divisions. However, no matter to what extent division management is permitted autonomy in operating decisions, the central company management must retain responsibility for the establishment of over-all objectives and policies, development of the company organization structure, and review and approval of the general programs and budgets formulated by the operating units to reach their objectives. Coordination of the activities of the various divisions and departments and over-all control of company activities must also be centralized.

Both the product and geographic division types of structure are amenable to effective control because they are divided into measurable administrative units. Both divisionalized types of structure also facilitate other activities which are an indispensable part of decentralization. Separation of organization units, for example, stimulates morale and productivity by forming relatively small groups in which interaction takes place most readily. Full discussion of this process will be found in the chapters dealing with delegation and decentralization.

Management Development

Each product and geographic division, when also decentralized on a profit center basis, is managed and operated as a small business in itself. Each competes in the open market with companies manufacturing similar products. This takes managers of competitive caliber; as a result, demand for people who are capable of planning, organizing, coordinating, motivating, and controlling is multiplied in proportion to the number of product or geographic divisions created.

Training of managers to *manage* is a long-term project. It should either be initiated several years before the organization change, or the company should face up to the need for hiring qualified managers from the outside.

Cost

A divisionalized organization is more expensive to initiate and to maintain than a functional. Additional capital is needed to build plants and facilities. Administrative costs are greater. There is also the probability that operating expense will be higher per unit in each of several smaller plants than would be the case if all production were concentrated in one or two plants.

A company with heavy capital investment in machinery and equipment might hesitate to make the investment necessary for separate product divisions unless it could show clearly that profit advantage would result. Also, the company might hesitate to put on a complete sales crew to service the West Coast from San Francisco if it thought it might accomplish the same purpose with salesmen traveling out of the headquarters office in Chicago.

The initial investment in divisionalization is largely a matter of faith in the increased effectiveness of this form of organization and that greater returns will be secured from improved motivation and greater market and product emphasis. Most companies that have undertaken the move with foresight and proper administrative preparation have found this faith more than justified.

Coordination

Since each of the product or geographic divisions in a divisionalized organization is primarily concerned with its own operating objectives, it is usually difficult to secure effective coordination among the divisions. Company objectives, policies, and central specialized staff are special means of achieving the necessary coordination. United Parcel Service, for example, has formulated detailed policies covering all major aspects of the business. Extensive participation was secured from supervisors and managers at all levels in preparing these policies, so that they accurately represent the needs of the people accountable for results. These policies help ensure unified and integrated action in the eighteen geographic divisions of the company in the handling of finance and accounts, plants, equipment and ·supplies, personnel and delivery operations, and service.

United Parcel Service has a central staff group which travels constantly among the divisions. On their visits they observe operations, pass along ideas for new developments, suggest improvements, and assist the accountable managers in coordinating their activities on a company-wide basis.

It should be noted that coordination *within* the divisions of a divisionalized structure is usually easier to achieve than within a functional organization. Instead of having sales, manufacturing, engineering, personnel, finance, and other major functions operating as independent entities, coordinated only at the level of the chief executive, the divisionalized structure brings the point of coordination lower in the organization and tends to bring the functional heads into closer contact. More than this, focus on one specific product or geographic area engenders a competitive attitude toward other divisional groupings. This stimulates group cohesiveness and establishes a favorable psychological climate for coordinated, informed group effort.

As the division manager of a processing company put it:

When we operated under the old functional basis, the only way we could get people in other functions together to find out what they were doing or to coordinate our work with theirs was to call a committee meeting or have a conference of some sort. Now we all work right down the hall from one another at division headquarters, so all we have to do is to drop in and clear the matter up in person. Since we're all being measured and rewarded by the results we achieve from the business we manage and judged in terms of the same yardstick, we find it a lot easier to keep the other fellow informed. I notice now, too, that people are more willing to go out of their way to help the other fellow with his problems.

Controls

Adequacy of the control system is one of the major limiting factors in both divisionalization and decentralization. Self-sufficient business units can be created within the framework of an integrated organization only to the extent that the central management of the company makes provision for measuring and evaluating operating results. An effective system of budgeting, measuring performance, and interpreting results accomplished should be instituted before divisionalization is undertaken.

Time

A final element essential to successful divisionalization and decentralization is time. Companies of over $100 million sales seem to require a minimum of about five years to complete their reorganization. Where there is inadequate preliminary planning, or where the company is especially large or has complicated production or marketing problems, the change may require eight to ten years of constant planning and effort.

Sequence of Divisionalization

It is not always practical or efficient to break out complete product divisions all at once. As will be described later, reorganization is best undertaken by means of interim or phase steps designed to implement an over-all master plan of organization. An effective sequence of divisionalization usually involves first breaking out the most easily separable of the line functions, together with a minimum of associated specialized staff groupings. In some cases, manufacturing is first divisionalized, together with allied functions such as engineering and maintenance. As was true with Sylvania and General Foods, sales may remain on a functional, centralized basis until the manufacturing function is matured and safely established on a divisionalized basis. In other companies, just the opposite is true and marketing is first divisionalized.

Specialized staff functions also tend to be divisionalized in sequence, rather than all at once. In some companies, purchasing and traffic are broken out of the functional grouping to the divisions rather early in the reorganization, later followed by personnel and finance. In many otherwise highly divisionalized companies, finance may remain quite highly functional and centralized. The legal, public relations, and, of course, secretary functions most commonly remain on a functional basis, with no equivalent groupings in the divisions.

HYBRID STRUCTURES

The grouping patterns already discussed have two characteristics: They apply to the over-all company structure, that is, to the first breakdown below the chief executive; and they are relatively pure, or theoretically perfect, groupings. In practice, most companies have a composite or hybrid organizational structure, both at the company level and at levels below the top. This hybridization leads to flexibility. It enables the company to meet special problems by appropriate adaptation of its organization. However, there are also distinct dangers involved in hybridization. Dissimilar groupings *within the same accountability center* tend to encourage overlap, duplication, and friction because of incompatability of interests on the part of the managers involved. For example, if a sales department is grouped on both a product and a geo-

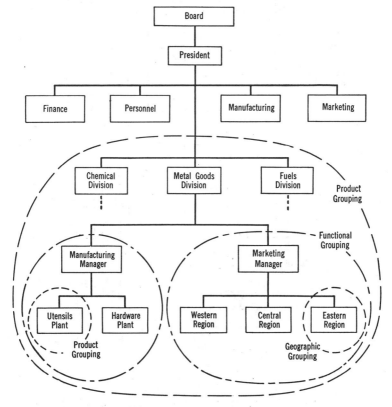

Figure 5–5. Hybrid Groupings

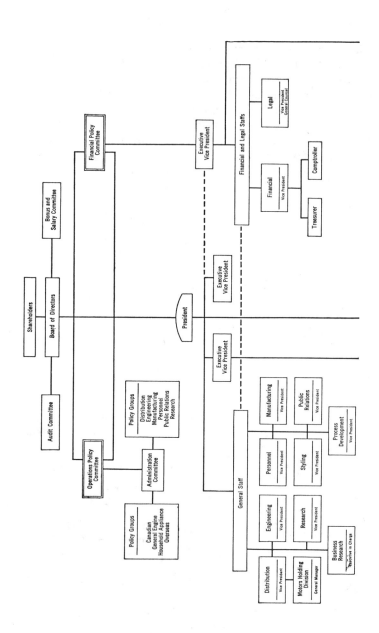

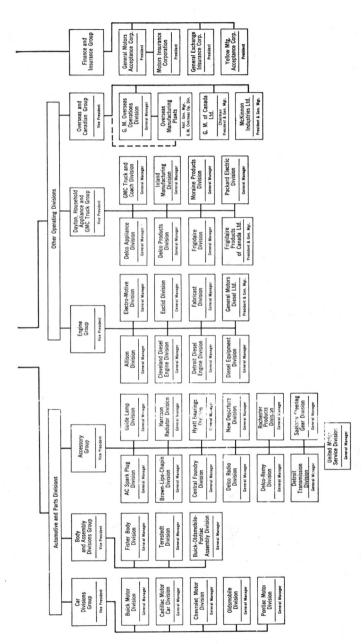

Figure 5–6. General Motors Corporation, Organization Pattern

graphical basis at the same level, there is always the question of who is accountable for selling the customer and what happens when customers in one salesman's district can be served effectively only by a product salesman covering all districts.

Again, if the maintenance department is grouped on both a functional and geographic, or zone, basis, where does the accountability of the zone plumbers and electricians leave off and that of the functional people begin?

The possible hybrid combinations are almost endless. Typical is the situation shown in Figure 5–5, page 109. Here we have a manufacturing company organized on a product basis, with chemical, metal goods, and fuels divisions. Each product division has its own specialized staff and line manufacturing and sales departments.

The manufacturing department of the metal goods division is in turn divided into production departments devoted to the manufacture of utensils and hardware. The sales department, which is part of a functional grouping, in turn forms a geographic grouping of three sales regions, eastern, central, and western.

The General Motors Pattern

Typical of the many combinations that may exist within a basic product division are the various groupings within General Motors. General Motors is organized at the company level on a product division basis. However, at this level there is also one geographic grouping— the Canadian and Overseas Group, which contains the G.M. Overseas Operations Division and G.M. of Canada, Ltd., together with McKinnon Industries, Ltd. There is no overlap, because the Overseas and Canadian product divisions are fully accountable for manufacture and sale of all products in their respective territories (Figure 5–6, page 111).

If we examine one of the product divisions, we find further product geographic, and functional breakdowns. For example, in the Allisor Division of the Engine Group, Transmission Operations, Aircraft En gines, and Aeroproducts Operations are actually product divisions i, themselves, with their own manufacturing, engineering, and sales and closely allied staff groupings. Planning and coordinative staffs report to the general manager.

Each subordinate product grouping is, again, divided into functional, product, and geographic groupings, as appropriate. Transmission Operations, for example, has a separate Bearing Department, which designs and manufactures bearings for the production departments. At the same level, manufacturing, engineering, sales and service, and quality control are functional. We find, in turn, that the Bearing Department is divided into functional manufacturing groups, manufacturing into both product and functional subgroupings, and sales into geographic groupings.

SUMMARY

When the company outgrows its functional organization, reorganization should be undertaken to divide the large, functional structure into smaller units that can be managed as relatively independent administrative units, each accountable for its own objectives. Divisionalization may be either in terms of product or geography.

Product divisionalization involves grouping in a division all functions related to each product or closely related group of products. This is the organization of choice when maximum emphasis is to be placed on product expansion and diversification and when the product and market characteristics are favorable.

Geographic divisionalization should be selected when the special characteristics of the market and product indicate regional emphasis.

Divisionalization is a radical procedure, involving dismemberment of the existing structure. Administrative preparation for divisionalization should include a full measure of decentralization to vitalize the management of the divisionalized units; adequate management talent must be developed or recruited to staff the organization; increased capital and administrative costs must be anticipated. Also, provision must be made for coordination of the separate divisions and an adequate control system must be developed. Above all, the company planning to divisionalize must provide adequate time for the change to be consummated.

CHAPTER 6 *The Process of Delegation*

"Has anyone given you the law of these offices?" asked John D. Rockefeller of a bustling subordinate manager. Answered in the negative, the builder of one of the most effective organizations in the history of business endeavor went on to outline his philosophy: "It is this: nobody does anything if he can get anybody else to do it. You smile; but think it over. Your department is the testing of oils. You are responsible; but as soon as you can, get some one whom you can rely on, train him in the work, sit down, cock up your heels, and think out some way for the Standard Oil to make money." [1] This is a practical philosophy. It points to what is probably the most important of all the skills a manager must possess—delegation, the ability to get results through others. Delegation is important because it is both the gauge and the means of a manager's accomplishment. Once a man's job grows beyond his personal capacity, his success lies in his ability to multiply himself through other people. How well he delegates determines how well he can manage.

The overworked manager, who carries a full brief case home, is often overloaded because he does not know how to delegate. Medical directors point out that ulcers, cardiac conditions, and many of the psychosomatic illnesses that result from strain, tension, and unresolved worries begin and persist because the afflicted manager is not able to distinguish between what is important on his job and what is not. As one railroad executive put it, "Instead of just trying to run the railroad, many managers also insist on collecting tickets, oiling bearings, tooting the whistle, and showing the chef in the dining car how to make his salads. No wonder they break down early."

The manner of delegation not only marks the effectiveness of the manager, it also influences the relationship between the subordinate and

[1] D. Woodbury, "Rockefeller and His Standard," *The Saturday Evening Post*, Oct. 21, 1911.

114

his superior. It inevitably has a profound effect on the performance of his subordinates. The person who is unsure of his job, who receives orders from several people, who does not understand the standards by which his performance is judged, is almost certain to be unhappy in his work.

The Atlantic Refining Company, which made a thorough analysis of the administrative practices of its managerial force over a period of six years, concluded that delegation is one of the mainsprings of effective management. Atlantic Refining points out that no manager and no company can function effectively without delegation. Lack of courage to delegate properly and of knowledge of how to delegate is one of the most general causes of failure in organization.

Companies stress repeatedly that they select men for management positions largely on their ability to delegate. To illustrate: the United States Rubber Company selects for promotion those managers who can delegate effectively. U.S. Rubber looks for people who can recognize broad objectives clearly and arrange for most effective accomplishment by delegating responsibility and commensurate authority to their subordinates. Dresser Industries identifies capable managers by their ability to get results through others. Westinghouse Electric Corporation rates high the manager who can work with and through people. Westinghouse expects its executives to recognize and evaluate the ability of others and to get peak performance without close supervision of the work of each individual.

Lounsbury Fish, Assistant to the Chairman of the Board, Standard-Vacuum Oil Company, graphically summarizes the need for delegation when he says, "An individual is only one manpower. Singlehanded, he can accomplish only so much in a day. The only way he can achieve more is through delegation—through dividing his load and sharing his responsibilities with others." [2]

WHAT IS DELEGATION?

Delegation often fails because the manager attempting to delegate does not understand what is involved in the process. This misunderstanding is natural, because the common concepts of delegation are confused and often contradictory. Not only does delegation mean different things in different companies, it is defined and interpreted in conflicting terms in the literature. Depending upon your reference, you can find that delegation means the conferring of authority and the correlation of authority and responsibility; you may discover that responsi-

[2] Lounsbury Fish, *Organization Planning*, American Management Association, General Management Series, no. 142, New York, 1948, p. 17. Also see other related points in this article.

bility is accountability and that it is an emotional condition. Responsibility and authority can be delegated and they cannot be delegated, according to various sources.

Most of these differences are semantic. Whatever terms we use, we are attempting to describe a management process that readily can be identified. To establish a consistent vocabulary for our discussion of delegation, we shall first describe what takes place and then attach to the activities we isolate the most appropriate terms.

Delegation is the dynamics of management; it is the process a manager follows in dividing the work assigned to him so that he performs that part which only he, because of his unique organizational placement, can perform effectively, and so that he can get others to help him with what remains. How can he best share his burden? First, he must entrust to others the performance of part of the work he would otherwise have to do himself; secondly, he must provide a means of checking up on the work that is done *for him* to ensure that it is done as he wishes.

If he wants to get others to help him, the manager must first divide his *work.* If he requires his subordinate to perform the work as he would do it himself, the manager must entrust him with part of the *rights and powers* he otherwise would have to exercise himself to get that work done. If the subordinate needs to spend money, hire people, use materials or equipment, the manager must permit him to do so or the subordinate cannot perform the work.

The manager must have some means of checking up to make sure that the work is done the way he wishes. This means he must create an *obligation* on the part of the person doing the work to perform in terms of any standards or conditions established. If he sets these standards properly, the manager can use them to appraise how well the work is being done.

We have now described the three essential aspects of delegation: the entrustment of *work,* or *responsibility,* to another for performance; the entrustment of *powers and rights,* or *authority,* to be exercised; and the creation of an *obligation,* or *accountability,* on the part of the person accepting the delegation to perform in terms of the standards established.[3]

---

[3] Possible semantic confusion should be anticipated here. Most authorities recognize the separate activities which go to make up delegation. However, there is considerable variation in the terms used to describe these activities.

Lyndall Urwick, in *The Elements of Administration,* Harper & Brothers, New York, 1943, pp. 41–42, uses this vocabulary: "*Duties,* which are the activities which the individual is required to perform by virtue of his membership in the organization. *Responsibility,* which is accountability for the performance of duties. *Power,* which is the ability to get things done [note here that power is considered a personal, individual quality]: that is to say, it is a function of knowledge,

ELEMENTS OF DELEGATION

Delegation is the entrustment of responsibility and authority to another and the creation of accountability for performance. It is to be noted that delegation is not a process of abdication. The person who delegates does not divorce himself from the responsibility and authority which he entrusts. He remains obligated for performance to the person or position from which he received his delegation. As American Enka defines it, delegation means "to entrust to the care or management of another." Lockheed Aircraft Corporation looks upon delegation as the process of entrusting responsibility and authority and creating accountability.

Responsibility

Responsibility is the work assigned to a position. Responsibility refers to the mental and physical activities which must be performed to carry out a task or duty. Responsibility can be delegated.

Ford Motor Company defines responsibility as the duties of a position or function. Bemis Bros. Bag Company looks upon responsibility as the work assigned to an individual or position. Standard Oil Company of California defines responsibilities as the components of the function which an individual is required to execute, or the duties of a position. Chance Vought Aircraft, Incorporated, defines responsibility as the work required to be accomplished.

Every person who performs any kind of mental or physical effort at an assigned task has responsibility. This is as true of the president of

---

skill and personal qualities. *Authority*, which is the right to require action of others."

Alvin Brown, in his incisive analysis, *Organization, a Formulation of Principle*, Hibbert Printing Company, New York, 1945, p. 16, says, "Responsibility is capable of being understood in two senses. In one, it denotes the *definition* of a part to be performed in administration. In the other, it denotes the *obligation* for the performance of that part. The definition is that which is to be done; the obligation is the duty of doing it. The two meanings are reciprocal. In most circumstances there is so little difference between the concept of the part and the concept of the obligation that it is more useful to view them as inseparably-related aspects of the same concept, and to refer to them by a single term. When it is necessary to consider responsibility especially in its aspect as an obligation, it may be so called."

The distinction is here clearly made. Since we intend to emphasize the *obligation to perform* which Brown mentions when we discuss delegation, decentralization, and staff and line, we shall isolate it from its correlative meaning by assigning to it the term "accountability." The part to be performed we define somewhat more narrowly than Brown as *the work assigned to a position* and give it the term "responsibility." The three concepts we have identified must be clearly distinguished; choice of terms is necessarily arbitrary.

the company as of the machine tender in the shop. For example, the president of Thompson Products, Inc., has the following among other responsibilities; that is to say, he is assigned the following work:

1. Maintains an up-to-date plan of organization for the entire company.
2. Appoints members of and directs the activities of the Central Policy Group.
3. Approves all staff budgets. . . .

In a manufacturing company, a machine tender is delegated such specific responsibilities as the following:

To operate his machine economically and effectively.
To notify the foreman of any requirements of maintenance that should be scheduled.
To keep machine and machine area clean and orderly.

Authority

Authority is the sum of the powers and rights entrusted to make possible the performance of the work delegated. Authority includes such rights or powers as those of spending specified amounts of money, of using certain kinds or quantities of materials, of hiring and firing people. It may involve the right to decide or act. However, authority often falls short of decision and action and may be limited to the power to advise, consult, and provide service. Authority also implies the right *not* to act, or decide.

As Koppers Company, Inc., puts it, authority is the power of an individual to carry out his assigned responsibilities. Every person to whom responsibilities have been given must also have certain implied or expressed authority if he is to perform. Boeing Airplane Company defines authority as the right to originate, direct, act, decide, and control.

We have seen that the authority, or powers and rights necessary to perform a given responsibility, may vary from one situation to another. Line authority, staff authority, and other aspects of organizational authority will be discussed in later chapters. At present we should also note the authority of knowledge, authority of position, and legal authority.

Authority of Knowledge. Some people have authority because of what they know. If a company hires a consultant to provide guidance, counsel, and advice on the installation of an executive compensation plan, the consultant gets his work done through the authority of knowledge. He knows more about executive compensation than the people he serves; consequently, he can strongly influence their thinking and actions without giving orders. Most staff positions operate through exercise of the authority of knowledge.

Authority of Position. Some individuals assume authority because of proximity to persons with line authority. For example, a staff assistant has no line authority. Literally, he has no power or right to give orders, except in the name of his principal. However, because of his proximity to the executive he serves, the staff assistant frequently has very real power to secure action from line subordinates of his principal. A suggestion or implied preference by the staff assistant may be tantamount to an order because the person with whom he is dealing knows that his suggestions and recommendations carry great weight with the top man and will be given priority by him.

In a Southern plant of a food company, the plant manager was delegated authority to approve all travel requests. The plant manager had a staff assistant, who possessed no authority for such approvals. From experience, the staff assistant knew precisely what travel requests his chief would authorize and which he would turn down. Over a period of years, subordinate managers became accustomed to bringing their travel requests directly to the staff assistant. If the assistant thought the request was in line, he would so imply. The manager would proceed on his trip, leaving the request with the assistant for the formality of signature. This was authority of position.

Both the superior and subordinate in an organizational relationship carry authority which stems directly from their relative positions. The principal has the implied authority of the ranking position, the privileges of rank. Because he *is* boss, he may reasonably expect that a preferred parking space or the best office will be assigned to him without his claiming it. If he and one of his section managers are discussing a matter with the executive vice president, the principal may expect his section manager to defer to his opinion or judgment and not to press his own personal viewpoint.

The subordinate also has power peculiar to his position. He has the capacity to weaken or actually limit his chief's authority by refusing him wholehearted obedience or compliance. If he cares to exercise it, he possesses an opposing power of considerable magnitude which can markedly affect the capabilities of the man he serves.

Legal Authority. This refers to the powers or rights conferred by law. The corporation is a legal person in the sense that it is authorized by the state to act as an individual or unit. The power or authority of the corporation is defined and limited by the general laws of the state which affect it and by its own charter. The charter outlines the nature of the corporation and its purposes. Once it is approved by the state, the charter has legal authority. It gives the corporation the right to engage in a specified line of business, to buy, sell, and lease property, and so forth.

For example, Merck & Co., Inc., is organized as a corporation under the general laws of New Jersey. Article II of its charter outlines the objects and purposes of the Corporation as follows:

To carry on the business of manufacturers, importers and exporters of, and dealers in chemical, pharmaceutical, biological, medicinal and other products, and goods, wares and merchandise of all kinds;

To construct or otherwise acquire, maintain or alter any buildings, works or mines necessary or convenient for the purposes of the Corporation;

To act as commercial or general agent for individuals, partnerships or other corporations engaged in any business similar or allied to that hereinabove described or in any business in which any product of this Corporation is employed;

To purchase, acquire, hold and dispose of the stocks, bonds and other evidence of indebtedness of any corporation, domestic or foreign, and to issue in exchange therefor its stocks, bonds or other obligations.

The Corporation may also establish and maintain offices and conduct its business or any portion thereof and may own, hold, lease and dispose of such lands and other property as the purposes of the Corporation shall require (subject to such limitations as may be prescribed by law), in other states of the United States of America and in the Territories thereof and the District of Columbia, and in any or all dependencies, colonies or possessions of the United States of America and in any or all foreign countries.

The foregoing clauses shall be construed both as objects and powers, but without in any particular limiting any of the powers which may now or hereafter be conferred upon the Corporation by the laws of New Jersey or any other law now or hereafter applicable to the Corporation.

Accountability

Accountability is the obligation to carry out responsibility and exercise authority in terms of performance standards established. Just as a person who is loaned money has an obligation to the lender, in terms of any conditions placed upon the loan, the person who is delegated responsibility and authority has an obligation to perform in terms of established standards. He must stand ready to report on demand and to answer for the success or failure of his activities. Accountability is most meaningful if standards for performance are predetermined and if they are fully understood and accepted by the subordinate. It should be noted that accountability applies both to the obligation to perform work and to exercise authority.

As defined by Jones and Laughlin Steel Company, accountability is the obligation to account for, and report upon, the discharge of responsibility or use of authority. Standard Oil Company of California, in its Management Guide, describes accountability as "the obligation of an individual to render an account of the fulfillment of his responsibilities to the principal to whom he reports."

Accountability Cannot Be Delegated. Accountability is incurred as the result of delegation of responsibility and authority. But accountability in itself cannot be delegated. The person making the delegation always remains accountable to *his* superior for that which he has delegated.

For example, the President of Pitney-Bowes, Inc., delegates to the Vice President for Manufacturing responsibility and authority for directing the manufacture of the products of the company. The Vice President for Manufacturing, in turn, delegates parts of his responsibility and authority to the plant superintendent, methods and tool manager, production control manager, and time study engineer. However, the President holds only the Vice President for Manufacturing accountable if discrepancy or error occurs in any of these subordinate departments. The Manufacturing Vice President cannot delegate the accountability he owes the President when he delegates responsibility and authority to his subordinates.

Since accountability cannot be delegated, the accountability of higher authority for the acts of subordinates is absolute. Most companies agree to this principle, although in practice it is sometimes violated. Typical of the best thinking is that of Johnson and Johnson. In this company, the head of an organizational component is completely accountable for everything done in all his departments. The executive or foreman alone is accountable for a weakness in his organization, no matter which of his subordinates caused it. Such rigidity of principle is, of course, modified by common sense in any particular instance.

Accountability Is Always Upward. We have seen that a person is always accountable to the person who delegated responsibility and authority to him. Accountability always flows upward. On the other hand, the flow of responsibility and authority is downward because both are delegated to subordinates.

Extent of Accountability. A person can be held accountable only to the extent that he is delegated responsibility and authority. If, for example, the sales manager is given responsibility for selling the company's product line but the personnel department is given responsibility and authority for the training of salesmen, the sales manager cannot be held accountable for the selling techniques or proficiency of his sales crews.

A subordinate clearly cannot be held accountable if he is not given responsibility, that is, if he is not delegated the work itself to perform. However, it is not always recognized that the same principle holds true with authority. Withholding authority automatically restricts accountability in an equivalent amount. As Standard Oil Company of California puts it, "Accountability is, by the act which creates it, of the same quality, quantity and weight as the accompanying responsibility and authority."

Accountability Is Unitary. Each person can be accountable only to one superior for delegated responsibility and authority. If an individual reports to two principals on the same responsibility, confusion and friction inevitably result. When this occurs, the subordinate is never certain who will call him to account for a specific activity; and since the personalities and demands of different individuals vary widely, he can never hope to satisfy two different people with the same handling of the problem. He may find that one likes to be kept constantly informed; the other prefers to be contacted only on exceptional matters. When reporting to two principals, the subordinate also finds himself frequently receiving conflicting orders. When this is the case, his only hope is either to get his two bosses together or to run the risk of displeasing one or both.

Sometimes the subordinate is clever enough to take advantage of the dual relationship to play off one boss against the other. If one principal attempts to call him to account for a mistake or omission, he explains that he understood from his other principal that it was to be done another way. If he gets behind on his work for one man, he points out that the other is keeping him so busy he can't satisfy both.

Standards of Accountability. Inherent in accountability is the obligation of the delegator to set standards of performance, unless such standards are explicit in the delegation itself. For instance, if the production superintendent is accountable to the plant manager for maintaining production schedules, he can be called to account when the established production schedules are not met. As we have seen, this accountability is limited only to the extent that the production superintendent is denied authority in setting the schedules or in performing the work required to meet them. In this case, the standard of performance is explicit in the delegation. In many instances, however, accountability tends to be diffuse because clear-cut standards of performance are not established. For example, to hold a person accountable for carrying out company policy in "quality control" or "planning" is as broad as the ocean and as deep as the sea. Accountability is meaningful only if the measure of performance can be spelled out in specific terms.

As an illustration of the development of standards of accountability, in one company the marketing manager is held accountable for providing the customer with dependable shipment and delivery of merchandise. To spell out what it means by "dependable shipment and delivery of merchandise," the company has established definite standards of accountability. As one example, the time standards for processing regular orders are as follows:

1. All orders received in the morning mails will be processed and sent to the traffic department or mailed to the warehouse the same day.

2. All orders received in the afternoon mail will be processed and sent to the traffic department or mailed to the warehouse by 2 P.M. of the following business day.

Continental Can Company provides standards of performance for major responsibilities delegated to managers. To illustrate: A major responsibility of the Staff Control Analyst in the Control Office is that of report analysis and interpretation. The key duties involved are as follows:

1. Work closely with the Control Officer and/or other specified department personnel in planning the major scope and nature of material and types of analyses and interpretations to be included in assigned regular and special reports to management.

2. Analyze reports on Company operations and prepare interpretative commentary and/or edit comments submitted concerning salient features of interest to management.

3. Evaluate over-all Company attainment of forecast objectives and prepare analysis of results.

4. Review prepared commentary, as necessary, with Control Officer to ensure agreement on soundness of conclusions drawn.

5. Work closely with other specified Department personnel in final editing and proofreading of assigned regular and special reports to management.

6. Explore, continuously, the possibilities of developing and applying new techniques to facilitate the communication of information on Company operations to Top Management and recommend their adoption to the Control officer.

7. Supervise Control Office personnel as specified by the Control Officer in the preparation and assembly of information to be used in reports for Top Management.

The standards of performance for this responsibility are met when "reports on company operations are analyzed and interpretative commentary prepared for inclusion in specified reports and analyses to management in a manner which contributes to understanding of the significance of the data being presented and provides basis for taking remedial action, as appropriate."

In Koppers Company, Inc., the standards of accountability for the president are as follows: "The operating profits earned (both in dollars and as a percentage of investment), the net earnings to common stock, the relation of these factors to objectives and programs, and the general stature of the company among the public, competitive enterprises and other industry."

INFORMAL DELEGATION

The process of delegation which has been described is formal delegation. It rests upon the exercise of formal authority, that is, authority defined by organizational role. Formal delegation is effective to the extent that people are willing to forgo their option of choice *to obey* or *not to obey* and are compliant to the commands given by their superiors.

Informal delegation occurs because people "want to do something" and not because they are "told to do it." Informal delegation takes place when an individual, or a group of people under an informal leader, decide they will carry out some activity and invest themselves with authority to do it.

In one large chemical company in New York, for example, a personnel specialist in the Employment Department had been delegated responsibility and authority for receiving, classifying, analyzing, and forwarding applications for employment from outsiders. This was formal delegation. It so happened, however, that this company had a large turnover of junior and middle management people. A number of section and unit heads who were trying to find jobs in other companies knew of this specialist's skill in writing and his acquaintance with the job market. Over a period of several months, these section heads prevailed upon the specialist to write and criticize resumés for them and provide them with lists of companies to contact. This was informal delegation.

Informal delegation often takes place because people want to cut "red tape" and "get things done." If the formal organization provides only a time-consuming or circuitous route for securing permission to do work and to get approval of work already done, or if people dislike or resist the source of authority, informal delegation invariably comes into play.

Bottom-up Delegation

In spite of delegation of specific authority and responsibility by the formal organization, delegation takes place, in fact, only to the extent that the subordinate is willing to carry out the orders he receives. This may be a willingness to do the job itself or to comply with the standards for the job established by the supervisor.

A large multiplant metalworking firm, for instance, finds that an informal leader or group, which is not recognized in the formal organization, may make decisions and establish patterns of conduct. In production departments of this company, workers sometimes exercise informal delegation and assume for themselves authority to restrict output. Even though piece-rate or wage-incentive plans are in effect, the people in the group, by their own authority, will hold down production to the level which the group considers "fair." This may occur even in defiance of the expressed wishes of the supervisors, who have made formal delegation of different authority and standards of accountability.

Lateral Delegation

Delegation has a third dimension. This is the process of entrustment that occurs when teamwork develops among the members of a group. In modern business, few jobs are independent. The person to whom responsibility and authority are delegated must, in a very real sense, informally delegate to others on his own level if he is to get his job done. Thus the responsibility and authority delegated to a personnel supervisor to make a wage and salary survey may be shared by that supervisor with the personnel research supervisor to secure salary data, with the training director to train a survey team, and with supervisors in the sales, finance, and production departments whose jobs are being evaluated.

Teamwork may be negative as well as positive. In one Middle Western food company, the sales promotion manager for one product line was responsible for reporting the effectiveness of the various displays his unit developed and installed. In an attempt to secure factual data, he asked each district sales supervisor to prepare a daily report covering all the stores visited by the salesmen. From the beginning, compliance was poor. The sales promotion man tried wheedling, cajolery, and finally turned to the Director of Marketing for support. However, even this additional pressure could not get him the cooperation he needed. Finally he had to resort to personal survey on a sampling basis. The sales supervisors had been able to balk him by use of informal authority.

Making Use of Informal Delegation

Most managers find that while they can be delegated formal authority to direct others, they must "earn" informal authority to lead others.

Nationwide Insurance has looked carefully into the factors that enable a manager to make use of informal delegation. This company concludes that a manager can earn authority from subordinates only to the extent he earns respect, loyalty, willingness, and, in other words, shows ability to lead others. In designing its organization structure, Nationwide Insurance finds that some positions do not carry their own weight because the people in those positions, even though delegated broad responsibility and authority, are incapable of "earning" the informal authority necessary to make the formal delegation effective.

Many managers who have identified informal delegation in their own groups and try to make use of it feel that the important consideration is to make sure, as far as possible, that formal and informal delegation support and reinforce one another and are not antagonistic.

How can this be done? A first step, before making a delegation, is to find out what subordinates are capable of doing and are willing to do. The techniques of consultative supervision are appropriate at this point. If the manager discovers that his subordinates are unwilling or unable to conform, he has two alternatives. He can try to change the attitudes and abilities of his people or change himself. The first alternative is difficult, the second, improbable. The best solution is application of the principles of motivation and training or amendment of the delegation to conform to the realities of the situation.

WHAT CAN BE DELEGATED?

A critical problem for every manager lies in determining what parts of his job he should entrust to others and which he must perform himself. If the manager tries to perform duties which might better be delegated, he finds himself buried in detail and continually overlapping the work of his subordinates. On the other hand, if he delegates responsibility and authority which he should exercise himself, he is certain to find his leadership in jeopardy and his subordinates constantly in conflict with him and with one another. A basic step in effective delegation is for the manager to analyze his job and to determine, in principle, what he should or should not delegate. With a logical pattern in mind, he can delegate with more assurance. For the purpose of this discussion, the personal skills and abilities of the manager himself are not considered.

RESERVED RESPONSIBILITY AND AUTHORITY

Reserved responsibilities and authorities are those which the manager withholds for his own performance. He may secure participation in formulating his decisions. He may make use of both line and staff subordinates in collecting information, analyzing data, weighing alternatives, and making recommendations. But he cannot effectively delegate responsibility and authority for *initiating* and making *final decisions* for planning, organizing, coordinating, motivating, and controlling the activities and positions that report to him. The manner in which this reservation is made is described below.

Planning

The manager reserves responsibility and authority for establishing and interpreting plans, at his level, for his subordinate units. This includes all the elements of management plans that we have already discussed—

objectives, policies, programs, procedures, and budgets. Only the manager himself is organizationally placed so that he can plan, objectively and with balance, for all subordinate elements. The manager will undoubtedly secure a great deal of participation and assistance from both line and staff subordinates in formulating his plans. However, if he delegates authority to make final planning decisions to any one subordinate, whether line or staff, he is running constant risk of distortion and slant in terms of that subordinate's special interests.

It is typical of the well-managed company that managers at all levels constantly plan ahead to ensure maximum return from the facilities and investment entrusted to their care. Every manager should prepare long- and short-range objectives, policies, and programs, appropriate to his position, aimed at producing the most profitable results attainable from his assigned area. When these plans have been approved, the manager interprets them to his organization and directs day-to-day operations so as to attain these objectives. To round out his planning activity, the manager submits budgets realistically reflecting the anticipated income or expenditures of his activity and, in operating, conducts his activity within approved budgets. This pattern is observable in Jones & Laughlin Steel Corporation. Here each manager is responsible for formulating clear policy within areas under his jurisdiction to permit assured, positive action and for interpreting corporate policy to his subordinate organization.

Organization

The manager himself must decide what organization he needs to accomplish the purposes of his unit. Starting with the chief executive of the company, each manager must reserve the responsibility and authority for developing an organization structure, defining responsibility and authority, and establishing relationships for his unit.

The manager himself must plan the organization he needs to accomplish the objectives he has set for his unit. In United States Steel Corporation, every manager reserves the responsibility for planning and recommending the organization structure required to perform assigned functions. This responsibility is also reserved by each manager in Creole Petroleum Corporation, who recommends the assignment of functions, changing of his departmental organization structure and the structure of field organizations assigned to his department for administration. He determines the activities of units and individuals within his department, delegates responsibility and authority to subordinates, and requests the organization planning specialized staff to publish organization descriptions reflecting these determinations and delegations. This is a basis for effective management action.

Motivation

The manager himself must withhold responsibility and authority for initiation and final decision in selecting, compensating, training, and inspiring the people who work for him. No matter how much assistance he may secure from the personnel staff, only the manager himself can decide the kind of people he wants in his department, who merit pay increases, counsel and coach his subordinates, handle grievances, and provide the example and leadership prerequisite to high productivity. In other words, only the leader himself can lead.

Characteristic of the best management thinking with respect to motivation is that of General Foods, where every manager is responsible for motivating his people to put forth their best efforts toward accomplishment of group goals. The General Foods manager is personally responsible for appraising performance, correcting poor performance, and rewarding outstanding performance. He advises, coaches, and provides work experience opportunities for subordinates so as to improve their abiilty to discharge their responsibilities with a minimum of detailed supervision and to expand their capacity to assume greater responsibilities.

The same pattern holds true in Standard Oil of California, where each supervisor is responsible for encouraging and supporting his subordinates. He guides, spurs, increases, limits, and requires action by his subordinates. When necessary, he takes corrective action, passing his corrections down through the chain of command, rather than delivering his comments personally to the subordinate directly concerned, except in an emergency. He visits and observes all levels of his own organization to determine the mental state and morale of his subordinates, their working conditions, their accomplishments, their desires, and their needs and personal requirements.

Coordination

All activities which report to a manager must be balanced, timed, and unified so that they take place as an integrated whole. The responsibility and authority for this coordination must be reserved because only the accountable manager is in a position to know, assess, and reconcile all the interests involved. As a general rule, the responsibility and authority for coordinating the interests of two functions must rest at a level higher than either of the interests involved.

If over-all company objectives are to be attained, the efforts of each part must be coordinated toward the common end. Cleveland Electric Illuminating achieves this coordination by operating on the basis that management is best accomplished in terms of over-all objectives and that every element in the organization has one or more objectives which are also common to other elements. Responsibility for coordination is placed at the point where the decisions are made, with the result that the manager who reserves authority to decide must also coordinate the actions resulting from his decisions.

In Ford Motor Company each manager has reserved responsibility and authority for coordinating, where appropriate, the functions performed under his jurisdiction with those performed under other executives and supervisors. Coordination is most effective when managers make consistent effort to keep themselves informed on matters that concern their work and the people who report to them. In West Penn Electric, managers coordinate the activities of their units with those of other units and render assistance to others as required. In addition, the West Penn manager has responsibility for keeping himself fully informed and up to date on all matters that contribute to the efficiency and progress of his unit and of other units of the company. Managers in American Enka carry similar responsibility. Here each manager coordinates his plans with other organizational units as required to ensure a coordinated approach in carrying out interdepartmental functions. He also cooperates with other organizational units in the exchange of ideas and information and in carrying out programs in which more than one organizational unit is interested.

Control

Just as the manager must reserve responsibility and authority for planning those activities for which he is accountable, he must also reserve responsibility for control, that is, for evaluating the work accomplished. As we have seen, control involves the development of standards, the measurement of work, analysis and reporting of results, and corrective management action.

Managers may make use of various agencies in accomplishing control. They cannot delegate active leadership and participation in developing the system of standards, records, and reports and in acting on exceptions and variances that are brought to their attention. This is shown graphically in Lever Brothers, where every manager reserves responsibility and authority for measuring performance against predetermined standards. From the data he secures, he is responsible for adjusting plans as required to achieve maximum effectiveness, holding costs to a minimum and within approved budgets. In American Enka, each manager also is responsible for keeping his superior informed of progress, deficiencies, irregularities, or other significant factors affecting his assigned responsibilities. This ensures effective over-all control and consistent direction of operations.

DELEGABLE RESPONSIBILITY AND AUTHORITY

What part of his responsibility and authority can the manager safely entrust to others? This is a vital question to every manager. To the extent that he answers it satisfactorily, he is enabled to concentrate on the important aspects of his own job and to give adequate time and attention to his subordinates. If he does not find the right answer, he is overwhelmed with detail and confronted with inefficiency and discontent on the part of his subordinates.

A plant manager, for example, is given responsibility and authority to run his plant. This includes production, maintenance and operation of facilities, inspection, accounting, engineering, personnel administration, and many other activities. In determining what to reserve and what to delegate, the plant manager is confronted with the impossibility of *doing* these functions himself. Accordingly, he reserves to himself only responsibility and authority for developing plans, establishing appropriate organization, coordinating, motivating, and controlling these functions as a group. His day-by-day, hour-by-hour work must be concerned primarily with these administrative activities if he is to do his job.

Detail and routine invariably should be delegated. A large part of the work in every management position consists of activities that are repetitious or are secondary to the primary purpose of the position itself. These lend themselves readily to delegation. It is to be noted that, after being delegated, these routine details often become major items of work when performed by subordinates. For instance, the company sales manager is responsible for selling the company's products. A matter of detail to him is the training of the sales crews, preparation of travel schedules, development of display pieces for sales promotion, and the process of calling on customers. However, at the appropriate level, each of these responsibilities becomes a matter of major concern to a subordinate manager or employee.

Managers in Ansul Chemical Company find they can get their own jobs done most effectively by providing over-all planning, coordination, and control and by restricting their own participation to advising, counseling, and guiding their subordinates. The more they concern themselves with the details of operations, the less they are able to manage. American Enka Corporation instructs its managers to delegate to the maximum the details and routines to be performed in the ordinary course of business so that they will be free for the demands of *managing* their jobs.

Matters of concern to only one subordinate element normally should be delegated. It is the business of the manager to occupy himself chiefly with problems that apply to several or all of the units reporting to him. When he concerns himself to a large extent with matters that are peculiar to only one of his subordinate units, he can be reasonably certain he is doing work the subordinate manager might better do himself. A manager delegates to his subordinates. He does not do their work for them.

How Much Should Be Delegated?

A corollary question to *what* responsibility and authority should be delegated is *how much* should be delegated. Just as a man's legs should be long enough to reach the ground, and no longer, enough responsibility and authority should be delegated to a position to enable the incumbent to accomplish whatever objectives are set for him. Much depends upon objectives. If the marketing manager is given the objective of simply selling the company products, he needs to be delegated responsibility and authority primarily for managing field sales activities. Such activities as long-term economic analysis, study and survey of consumer trends, and motivation research might be properly delegated to the Development, Economic Analysis, or Research Department or to some other function. If the objective set for the marketing manager, however, is to discover or create markets for existing products and to recommend potential markets for new products, he must be delegated all the activities necessary to accomplish this goal.

The question of how much authority should be delegated often gives more trouble than that of responsibility. The best answer is that enough authority should be delegated for the individual to reach the performance standards that have been set for his work. A salesman who is given the responsibility of selling a product line, for example, must have the right to approach customers in the name of the company. He must have the power to offer the company's wares for sale, with promise of delivery. He also needs the right to approve a sale if he consummates it in accordance with the prices and terms established by the company.

Beyond this minimum of authority, however, there is a considerable range for discretion on the part of the manager who delegates. For instance, should the salesman be permitted to approve requisitions for supplies? To hire other people to help him? To rent an automobile? To commit the company to a larger quantity of goods than current inventory levels warrant? These questions all require decision as to the amount of authority that should be delegated for effective performance of responsibility.

Authority Never Equal to Responsibility

A rule of thumb often cited is that "authority should always be delegated equal to responsibility." However, this is a misconception. If sound management is to prevail, authority can never be delegated equal to responsibility. That is to say, a person can never be given exactly as much authority as the work he is assigned. Some authority must always be withheld and cannot be delegated. For example, if the personnel director delegates responsibility for wage and salary matters to the manager of wage and salary, he must always withhold the authority for over-all planning, organization, coordination, motivation, and control with respect to wage and salary matters. Authority can only be delegated *commensurate* with responsibility.

How Far Down?

To what levels in the organization can responsibility and authority be delegated? If work is to be done, responsibility must be delegated to the people who will do the work. And if the principle of accompanying responsibility with commensurate authority is to be followed, it will be necessary to delegate authority to the place where the work is being done. Many companies have adopted a policy of pushing authority as far down in the organization as possible. When consistently and systematically practiced, this constitutes decentralization.

Food Machinery and Chemical Corporation follows a distinct policy of delegating as much authority as possible to its operating levels. FMC believes that decisions should always be made at the lowest possible level, as close as possible to the action to which they apply. Crown Zellerbach Corporation finds that maximum delegation of authority is sound not only organizationally but also from a developmental point of view. Crown Zellerbach finds that by delegating authority to the lowest possible point in the organization, it enables managers to make more decisions on their own initiative. This encourages the development of management talent at lower levels of the company, while at the same time freeing higher level managers to devote additional time to more important management problems. The Electric Storage Battery Company finds that delegation of authority to the point of actual performance of work helps managers to learn to manage and in doing so provides a training ground to qualify replacements for all positions.

SUMMARY

Delegation is probably the most important of all the skills a manager must possess. Delegation is the process the manager follows in dividing up his work, entrusting part of it to his subordinates, and establishing the conditions that will enable him to hold them accountable for performance.

Both formal and informal delegation must be recognized. Formal delegation involves entrustment of specific responsibility and authority to a position and creation of an obligation for performance of the work and exercise of authority. Informal delegation is the performance of work and exercise of authority because people want to do it and not because they are compelled to do so by the organization.

The process of delegation must be sufficiently flexible to provide for both formal and informal types.

A key question in delegation is: What work can a manager safely entrust to others and what must he perform himself? Because of his unique organizational position, the manager must always reserve responsibility and authority for initiation and final decision with respect to planning, organizing, motivating, coordinating, and controlling the work of those who report to him. He can safely delegate the detail and routine leading up to final decisions and the operating work he otherwise would perform himself.

CHAPTER 7 *Better Methods of Delegation*

Delegation is one of the most important of management skills; it is also one of the most difficult. The reasons a manager does not delegate effectively may be entangled with his personality make-up, his aptitudes, his training and experience. Delegation demands expression of some positive human traits. To delegate effectively, a manager must be prepared to give of his time, his interest, and his effort with no promise of immediate return. Humility is required. The person who delegates needs to accept the fact that others may be able to do all or part of his own job as well or better than he can.

The true nature of delegation and a measure of its difficulty is perhaps best described in a statement made by Lao-tzū. "Of the best leaders," said this wise Chinese, "when their task is accomplished, their work done, the people all remark, 'we have done it ourselves.' " [1]

PREREQUISITES

The problem of delegation is essentially one of human leadership. Delegation is not only a technique of management; it is part of the attitude of the business itself. This general attitude depends on such factors as the management climate and the willingness of key managers to let go of authority and responsibility.

Climate

The climate most favorable to delegation is forward-looking, optimistic, and expansive. The delegation-minded company has its sights focused on the future. It has measured for itself a broad swath of accomplishment five, ten, and twenty years to come. Because of this orientation, the company is willing to bet its future on people far down the management ladder—the juniors who show promise today but who will need encouragement and assistance if they are to be ready to step into positions of leadership. The company recognizes that capable managers are developed primarily on the job. The budding manager has to be

[1] *The Wisdom of Lao-tzū*, Modern Library, New York, 1954, p. 114.

134

given important work to do, he must be permitted to make decisions, and he grows best in making mistakes and learning how to do better after he recognizes where he failed.

A climate favorable to delegation can exist only when teamwork is prevalent in the management group. This rests on mutual confidence, a sense of interdependence in the achievement of common goals, and a free interchange of ideas and suggestions. The management that wishes to develop effective delegation must first establish sound personal relationships and thorough knowledge of the organization by all its members. This, in turn, is a product of careful personnel selection, motivation, and, in largest degree, time and patience.

Willingness to Let Go

Some of the major hurdles in delegation are psychological. The manager may find himself unable to let go. He may delegate but continue to breathe so closely down the necks of his subordinates that he makes effective work impossible. He may maintain a follow-up so detailed that every action takes place under close scrutiny, or he may delegate responsibility but continue to make all the decisions himself. Only after the reasons for this inability to let go have been identified can corrective action take place.

Lack of Faith. This is one of the primary reasons why managers find it difficult to let go. The manager does not feel that his subordinate is capable of doing the job. The crux of the difficulty may be that he believes subconsciously that nobody could possibly do the job as well as he can. This is particularly true if the manager himself has come up through the business and is an expert in some part of the function which he supervises.

Take, for instance, the sales manager of an appliance firm in the Middle West, who started his career as a field salesman. He had developed many special customers and invented many sales gimmicks of his own. What was his attitude after he became sales manager? If sales results were not up to par or if some particularly difficult dealer problem arose, he was sure he could set the matter quickly to rights if he were to take care of it himself. Frequently he did. And to the extent that he succeeded, he managed to reinforce his own lack of confidence in his subordinates and to diminish their chances of learning. As a result, he complained continually about the inefficiency of his sales crews and the long hours he had to put in "to see that the job was done right."

This lack of faith may have solid foundation. It is often true that the principal can get the job done more quickly, more effectively, and with less trouble if he does it himself. But he forgets that he went through a period of trial and error himself before he became proficient in the task.

In the final analysis, delegation is a process of entrustment and hence of faith. Merck and Company emphasizes some of the aspects of this attitude of trust. For one thing, when the manager delegates, he must be prepared to back up his man. When the principal leaves the decision on a matter to a subordinate, he must be willing to give him the latitude he needs. If the subordinate's decision must be reversed, the revision itself should, if possible, come from the subordinate. Merck and Company believes that delegation requires not only faith in subordinates on the part of the principal, but also a strong faith in himself.

Fear. This is a most pervasive reason why some managers find it difficult to let go. The manager may be afraid that his subordinate will outshine him and hence secure more attention and recognition than he himself. The principal may be afraid that if he delegates too much, he won't leave enough for himself to do; in other words, he will work himself out of a job. Most such fears are an expression of insecurity and a reflection of the climate of the company itself. It is difficult for the manager to accept the usual clichés about earning promotion by developing subordinates if he knows two or three company executives who have literally worked themselves out of a job by bringing along men more capable than they. He is certain to fear outstanding ability in his subordinates and to regard it as a threat to his own position unless he knows from experience that the company has developed a system of transfer and rotation and will be able to place any stars he may develop without endangering his own position.

THE ART OF DELEGATION

Delegation is an art, not a science. The manager who wishes to perfect his skill in delegation has no infallible principles to draw upon. If he performs certain prescribed actions, specific results will not necessarily follow. The experience of a great many executives provides the foundation for certain guides which have been tried and proved in company administration. The manager who wants to evaluate his own thinking and approach to delegation will find these helpful. The steps in delegation are part of the process of management itself. As is true of all management activity, the initial phase is that of establishing the objectives for the responsibility and authority that are to be delegated.

1. ESTABLISH GOALS

The person to whom work is being delegated wants to know, "Why am I asked to do this?" Blind obedience is not characteristic of modern business. While the principal may clearly see the total picture and where this particular work fits in, his subordinate probably has little idea of why it is required or important. And if he is to accept the delegation enthusiastically, he needs to know that his work is both necessary and important.

Just as effective management can truly be said to be management by objectives, successful delegation can also be characterized as delegation by objectives. The machine operator is not content just to be operating a machine. He wants to know he is making something that has utility and will fill a real need. The tax accountant wants to do more than figure taxes. He will be much more interested in the work delegated to him if he feels that he is helping determine the company's tax obligations and that he can contribute materially to its success by ensuring that these obligations are discharged for the minimum amounts the tax settlement process will permit.

Personal Goals

People want to know the goals toward which they are striving. As H. P. Hood & Sons points out, it is the responsibility of the company to spell these out for its employees. No matter how routine his job, every manager has something to contribute to the company's dealings with customers, producers, fellow employees, and the general public.

The individual manager also wants personal goals. What is he expected to accomplish? What constitutes good performance for the kind of work he is given to do? Many companies set objectives for managers at all levels. For example, Aluminum Company of America gives each foreman a budget for direct and indirect labor and indirect materials. This, in effect, makes him a businessman in his own right and gives him a profit objective for his operation. The company reports to him his performance, whether over or under his budget. Superintendents and department heads establish similar goals, as do plant and division managers, and are kept currently informed of their performance. Each manager thus works toward a clearly defined goal. He is kept informed in terms of dollars and cents of how effectively the responsibility and authority he has delegated are being carried out.

2. DEFINE RESPONSIBILITY AND AUTHORITY

If a manager is to perform efficiently, he needs to know what his job is and how much authority he has to perform it.[2] Companies that have

[2] Says John M. Pfiffner, Professor of Government, University of Southern California, "There is no complaint more widespread among supervisors than that they do not know their authority. . . . The supervisor who is not sure of his ground will evade issues or take every question to his chief for decision." "How to Delegate Authority," *Public Management,* December, 1943, pp. 351–353.

made a serious study of delegation find that a desirable preliminary is to put in writing the authority, responsibility, and relationships of each manager. AMI, Incorporated, for example, uses written position guides to provide a basis for agreement between each supervisor and his superior as to the objectives, responsibilities, relationships, and limits of authority of each position. AMI finds that, from the subordinate's point of view, it enables him to understand what his superior expects of him; from the standpoint of the boss, it helps him to balance the requirements of the work he is assigned and the manpower he has available to do it. American Air Lines also finds that clear definition of responsibility and authority helps to facilitate delegation and to eliminate confusion by identifying jobs that have been delegated to more than one person. This eliminates much duplication and overlap.

3. MOTIVATE SUBORDINATES

The effective manager is one who can get results through others. It follows that the manager who wants to delegate should be able to motivate people to do what he wants done, willingly and enthusiastically. Motivation is the moving force in delegation.

Although people have been working for others all down through recorded history, we still do not know much about what makes people *want* to work. As business and industry have grown and developed, attitudes about motivation have also changed.

Early in this century, it was assumed that people would produce more if the mechanics of production were improved. Make it easier for a man to work, give him better tools, and his production would increase. This proved true up to a point. Early in the century, Frederick Winslow Taylor, the pioneer in scientific management, found that study and improvement of work methods would accelerate production tremendously. Working with coal handlers in the Bethlehem Steel Company, Taylor was able to boost production per man by 80 per cent. Taylor assumed at first that if a man used the largest shovel and scooped it heaping full, he would shovel the most coal in a day. However, Taylor observed that this did not necessarily follow. Men who used small, short shovels often loaded most in a day. Experimenting a little, Taylor found that if he decreased the size of the shovel a man used he could increase the tonnage shoveled. However, once the shovel load fell below 21 pounds, production also fell.[3]

Taylor demonstrated that great gains in production could be made through improvement of work methods and through specialization. He

[3] Frederick Winslow Taylor, *The Principles of Scientific Management*, Harper & Brothers, New York, 1942, pp. 64–76.

believed that the paramount objectives of a business organization should be high wages, low unit costs, and improved and standardized working conditions.[4]

Taylor's thinking had a widespread impact upon business. Following a similar line of thinking, Henry Ford startled the business world early in the century by being able to put out a standardized, low-cost automobile, take the lead in the industry, and yet pay the unheard-of sum of $5 a day to workers in his plants. Many other companies have followed this same basic formula with great success. However, we are now beginning to discover that the internal relationship among these three factors of high wages, low costs, and standardization is not as predictable as we had once assumed.

Stimulus of Challenge

Many companies have found that it does not necessarily follow that people will work harder if work is made easier and simpler to perform. Overspecialization can devitalize work and kill motivation. International Business Machines has done pioneering work in demonstrating that people react well and production actually increases if work is purposely made more complex and challenging. For example, in one factory of 7,400 people, IBM is engaged primarily in machine processing and assembly. In 1943, this plant, following Taylor's basic idea of specialization, had different people specializing in machine setup and machine operation. The setup would be made by the setup man, working with the machine operator. The setup man would then make a test run, check it, and leave the worker to operate the machine. The ratio was one setup man to every eleven operators.

However, mounting indirect labor costs and higher unit costs resulting from this plethora of setup men stimulated the company to study the situation carefully. IBM concluded that the setup job was not complicated enough to warrant a specialist. If the typical operator could be trained to operate a machine such as a horizontal miller in five hours, he could also be trained to make a setup and test it.

Some interesting motivational forces were put into action following this conclusion. The company now trains a machine operator to set up his own tooling. He operates his own machine. When he has made his run, he inspects his own tools, checks wear, decides whether the tools should be reground or discarded and replaced. He also inspects his own work. The number of setup men was cut to one in forty-eight by 1946. By 1954 there were only four setup men in the entire factory. Evidence of the motivation resulting from this change toward complexity is the

[4] Frederick Winslow Taylor, *Shop Management*, Harper & Brothers, New York, 1911, p. 27.

fact that production has gone up steadily. Costs have come down. And the machine operators show more interest and pride in their work.

There is almost daily evidence that refinement and specialization of operating methods is not the whole answer in motivation. Many times the challenge of a complex and difficult job is motivation in itself and a stimulus, not a deterrent, to productivity.

Diversity of Motivation

What *does* motivate people in an organization? As is to be expected, the answer is as complex and various as people themselves. The latest findings indicate that true motivation is internal. The way we react *inside* to various incentives determines to what extent we will be motivated.

One person will work hard and long for money, another is greatly concerned with the size of his office, a third will work hardest for a word of approbation from his supervisor. As Gracian, the Spanish Jesuit, put it some three hundred years ago, "Every volition has a special motive which varies according to taste . . . knowing any man's mainspring of motive, you have, as it were, the key to his will." [5]

Different people are motivated by different incentives. As a general rule, however, all of us have one internal need in common, and that is a desire for recognition—a feeling of importance. We want to be thought worthwhile and of some consequence by others with whom we come in contact. Dr. Rensis Likert, Director of the Institute for Social Research, University of Michigan, believes that this desire for recognition or ego satisfaction is central to other incentives in motivating people.

Money, for example, is effective as a motivator only in terms of how much it means to the individual and his ability to convert it into marks of status and prestige. Money can provide the fine clothes, large home, and expensive automobile which mean recognition and success to many people. The effectiveness of each as an incentive depends upon the personality make-up of the individual concerned.

To know what motivates a subordinate, it is important for his supervisor to find out what incentives mean most to him—which he can most readily convert to a feeling of recognition and importance. Some managers make it a practice to discuss goals and desires with the people who report to them. By finding out what a person really wants from his life and his career, by evaluating the importance to him of security, status, money, and other incentives, the manager can more easily determine how best to motivate him.

[5] Balthassar Gracian, *The Art of Worldly Wisdom*, The Macmillan Company, New York, 1955, p. 15.

Group Factors

Recent research points to an additional source of motivation that has largely been overlooked. This is the fact that individuals can be impelled to action because of their relations with other people—their membership in a group. Since business organizations are essentially collections of groups, it is obvious that this aspect of motivation is of great importance.

Research in group motivation has been done at many universities, including Harvard University, University of Michigan, University of Illinois, and Massachusetts Institute of Technology.[6] According to these findings, an individual may secure satisfaction and recognition from his interaction with the group. All individuals are not affected to the same extent by group membership. Some never "belong," others are accepted by some groups, rejected by others.

The extent to which an individual can be "pressured" by his membership in a specific group is determined by the degree of loyalty which he and other members of the group feel toward one another. This is known as group cohesiveness. Members of a cohesive group see themselves as part of the team. Other things being equal, they would rather stay with the group than leave it. They tend to think their own group better than similar groups.

Group Cohesiveness

This desire to feel one with the group is a powerful influence in successful motivation. The individual members of the group tend to act together and to be influenced by the group as a whole in proportion to the loyalty they feel toward one another. This helps to explain why, in some companies, employees will refuse to exceed the production standards they set themselves, even though by so doing they could easily make a large amount of incentive pay. The individual feels more loyalty toward his own group and its standards than toward the company and the standards it sets. As Robert L. Kahn and Nancy L. Morse of the Survey Research Center, University of Michigan, put it,

If a supervisor is rigid and refuses to recognize individual or situational differences, the work group will tend to set a norm which is attainable by most of its members, and to penalize an individual who produces in excess of that norm. Thus, his motivation to high production comes into immediate conflict with his motivation to be accepted by other members of the group.[7]

[6] See Dorwin Cartwright and Alvin Zander (eds.), *Group Dynamics: Research and Theory*, Row, Peterson & Company, Evanston, Ill., 1953, for a summary of research findings.

[7] Robert L. Kahn and Nancy C. Morse, "The Relationship of Productivity to Morale," *The Journal of Social Issues*, vol. 7, no. 3, 1951.

The highly cohesive group tends to set its own standards and to operate in terms of them. It is significant that the cohesive group will accept the standards of the manager to the extent that he is a member of the group itself. In other words, the manager can secure highest motivation and productivity if he is loyal to his own group and supports it. To motivate his people strongly, the manager needs to work *inside* the group as a member of the team, not *outside* issuing directions and commands. The research findings indicate that if he is confronted with the choice of pleasing his own group and pleasing higher management, the manager is likely to accomplish more, productivitywise, by catering to the needs of his own group.

Improving Group Cohesiveness. The important question at this point is: What can the manager do to help increase cohesiveness of his group? That is, how can he be sure that he is one of the group and that his standards are being accepted? He can do this by helping the individual members of the group satisfy their own needs. To the extent that he convinces the members of the group that their needs, his own, and those of the company coincide, he can motivate them to produce according to the standards he sets. What should the manager do to develop motivation? He can make use of both organizational and leadership factors.

Organizational Influences

Motivation in the company is largely motivation of people in groups, and groups can be organized to facilitate group cohesiveness and hence motivation. The two factors most readily influenced by the organization design are the size of the group and the opportunity for interaction by its members.

The fewer people in a group, the more opportunity there is for communication and participation and the more quickly the people involved come to know one another and to understand their common problems. This leads to a high degree of group loyalty. The Procter & Gamble Company is an advocate of this principle. Procter & Gamble tries to keep to a minimum the number of people reporting to supervisors at all levels of management. On the average, only about fifteen people will report to a foreman, about five foremen to a supervisor, and so on up the line. Procter & Gamble finds that this enables the members of the group to get to know one another well. The manager can find out about the ambitions and hopes of his people, their worries and problems. He can discover who are the natural leaders, and those upon whose influence he can count in his day-to-day explanation and handling of new problems and policies.

The organization structure itself can isolate people or it can provide opportunity for them to work together and hence directly affect motivation. Some companies make organizational provision for interaction by establishing formal working relationships. For example, the staff and line relationship as established in many companies makes it mandatory for the line to utilize staff services to the fullest. Other companies make use of scheduled meetings, work teams, task forces, and committees.

Departmental and staff meetings encourage close interaction of all members of the group by providing for discussion of operations and problems. Work teams, in which several members of the same department are assigned a common problem, require teamwork in the accomplishment of a common objective. Task forces, made up of members of various departments and functions within the company, accomplish the same thing on a broader scale.

Many companies make use of Junior Boards of Directors, in the pattern of "multiple management," first introduced by McCormick and Company, Incorporated, Baltimore, Maryland. Through membership on such boards, promising representatives of middle management are provided the opportunity to participate in the solution of over-all operating and policy problems of the company before full top-management responsibility is placed upon them. Junior Board participation thus contributes (1) to the development of individual members by strengthening a feeling of belonging, by developing attitudes of cooperation, and by stimulating individual initiative and ingenuity; and (2) to the improvement of the business by assuring the continuous flow of new ideas to top management.

Leadership Factors

Individual managers can encourage and develop motivation through their methods of leadership. Two of the most effective leadership activities are providing for participation in the decision-making process and the development of effective methods of communication. People are most interested in action which they have helped plan themselves. This is true from the president of the company to the worker at the bench. Giving subordinates a chance to be heard and to offer their own ideas and suggestions helps to establish the feeling of proprietorship which leads to self-motivation.

Consultative Supervision

Some companies secure participation by encouragement of consultative supervision. Esso Standard Oil Company believes that employees at all levels should be invited to discuss matters affecting them, that they should be given an opportunity to share the problems in their groups, and that their views should be given full consideration in working out problems. When participation takes place, subordinates accept the principal's decisions more understandingly, and the decision itself is likely to be more sound and balanced because it reflects the views of all who will be affected. More than this, it helps to bring into the open differences of opinion and to reconcile conflicts before the die is cast.

In his research, Dr. Likert has found that one of the best ways to have supervisors accept delegation and the accompanying accountability for responsibility and authority is to involve them in the process of making decisions.

Communication

Motivation is dependent upon communication. But what is involved in communication is often misunderstood. It is often thought to be a matter of techniques—of knowing how to speak clearly, of putting up bulletin boards and sending out announcements. This is but scratching the surface. Communication is the sum of all the things one person does when he wants to create understanding in the mind of another. Communication is a bridge of meaning. It involves a systematic and continuing process of telling, listening, and understanding. The significant fact in motivation and delegation is that whenever possible, communication should be accomplished first, not secondhand. Most companies agree that people listen and understand better if new information is imparted to them by their boss, on the job. This gives the information the stamp of authority. It relates it to their day-by-day work and problems. And the boss is always available to further explain, interpret, or suggest.

Procter & Gamble places greatest reliance on this face-to-face communication. The company believes that personal-communication is not only more immediate and flexible but also the most effective in terms of employee response and interest. This close, natural channel of communication helps the Procter & Gamble manager to let his people know where they stand, with relation to both their own jobs and the business as a whole.

Face-to-face communication is most often a matter of informal contact while the work is in progress. Some companies make provisions for planned meetings of a relatively informal nature to facilitate this process. Aluminum Company of America, for instance, in its Conference Plan for Management, trains all members of management to talk effectively to individuals and with groups they supervise. Unit and department heads meet frequently with their subordinates in information meetings, to present and discuss material of importance and interest. In some cases, a new product or the installation of new equipment is discussed. On other occasions, the annual report of the company is reviewed and analyzed. In addition, programs of basic economics, human relations, or supervisory techniques may be presented.

What Should Be Communicated? The manager should first communicate matters he wants his people to know about. This information may range from changes in daily operating procedures to discussion and interpretation of company policy and objectives. It includes information funneling down from top management for relay and interpretation to all members of the group. Members of management need to be constantly aware of what the company is trying to accomplish, the major problems it is trying to solve, and the nature and meaning of company policy. Unless they are told these things, they are likely to feel on the outside looking in, and not really members of the team. It is possible that this information may not have intrinsic interest to the people who will hear it. The manager doing the communicating then has an obligation to relate it to their personal welfare, their work and problems, or other matters that are of personal interest.

Only one part of the process of communication is completed when the principal gets his ideas across. Subordinates invariably want to know many things the supervisor would never think to tell them. For example, American Air Lines recently conducted a survey to find out what kind of information their people would like to have. The response shows a keen interest in the company and its welfare. Specific items included:

Information about the company's future plans. This included general growth and expansion and such specific items as new equipment and maintenance and sales programs.

Company policies and policy changes. There was greatest interest in those policies and changes which would directly affect the individual in his position.

Company income and its profits and losses. People within the company were interested not only in its year-end financial statement but also in more frequent reports on the success or failure of the entire business, covering passengers carried, sales, freight hauled, and claims paid.

Desire for this kind of information is present, but frequently it is not voiced. It then becomes the responsibility of the manager to find out what his people want to know and to provide the answers and the information in fullest possible measure.

4. REQUIRE COMPLETED WORK

Delegation does not always cut down a manager's work load. Sometimes it increases it. This may seem paradoxical, but it proves true when the subordinate keeps on referring back with questions, problems, and requests for interim decision. The more difficult the delegation, the greater the impulse for the subordinate to ask his superior what to do. The subordinate cannot be cut completely adrift. How much should he be allowed to check back after he has received the delegation? How can the principal get maximum performance while still conserving his own time to the utmost?

There are three alternatives. The first is to permit the subordinate as much contact with his chief as he wishes. This is impractical because the manager ends up doing most of the work. Another alternative is to put the subordinate completely on his own and refuse him access until he has completed the job and is ready to present his solution or recommendation. Carried to the extreme, this denies to the subordinate the advice and guidance he needs from his chief. It reduces the opportunity for participation, face-to-face communication, and personal interest which are at the heart of motivation. Most companies find that the reasonable solution is a compromise. The doctrine of completed work, as adopted by such companies as Chance Vought Aircraft, American Enka, and Minneapolis Honeywell, provides for necessary supervisory and motivational interaction but limits the demands made upon the principal.

The doctrine of completed work embodies a two-way relationship between the superior and his subordinate. It requires that the principal make a clearly understood delegation. He consciously plans for guidance, coaching, and communication. Over and above this, he insists that his subordinate must do the work. Completed work involves several distinct steps.

a. Make a Clear-cut Assignment. One reason subordinates often check back is that they have not clearly understood the delegation made to them. The principal overestimates how much his people know about what he wants done. The manager has a very clear idea of the total picture. But he forgets that transmitting his thinking to the mind of his subordinate is a major undertaking in itself. Incomplete communication at this point is often a primary deficiency in delegation. Many executives emphasize that if the principal will take the time to explain patiently exactly what he wants done and how he wants it, he will have the best possible assurance of completed work. To make everything clear, provision should be made for feedback. Questions such as "How do you plan to go at this?" or "What is your understanding of how this is to be done?" will encourage the subordinate to repeat the assignment back. If a time schedule is part of the assignment, this is best transmitted in writing.

b. Delegate the Details of Coordination. While the manager himself must reserve responsibility for over-all coordination, the subordinate will know what he should coordinate if he will ask himself these questions: Who has to know about this work? What does he have to know about it? Who has to agree to whatever action we take and what is the nature of the agreement required of him?

If the superior will specify what coordination is necessary for satisfactory completion of the work, his subordinate can take the necessary steps, within the limits of his own authority, to get whatever prior agreement from them he can. If the subordinate can say, "I talked this over with Mr. Jones's assistant and he agrees to it," it is better than if he had not coordinated with Mr. Jones's department at all.

The doctrine of completed work does not preclude the subordinate calling a committee meeting for purposes of coordination *at his level,* provided he has the authority to do so. Instead of putting it to a meeting, the subordinate can do the coordination by personal contact. This involves more effort on his part, but it can help cut down the demands on his chief.

c. Specify Progress Information Required. The concept of completed work requires that the principal remain informed of the progress of work he delegates. It is the responsibility of the manager himself to determine what information he will need and how he wants it presented. Perhaps he will require formal reports; possibly an occasional verbal summary will fill his needs.

d. Provide Counseling and Guidance. No matter how much time the principal devotes to preliminary discussion of the delegation, there is always the possibility that he will have overlooked an important detail or his subordinate will have misunderstood something and want to check back. Every opportunity should be provided for this type of reference and for personal guidance. The manager will want to call his subordinate in to talk over what he is doing, to discuss various alternatives that he himself may have tried and found inadequate, and to provide as generously as he can of his own experience and knowledge.

The key consideration at this juncture is that these discussions should be at the initiative of the principal and should be for purposes of development and guidance. If the principal falls into the trap of giving or withholding approval of specific action the subordinate proposes to take, he will find himself doing work he presumably had delegated.

e. Require a Finished Package. The test of completed work is whether the subordinate works through his own problems to the point that the principal can indicate his approval or disapproval of the completed action simply by saying "yes" or "no." If the final product is a written report or recommendation, it is either acceptable or needs to be taken back and worked over. As Chance Vought Aircraft, Incorporated, points out, it is important for the subordinate to retain responsibility for a solution to the problem until he has worked it out in finished form, ready for approval. In discussing the problem, the principal's emphasis should be on the "how" of problem solving: how to get the necessary facts, what factors should be considered, and how to evaluate the various factors. If the principal disapproves the first completed solution presented to him, it is essential that he discuss with his subordinate how to ensure correct choices in the future.

If the subordinate writes a memorandum *to* his chief, this is not completed work. However, if he writes a memorandum for his chief to send to someone else, and if he so presents his views that his chief can make them *his* views simply by signing his name, this is in the best meaning of completed work.

When the work is in the form of a report, it should be presented as a complete, self-contained unit which can be forwarded, without explanation, simply by signature of the principal. If the proper result is reached, the principal will recognize it. If he wants explanations, he will ask for them.

Difficulties in Carrying Out Completed Work

Completed work is exacting. It requires discipline both of the superior and the subordinate. The manager must have faith and self-control. He must believe fully enough in his subordinate to allow him to go to the point of failure, if necessary, without interfering. At the same time, he must restrict himself to giving counsel and advice and insist that his subordinate make the choice of a course of action.

Advantages

Companies which insist on completed work find it has many advantages. First, it frees managers from detail. They can concentrate on the management aspects of their own jobs and not spend their time on details they had supposedly delegated. Completed work conserves effort. By ensuring that work is done by only one person, it helps to eliminate duplication and overlap. This technique is also an excellent means of development. If subordinates are to develop an ability to exercise good judgment, they must be given an opportunity to make decisions. Many companies find that completed work is one of the best ways of exercising the decision-making muscles.

5. PROVIDE TRAINING

The process of helping managers develop ability in delegation is often complex and difficult. Three different skills are involved. Subordinates must be trained to accept delegation. The manager must master the skill of delegation. He needs to be able to accept delegation.

Training subordinates to accept delegation is complicated by the fact that individuals vary greatly in capacity. Some people are constitutionally incapable of making decisions or of acting independently. No matter how much authority they are delegated, they are never able to exercise it properly. In some cases this is an acquired weakness. If the person has worked in the shadow of a strong and domineering principal, who insists on making all the decisions himself, the subordinate is almost certain to lack decisiveness himself.

In other cases the subordinate may be the "professional" type, who prefers to work by himself rather than as member of a team. Since this type of personality frequently has ability of a high order, the principal needs to find a method of delegation that will enable him to capitalize on his subordinate's unique abilities, while at the same time motivating him to highest productivity. Frequently this is accomplished by delegating relatively limited, highly specialized work to the "lone worker," so that it does not involve extensive participation and coordination with others.

Most managers find that, once the subordinate's weakness is identified and understood, he can be trained to accept delegation and to discharge responsibility and authority more effectively. Armstrong Cork Company, for example, has all new supervisors undergo a special course of training to prepare and condition them for gradual assumption of the full load of responsibility and authority delegated to the position they have been appointed to fill.

The manager needs to learn to accept delegation. To some, this is at once the most difficult and the most rewarding of the skills required. The manager who recognizes his own weaknesses is better able to understand and sympathize with those of his subordinates. When he learns to follow, he at the same time learns to become a better leader. In the words of Hamilcar, "My son Hannibal will be a great general, because of all my soldiers he best knows how to obey."

Training in delegation should follow three well-defined steps:

a. Appraisal of current performance in delegation

b. Counseling for improvement

c. Coaching on the job

Suitable modification of these steps permits development of managers in all facets of delegation.

Appraisal of Current Performance

The first step in training managers to delegate is to ensure that clear and well-defined concepts of delegation exist. By definition, delegation must proceed from the top down. If effective delegation is not practiced by the chief executive, and, in turn, the key officers of the enterprise, it is very unlikely that delegation will be effective farther down the line, no matter how much training is invoked.

Performance Inventory. The training process itself begins with an inventory of current performance. This requires that the work of each manager be appraised, with appropriate attention to evaluation of practices in delegation. The performance standards established as measures of accountability, which were described in the previous chapter, can readily be adapted to use for appraisal of management performance.

The Detroit Edison Company emphasizes the need for full participation and reconciliation of standards between both the manager and the subordinates whose work is being appraised. Detroit Edison makes extensive use of appraisal techniques based on performance standards derived from job responsibilities. A typical example is the standard developed to measure how well a superintendent is handling his responsibilities in organization and development.

Performance is satisfactory when:
1. An organization chart that presents the true picture of the department's organization exists and shows evidence that the following items have been considered:
    a. The nature of the work to be performed and its flow
    b. The number of people needed to perform the work
    c. The number of work groups needed
    d. The number of supervisors and levels of supervision necessary
    e. The salary grade relationship between employees and supervisor and other supervisors in the department
    f. The need for clear-cut lines of authority
2. Adequate provision is made for developing replacements at all positions
3. There is evidence of continual review and evaluation of departmental organization through consideration of:
    a. Technical developments
    b. Appraisal of subordinates
    c. Proposals for improvement

Performance Standards in Tremco. Effective methods of appraisal in these terms have been developed and are in use by the Tremco Manufacturing Company. Tremco first defines the work to be performed by the manager, securing his agreement and reconciling any differences with his superior or others concerned. Standards for performance are then set against these job responsibilities. It is significant that the standard is set by the individual whose performance is to be evaluated, not by his superior. This ensures his understanding and complete acceptance of the yardstick by which he is being measured. It is interesting that instead of setting standards too low, the subordinate more often tends to set them too high and they must be scaled down.

Tremco ensures that the standards are not vague generalities; where possible, numerical quantities or check points are used. For example, a market manager is measured in terms of dollar volume of new business in the United States and Canada, the percentage ratio between cost of sales effort in relation to volume, the dollar cost of research time, and the dollar cost of such items as instructor-mechanic and field application engineering.

Typical of the standards Tremco uses to measure the effectiveness of delegation are the following excerpts from the performance standards set for the Market Manager, Industrial Sales:

Satisfactory performance on the part of the Industrial Division Market Manager is achieved in respect to:

I. Training men who are devoting time to industrial business to be effective:

   A. Teaching planning

      1. In evaluating who is a prospect:
         When subsequent contacts or events indicate that he has selected in any one field the principal prospects from whom business can be secured and has made specific plans for the timing of his contacts upon them.

      2. In routing himself:
         When his plan for covering any area which includes all accounts to be seen in that area; and his analysis of his time during that period shows that he was able to contact these accounts he planned to see without too much loss of time or retracing his steps.

   B. Developing effective sales techniques
      When the planning for and the carrying through of an interview results in trial orders in a satisfactory proportion of his accounts; and when a satisfactory volume of business results where we are able to provide a product which meets the prospect's needs.

   C. Providing reports which give necessary information concisely and fully:
      When the reports give all information necessary for supervision to evaluate the progress being made with the account; the potential of the account; and the nature of the problem.

  Performance review is conducted either on an individual or committee basis. In the individual method, the review is completed by the superior alone, with possible review by *his* superior. This method has the advantage of being most rapid and economical of supervisory time. However, such speed and economy are usually at the expense of objectivity and balanced consideration and discussion of the total performance of the individual being appraised. In practice, when the superior conducts the appraisal by himself, it is usually more an expression of personal opinion than the weighing and analysis of specific actions. The conmittee method helps to overcome this bias by bringing together at least two, and perferably three, people who know the work of the man being appraised. Discussion of the man's performance by such a committee most often results in a relatively well-balanced and impartial appraisal.

Counseling

Counseling is the process of talking to the subordinate about his job performance. Properly done, this can be a most valuable part of the training process and can help to establish cordial and enduring relationships between the boss and the people who report to him. Handled improperly, the counseling interview can result in resentment, frustration, and weakened morale.

Counseling is undertaken to help subordinates help themselves. The emphasis is upon assisting the subordinate to recognize his own strengths and weaknesses, to aid him in determining what he himself can do to improve, and to leave him with a firm resolve to do something about it. Counseling is not the giving of advice; it is a means of helping a person to help himself.

Securing Data. Effective counseling depends upon adequate and acceptable data. Unless the counseling interview is based upon facts, that is, upon things that have actually happened, it is likely to deteriorate into an exchange of opinions. Most managers who undertake counseling sessions prepare themselves beforehand by gathering supporting evidence for every point they wish to make. It is not enough for the manager to state that the subordinate is "unreliable" or that his "costs are too high" or that he is "immature." Unless he is able to support his statements with examples of specific occurrences, he is dealing in opinions. Psychologists point out that such value judgments are sometimes a reflection of personal deficiencies which the superior himself may possess.

Some managers who do a sound job of counseling maintain a day-by-day record of significant events that occur on the job. If a person does something outstandingly good—or poor—the fact is recorded and can later be cited to qualify whatever points the supervisor wishes to make during the counseling interview. Dr. John A. Flanagan, Director of the American Institute for Research, has formalized this process of noting significant occurrences in an appraisal process known as the Critical Incident Method.

Another method of securing data is that of encouraging the subordinate to rate himself. Usually he is asked to complete the regular rating form and to cite any examples of significant performance, either good or poor. United States Rubber Company, which makes use of this technique, finds it has many advantages.

The subordinate is often more critical of himself than his superior would be. He starts off knowing that he needs help, and he has every chance for participation.

The Counseling Interview. During the counseling interview, the subordinate will frequently bring up points which the superior had not known about or had forgotten. He may provide reasons for discrepancies which change their character. In some cases, he may have evidence which shows that his boss is really the cause of an error or mistake in judgment.

Productive counseling depends upon a mutual feeling of respect and confidence. It arises largely from the feeling of the subordinate that his boss is interested in him and wants to help. Satisfactory experience and relationships on the job are prerequisite to this feeling. It can be encouraged during the interview by the attitude and method adopted by the superior. If he talks continually and is primarily interested in expressing his own ideas, he will not develop a cooperative attitude. However, if he does as much listening as telling, if he shows by his questions and remarks that he is trying to understand and be helpful, he will find that empathy really exists.

Positive Approach. People want to hear the good things about themselves. They automatically tend to rationalize or refute negative comments. The counselor can anticipate this difficulty and help to overcome it if he will try to assess weaknesses from a positive instead of a negative viewpoint. The boss who stresses "you are weak in delegation" or "you don't get out enough work" is immediately setting up strong opposition both to his ideas and to the development of a corrective program. However, if he will start with, "In order to be promoted you have to know how to get others to do a good share of your work for you," he creates a positive interest on the part of the person he is interviewing.

Coaching

Coaching refers to the activities the manager undertakes on the job to help his subordinate improve in ability to accept delegation and to delegate to others. Coaching is based on example. We tend to delegate as we are delegated to. The manager who wants to act as trainer must assure himself that he is doing a good job of delegation himself.

Coaching also includes the use of assignments which are specifically designed to help an individual improve his skills of accepting delegation. This means the manager should make every opportunity on the job for his people to undertake difficult assignments, to operate above their usual level. In other words, he should make every opportunity for his subordinates to succeed at new and demanding tasks or to fail and to learn by failure. Over and above on-the-job coaching, the company should systematically develop and create opportunities for managers to rotate among different management jobs. These rotational assignments should occur early enough in the man's management career so that by the time he and his family are well established in a given location, the company will not be under pressure to uproot him to give him management experience.

6. ESTABLISH ADEQUATE CONTROLS

If he is to remain accountable, the manager who delegates must be able to report quickly and accurately on the status of his obligation. Controls limit delegation. When the manager can determine by personal inspection the status of work in progress or completed, this limitation is minimal. However, when factors such as time, or the size or diversity of the job, or geography limit personal inspection, effective delegation requires a system of controls which will free the manager from routine inspection yet enable him to maintain his accountability. The more complete the delegation, the more comprehensive the system of controls required.

In establishing controls for delegation, the best approach is to give the subordinate the means of self-control. If the person to whom responsibility and authority have been delegated can measure and evaluate his own performance against a predetermined standard, instead of having it measured and evaluated for him, the task of the accountable superior is lessened considerably.

Certain prerequisites are needed for effective self-controls. The subordinate should participate in setting the standards that are to measure his performance, so that he will both understand and accept them. He needs a continuing supply of reliable information, and he must have personal access to that information. For example, the foreman who is given responsibility for the control of costs in his department is handicapped if he does not know and understand the standards that apply to his operation. And if he is to make sound control decisions to keep his costs in line, he must know what his cost performance is from day to day, how he is measuring up to standard, and if variances exist, the reasons for them.

SUMMARY

Delegation is facilitated if a favorable climate is first established by top management. The manager who wishes to delegate must prepare himself psychologically so that he can relinquish part of his responsibility and authority with freedom and assurance.

Delegation best proceeds in terms of a sequence of management activity. Our unified concept of management is the best basis for the activities involved. First is the need to establish goals; next, the responsibility and authority to be delegated should be clearly defined.

If delegation is to be effective, subordinates must be motivated to highest productivity. Motivation depends upon complex psychological and emotional factors, as well as such tangible incentives as money and promotion. Organizationally, motivation is encouraged by creating small work groups and providing for maximum interaction by group members. Leadership factors are also important, including adequate provision for participation and communication.

Effective delegation requires that the doctrine of completed work be observed, so that subordinates will undertake the job as a total package and not make undue demands upon the superior in getting it done. As a final step, managers who delegate must develop subordinates to perform at top efficiency by appraising, counseling, and coaching and making provision for appropriate training procedures.

CHAPTER 8 *Centralization and Decentralization*

Decentralization is one of the most confused and confusing of the administrative techniques that characterize the art and science of professional management. Decentralization finds many uses—some useful, some ambiguous, others downright contradictory. If a company wants to expand, decentralization is recommended to help develop new products, facilitate technological advance, and grow new managers in abundance. When the enterprise is in trouble, decentralization is prescribed for failing markets, poor product mix, or an overdose of diversification. And like some ideas with regard to medicine, there is belief that if a little decentralization is good, more is better. The company that is "completely decentralized" supposedly has reached the administrative Valhalla.

Every once in a while this optimistic note is muted. One West Coast company decentralized too far and too fast, without providing a proper balance of centralization. As a result, it found itself going in all directions at once, nearly lost a successful product line, and dropped several million dollars in profits. Another company found that decentralization encourages *too much* freedom of decision making. Top management, swayed by the optimistic predictions and aggressive promotion of one decentralized division vice president, committed almost all its capital funds to a new plant for a plastic product in current demand and neglected the potential of petrochemicals, to the detriment of the long-term profitability of the company as a whole.

MISUNDERSTANDINGS ABOUT DECENTRALIZATION

Decentralization can mean many things. Indicative are the semantic variations, which range from administrative, physical, and functional decentralization, through federal, product, and geographic. At one and the same time, decentralization is taken to mean separation of facilities, a type of organization structure, and the delegation of decision making.

Typical of this confusion is a statement published in a Detroit union paper to announce that a local company was "decentralizing." As the story had it, "This is the first step in moving the company out of the city. Office and executive personnel are shifting bag and baggage to Chicago and Milwaukee. Next we can expect the management to start sneaking machine tools out in the middle of the night. Decentralization means runaway shops and runaway jobs." Such confusion is typical. There are perhaps more misapprehensions and contradictory statements about decentralization than any other area of management activity.

Not a Type of Organization

In many quarters, there is belief that decentralization is a distinct type of organization and that a company decentralizes by changing its organization structure. This is not the case. A related error is the attempt to classify different kinds of decentralization where differences do not exist. For instance, decentralization within a functional structure is characterized as something different from decentralization within a divisionalized structure. The distinction is specious. It would be as meaningful to attempt to classify pneumonia found in men as "male pneumonia" and that found in women as "female pneumonia."

Centralization and decentralization are extensions of delegation. Delegation refers primarily to the entrustment of responsibility and authority from one *individual* to another. Decentralization applies to the systematic delegation of authority in an organization-wide context. It must be noted that centralization and decentralization are found in both functional and divisionalized organizations; in both cases, authority may be placed either high or low. It is true the divisionalized structure tends to facilitate decentralization; however, a clear distinction must be made between the structure itself and the characteristic placement of authority within that structure.

Should Not Go to Completion

The belief that "complete decentralization" is a desirable state of affairs is also fallacious. Neither centralization nor decentralization should be allowed to go to completion; an equilibrium is always necessary. Unless a central authority does the work of over-all planning, organization, coordination, motivation, and control and makes the decisions necessary to cement the operating units of the organization together, the company will disintegrate. At the opposite end of the scale, centralization can never be complete. There must be some decentralization of authority to the operating units of the company if action is to take place at all. If managers in the factory and the field cannot make decisions, paralysis will swiftly creep in from the extremities to the nerve centers of the enterprise.

Distinct from Dispersion

Decentralization is often confused with the separation of physical facilities. The two are distinctly different. *Dispersion* is the process of building plants and offices with physical distance between them. When a company with a head office in New Jersey builds one plant in Texas and another in California, it is dispersing, and not necessarily decentralizing. Decentralization can proceed without separation of facilities, and facilities can be separated without decentralization.

Because of the widespread misunderstanding that exists, a first step is clarification of the concepts of centralization and decentralization.

CENTRALIZATION

Centralization is the systematic and consistent reservation of authority at central points within the organization. Just as we find that a manager may perform work, or responsibility, that can be done as well or better by subordinates, we also discover that the manager may make decisions that could be made effectively by his subordinates. If the manager reserves work, he necessarily also reserves authority; however, he may delegate the work but not the necessary authority to carry it out effectively.

Centralization denotes that a majority of the decisions having to do with the work being performed are not made by those doing the work but at a point higher in the organization. As Fayol put it, "Everything that goes to increase the importance of the subordinate's role is decentralization, everything which goes to reduce it is centralization." [1]

Reserved Authority

Certain authority must be reserved by every manager. As we have seen in our discussion of delegation, this is the authority for over-all planning, organization, motivation, coordination, and control. Every manager must withhold authority for these decisions with respect to the work of the people he manages, because only he can make them with objectivity and perspective.

When authority is reserved by company top management, the decisions made should be expressed as largely as possible in the form of policy decisions, so that they will apply repetitively to problems that come up in the operations of the company. Below the top executive

[1] Henri Fayol, *General and Industrial Management,* Sir Isaac Pitman & Sons, Ltd., London, 1949, p. 34.

level, an increasing amount of operating authority tends to be reserved by managers for the same reasons that the proportion of operating work performed by managers tends to increase at successively lower levels of the company.

WHAT FACTORS DICTATE CENTRALIZATION?

The company, or the individual manager, may find it necessary to reserve authority under special circumstances to accomplish specific results. Centralization is indicated to facilitate personal leadership when the company is small, to provide for integration and uniformity of action, and to handle emergencies.

To Facilitate Personal Leadership

We have seen that personal leadership can be a potent influence in the success of the small company and during its early growth stages. When this is a factor, the organization form and the placement of authority should facilitate this type of leadership.

The success and survival of the small, young enterprise in the competitive market place depends upon aggressiveness, singleness of purpose, and flexibility. Under a talented, dynamic leader, who is able to assert personal command, centralization *in the small company* results in quick decisions, enterprising and imaginative action, and high mobility. The small, centralized company often shows a distinctive flair in styling or production or sales that puts it at a competitive advantage.

In 1945, for example, O. A. Sutton viewed with interest the static condition of the electric fan business, in which no significant improvements had been introduced for a score of years. He borrowed some ideas about moving air from the new science of aerodynamics and began to build his fan in a garage in Wichita. By advertising his fan as an "air circulator," equally effective for moving air in winter or summer, he was able to develop a year-round market. His innovation in design and marketing enabled him to meet and beat the giants of the industry in his specialty. Today the O. A. Sutton Corporation has a net worth of $9 million, manufactures air circulators and air conditioners and motors with annual sales of about $40 million, and is fast approaching a point where it will have to give serious consideration to both divisionalization and decentralization.

Paul D. Arnold had an idea that he could make bread more tasty and appetizing than the standard commercial loaf. In 1940, he started a small bakery in Greenwich, Connecticut, producing a "home baked" white bread that enabled him to compete successfully with the conventional loaf even though his bread sold at a premium price.

Motorola Incorporated, Chicago, the world's largest manufacturer devoted exclusively to electronics products, with annual sales over $225 million, shows a transition from operating to management leadership in its growth and development. Paul V. Galvin started this company in 1928 on a few hundred dollars capital to manufacture in volume a new product—a popular-priced automobile radio. Gathering together a few men talented in the embryonic science of electronics engineering, Paul Galvin directed the creation of an abbreviated product line. He established and supervised the first distributorships, arranged initial advertising campaigns, and supervised the accounting activities.

For some ten years the company grew successfully under his centralized, personal leadership. During the forties, Paul Galvin began to decentralize, divisionalize, and delegate. He instituted a strong research department to take work from his shoulders, built up engineering and sales. Later on, he strengthened the top management group and established a specialized staff to provide personnel, purchasing, financial, public relations, and operating controls. In 1957 a realignment took place which formalized an organizational structure divisionalized into Automotive Products, Consumer Products, Semiconductor Products, Industrial Electronics Products, and Military Electronics Products.

The small company can retain the advantages of centralization so long as it continues to function as one entrepreneurial unit; that is, so long as it can operate effectively as a projection of the personality and skills of one outstanding leader. It is to be noted that the large company, when it decentralizes, is in reality attempting to reestablish such small entrepreneurial units at its periphery.

To Provide for Integration

Most companies find that a certain amount of centralization is necessary to unify and integrate the total operation of the enterprise. Central direction is needed to keep all parts of the company moving harmoniously together toward a common objective. If decentralization proceeds too far, this integration is endangered.

Sun Chemical Corporation illustrates the need for integration through centralization. Sun Chemical, which was established as the General Printing Ink Company in 1929, grew to twenty-six divisions and wholly owned subsidiaries by 1945. The units of the company operated autonomously. As a result, there was expensive and wasteful duplication of both facilities and operations. There were eight chief chemists in the company, each in charge of a division laboratory. Several of the laboratories would work on the same problem. In one case, three continued their investigations after the fourth had already found the answer to the problem. Independent purchasing by each of the divisions led to small purchases at relatively high prices. Some divisions were forced to carry high inventories to cover their operating needs. Because of lack of coordination of the company's sales effort, two or more salesmen would often call on the same customer, selling him similar products. Since warehousing was independent, if the customer bought from two or more divisions, he might receive his purchases as separate small shipments from several warehouses.

Sun Chemical found that these independently proliferating divisions were rapidly getting out of hand. The company provided necessary coordination by consolidating and centralizing its manufacturing and selling organization into three groups—inks, textile chemicals, and paints.

The shift to requisite centralization enabled the company to achieve significant results; it affords unlimited stable market potential on the one hand and permits unusually close-knit, efficient production on the other. This has been of enduring benefit.

To Promote Uniformity of Action

To the extent that the company wishes all its units to do the same thing in the same way or at the same time, there must be centralization of the appropriate decisions. Only when the major management decisions are made by a central authority administratively higher than the operating units will there be uniformity of purpose, of planning, and of control.

When uniformity of action is desired, especially in a multiunit company, centralization of decision making is indicated. In Sears, Roebuck and Company each of the retail store managers is so highly decentralized that he operates almost as an independent businessman. The local store manager sets his own prices and arranges his store in a manner he thinks best. However, in certain activities it is to the advantage of the company to secure a high degree of uniformity. In those areas, authority in Sears has been centralized.

All buying in Sears, for example, is done centrally, from the Chicago headquarters. This ensures uniformity in the goods offered for sale through the thousands of company outlets. It also enables the company to schedule production most effectively in its own factories and to take advantage of volume purchasing from outside vendors. Store managers order the merchandise they wish in quantities they need from control stores or pool stocks maintained by the company and directly from factory sources developed by parent buying departments.

Sears relies heavily upon local newspaper advertising. To ensure uniformity of theme and of quality with respect to the type of advertisement, art work, copy, and design of the advertisement, the company has centralized the advertising function. There is available to each store manager a prepared mat service from the headquarters office and a standardized description of the various items offered for sale.

Uniformity of action in personnel matters is important, and this can best be assured by a degree of centralization. Burroughs Corporation, for example, which is both divisionalized and decentralized with respect to operations, centralizes personnel policy making to secure uniformity on such matters as hours of work, salary ranges, promotion, standards, and grievance handling.

Sylvania also illustrates the need for centralization to provide uniform handling of personnel matters. When a division in Sylvania Electric has an opening for a professional, administrative, or executive employee, the opening may be offered to any qualified employee from another division for whom the job would be a promotion. To provide a framework within which this can be accomplished, the establishment of salary job classifications and of salary ranges is a centralized function. If this were not the case, it would be difficult to establish, in many instances, whether an opening was a promotion for a given employee, and salary problems would be created when the transfer took place if the rate ranges or paid rates differed between locations.

To Handle Emergencies

When emergency decisions which affect all units of the company must be made, centralization of decision making is highly desirable. For instance, in Continental Can Company, management of inventory is largely decentralized. Most local managers decide how much inventory to carry. However, when commodity analysis by the central headquarters staff shows that there will be a cutback in customer buying in three or six months or a shortage of alloy steel, company and division management has to require that inventories be cut or increased, as appropriate to meet the anticipated emergency. The more acute the emergency or the more competitive the situation, the greater the need for centralized decision making.

DECENTRALIZATION

Decentralization refers to the systematic effort to delegate to the lowest levels all authority except that which can only be exercised at central points. Decentralization is concerned with the placement of authority with reference to responsibility. The placement of responsibility is not a primary concern, because work must be assigned to the place where it is to be done, or its accomplishment becomes a physical impossibility. The key question is: What decisions can be made by the people who are asked to do the work?

It should be noted that delegation can take place from one person to another and be a complete process. However, decentralization is completed only when the fullest possible delegation is made to all, or most, of the people who are delegated a specific kind of responsibility.

For example, the president delegates to each of his division managers authority for selling his division's products. At the same time, he delegates to him authority to hire salesmen at salaries up to $8,000 a year and to give salary increases up to 10 per cent of base salaries annually, at his option.

If this delegation is company-wide, we can say there is decentralization of this authority to the division manager level. If the division managers require that they personally approve hiring of field salesmen and all salary increases, the decentralization is limited. However, if the company encourages the division managers to delegate further, so that each sales supervisor is permitted to decide which salesmen he will hire and what increases he will give, within certain prescribed limits, we can say that this authority is highly decentralized. If delegation is practiced systematically in all functions and divisions of the company and for a wide range of authorities and responsibilities, we would say the company is highly decentralized.

Decentralization proceeds at a different rate to different levels and for different functions within the same company. Decentralization usually spreads level by level from the top. It is not unusual to find a company which has decentralized from the chief executive to the division manager level, but in which the division manager is still running all his plants in person with the help of a dozen or so personal assistants. The same may hold true at the next level. Many plant managers in highly decentralized companies run strongly centralized operations. It is the unusual case in which decentralization has proceeded in large measure down to the first-line foreman.

Degree of Decentralization

The extent of decentralization is determined by *what kind of authority is delegated, how far down in the organization it is delegated, and how consistently it is delegated.* For example, in a lumber company, the procurement manager is given the work of selecting and grading timber. Part of this he does himself, part he delegates to others. To perform effectively, he needs certain authority. Does he have the power simply to obtain a price quotation, which he must refer to a superior before he can commit the company to purchase? Can his superior approve amounts up to a given level and must he go yet higher for decisions involving greater amounts? Or can the procurement manager close the deal, issue orders, and pay for the timber after it is delivered? Answers to these questions help determine the degree of decentralization. If the procurement managers in the company are given the right to make decisions to spend up to $500 to purchase timber, there is less decentralization than if they are empowered to spend $1,000. And the $1,000 limit would signify even less decentralization than if they were empowered to spend any amount necessary, at current market prices, to purchase the volume and kind of timber requisitioned.

Different degrees of authority may be delegated. A manager may be given authority to make a final decision without need to refer to anybody else. Or he may be permitted to make the decision, but only after he has consulted with his superior. Or he may be required to refer to a staff manager or other person and give consideration to their advice and suggestions before he makes decisions.

A ready index to the degree of decentralization is the amount of money various levels of the organization are authorized to spend. For example, in one chemical company, the president can approve appropriations for capital expenditures up to $100,000 within the general limits of the budget. A department head is delegated authority to approve up to $25,000 and a division superintendent up to $10,000. In another chemical company, with an almost identical total budget, the president is required to refer requests of over $25,000 to the Board of Directors. In this company, department heads can approve up to $10,000 and division superintendents up to $2,500. It is obvious that the first company has decentralized this specific authority to a greater degree than has the second.

Other authorities may be used as yardsticks in determining the degree of decentralization. In each, the critical questions are: How much authority is delegated, how far down in the organization is it placed, and how consistently is it delegated? Some representative authorities are the following:

Hiring and firing employees
Approval of wage and salary increases
Approval of travel expenses
Promotion of personnel
Approval of purchase commitments
Acquisition of capital equipment
Employment of outside consultants
Leasing property or equipment
Sale of capital equipment
Approval of price quotations
Acceptance of sales orders
Approval of transportation contracts

Proper Structure Facilitates Decentralization

Decentralization can be accomplished to some extent in a functional structure. However, its best vehicle is divisionalization. The three largest companies in the automobile industry, General Motors, Ford, and Chrysler, have all changed from a basic functional organization to a divisionalized type as a basis for extensive decentralization. Westinghouse and Radio Corporation of America changed from a functional to a divisionalized organization in order to decentralize. Sperry Rand is decentralized on a product division basis. International Business Machines, which has been highly centralized on a functional organization pattern, has divisionalized in order to decentralize. In the aircraft industry, the three leaders, Douglas, Boeing, and North American, have all decentralized on a divisionalized basis.

WHEN TO DECENTRALIZE?

At what point should a systematic effort be made to decentralize authority to the lowest possible level in the company? What signs indicate the need to drain off decision-making power from top management? The decision to decentralize is critical because it involves a major change in the company's philosophy of management. It not only demands concomitant changes in attitudes and habits of individual managers but also may require drastic changes in the basic organization structure. The factors that point to need for decentralization largely parallel those that indicate divisionalization. These include easing the burden on top executives, diversification, product and market emphasis, development of managers, and improved motivation.

To Ease Burden on Top Executives

Centralized, personal management, as we have seen, in effect turns the administrative mechanism of the company into a funnel, which pours the full weight of problems, perplexities, and pressures from every part of the organization upon the chief executive and his immediate group. There are usually several very clear indications that the company has centralized too large a burden of decision making in its top executives.

Lack of planning and control for the over-all company can often be traced to a chief executive who is so busy fighting fires that he does not have time to plan ahead, anticipate problem areas, provide necessary coordination, and develop controls.

When the chief becomes habituated to making operating decisions and dealing with problems of immediate urgency he finds it almost impossible to adopt the relaxed and contemplative point of view necessary for planning and thinking ahead.

Proliferation of personal staff is often a sign that the manager is overburdened and is trying to find assistants to carry part of his load for him. The use of personal staff is never a satisfactory solution. The manager with assistants will invariably find work for them to do and in the process is almost certain to reserve for himself responsibility and authority which might better be delegated to subordinate managers.

Overdependence upon committees is another sign that the centralized executive is trying to get out from under part of his burden. Committees are used as crutches by some executives who are literally crippled by the dragging weight of the authority and responsibility thrust upon them. The committee can be of great value to the executive by bringing together a group of experienced managers who are qualified to provide real help in developing solutions. However, when the chief executive uses committees to make decisions he ordinarily would be able to make himself, he is adopting an expedient which is not only very expensive but which may also consume the time of subordinate managers so that they are not able to handle the administration of their own affairs properly.

To Facilitate Diversification

We have seen that divisionalization facilitates diversification and in fact is almost a necessary accompaniment. We can carry this one step farther by demonstrating that decentralization must accompany divisionalization if most effective diversification is to take place. There is plentiful evidence that a company can grow very large in sales volume and number of employees and still be within the management capacity of one man if the problems presented to that individual are limited in type and variety. A company selling thirty brands of distilled spirits, for example, presents a set of problems to the chief executive similar to those which confronted him when the company marketed only two brands.

Let the company diversify into chemicals, feeds, and pharmaceuticals, however, and the capacities of the centralized authority are immediately taxed. If all the varied products are to attain maximum growth, decentralization must proceed to the point where skilled and experienced judgment can be brought fully to bear on major problems as they occur. In many cases diversity, rather than size, is the impelling reason for decentralization. This is characteristic of the small enterprise as well as of the large, and of almost every type of endeavor.

To Provide Product and Market Emphasis

When a company begins to lose its markets to competitors, when its product lines fail to keep abreast of innovation and customer demand, a basic reason is frequently the inability of a highly centralized management to be as omniscient as it needs to be. The facts of life in a competitive market require each salesman to offer as new a style, as low a price, as high a quality as other salesmen who are calling on the same customer. The customer has no interest in the burdens of top management or the complexity of company administration; he is interested solely in price, quality, delivery, and novelty. The impact of decentralization on both product and market is shown in many company case histories. Representative are Johnson and Johnson, The Square D Company, Allis-Chalmers, and Scandinavian Airlines.

Johnson and Johnson. Up to 1930, Johnson and Johnson was highly centralized. The president ran the company as a one-man enterprise. He made most of the decisions personally, whether they had to do with production, sales, purchasing, or personnel. As the company began to approach the $20 million mark in sales, however, it became impossible for even the highly capable president to keep himself so well acquainted with the operating situation that he could make fast, effective decisions for every problem presented to him. Some parts of the business began to lag. Needed innovations in manufacturing, in some instances, were not introduced quickly enough to match competitors. Some products were neglected for the long pull and others overemphasized for immediate advantage. Product lines were commingled to such an extent that no one received proper emphasis and promotion. In short, the company had grown to the point that no single person could possibly meet and answer all the challenges and opportunities that were presented. More decision makers were needed to handle the multiplicity of problems at the time and in the place where they had to be answered if fast, effective action was to result. Under Robert W. Johnson, who became General Manager in 1930 and President in 1932, the company decentralized and dispersed its operations. The increase of world-wide sales from $20 million in the early 1930s to $296 million in 1956 is some indication of the success of the move.

The Square D Company. This company, manufacturer of industrial control and electrical distribution equipment, doubled in size over a ten-year period. To secure best return from its $12 million capital investment program, the company had to compete with much bigger companies, such as Westinghouse and General Electric. Square D found the answer in building regional plants and warehouses and decentralizing both responsibility and commensurate authority in as large measure as possible, so that Square D managers in each plant could give local customers an edge in quality and service. To secure the economies inherent in centralized manufacturing, the company manufactures and assembles the great bulk of its products in its three largest plants in Cleveland, Detroit, and Milwaukee. However, Square D's customers in California, Texas, New Jersey, and other parts of the nation frequently need specially designed equipment or modifications of stock items for their plant electrical equipment systems. To give them fast service and a high-quality product, Square D has built fifteen regional plants which are centered in major geographic areas of the United States, Canada, and Mexico. Supporting these nerve centers is a network of distributors and Square D field offices.

Because there is considerable decentralization, each of these regional plants can quickly deliver standard items or modify or design special equipment to the customer's order. It can match the speed and special service of small, local firms yet at the same time provide larger, more intricate systems which would ordinarily be available only from the larger manufacturers.

Allis-Chalmers Manufacturing Company. Operating under a centralized administration, Allis-Chalmers was aware that while product diversification contributed greatly to stability, special emphasis on engineering, manufacturing, and sales was necessary in order to compete with firms specializing in certain of its products, such as tractors, construction machinery, motors, and electrical equipment.

A program of decentralization and divisionalization was launched to give emphasis to its diversified product lines and to provide for concentrated sales effort to major lines. Six major operating divisions were established with three divisions in the Tractor Group and three in the Industries Group. Each of these specializes in its own product lines and concentrates its products and services directly to the special markets in which it is competing.

Scandinavian Airlines System. This company provides another example of a company which has decentralized to provide maximum customer emphasis. With headquarters in Stockholm, Scandinavian Airlines System has been able to compete successfully with American carriers. Instead of trying to run the United States business from Stockholm, SAS has decentralized to an American corporation, with headquarters in New York. Each of the twenty-six district offices in the United States can make a great many decisions that affect its own operations. The American offices of SAS develop their own sales promotions, cater to the preferences of regional customers, and offer special package travel deals to attract local customers.

It is clear that, no matter what the basic type of organization structure, as the company grows, operations over the long term will be improved if the growth is accompanied by a commensurate measure of decentralization of decision making. In a competitive economy, the victory goes to the enterprise that can bring the most to bear at the point of action. Fifteen master salesmen making decisions at the headquarters in New York are of little help to the company representative in California trying to sell an air-conditioning installation to a customer who is considering the offerings of four other firms and intends to make a decision this afternoon. The more decisions the company representative can make at the scene of action, the better he can meet the sales efforts of his competitors.

To Encourage Development of Managers

Most companies find lack of managerial talent a limiting factor in growth. It is evident that a company cannot expand effectively beyond the scope and abilities of its management group. The development of broad-gauged, capable managers comes not from programs and courses primarily but from giving managers a management job to do and delegating to them the authority to make important decisions. In this way, the manager who makes poor decisions learns and improves under fire or finds that he is not cut out for management responsibilities.

Sears, Roebuck and Company has long been a leader in the selection and development of management talent. As the company has expanded, it rarely has had to go on the outside for managers. The key to its successful promotion from within policy is a philosophy that managers and future executives develop best when they are given authority and responsibility to *manage* something, not simply lectured about management or permitted to observe others managing. Accordingly, Sears gives a manager responsibility and authority to run his own small segment of the business, even at a low level and an early age. Sears watches a manager carefully as he graduates from a smaller to a larger store and from management of a district to a zone, to a region. Each step of the way he is systematically appraised, counseled, and coached, so that he can be helped to carry out his responsibility and exercise authority more effectively. This is also true of promotable men in other areas of the company.

Prudential Life Insurance Company has found that decentralization gives managers freedom to try out new methods and techniques. It gives individuals within the company more chance to make decisions and thus to learn how to lead.

United States Rubber Company finds that decentralization helps develop managers because it spreads decision making to more positions. Managers who learn to decide develop at the same time. U.S. Rubber finds that by creating a great variety of decision-making positions, it can rotate managers among jobs more effectively and help to increase the scope of their effectiveness.

To Improve Motivation

Research findings at Harvard University, the University of Michigan, and other institutions demonstrate that the organization structure itself can influence the motivation of people within the company. These conclusions show that to the extent that the organization structure facilitates participation, communication, and delegation, it also motivates managers to highest productivity. The type of organization structure most favorable to motivation would tend to emphasize small groups, close interaction, and mutual interdependence.

Decentralization, while not a separate type of organization structure, tends to emphasize these desirable characteristics in whatever type of structure it is found. Decentralization stimulates the formation of small, cohesive groups. Since local managers are given a large degree of authority and local autonomy, they tend to weld their people into closely knit, integrated groups. Most decentralized managers discover that this type of leadership demands a high degree of participation, constant effort to communicate, and continuing personal interest in the welfare of the members of the team.

By forcing the manager to work more closely with his subordinates, decentralization enhances his ability to appraise their performance and counsel and coach to help them improve. This in itself is a potent source of motivation.

Sylvania Electric Products, which has decentralized to many small plants, finds that this brings managers closer to employees than is true in large plants. In Sylvania's experience, the relatively autonomous manager of the small plant is able to communicate quickly and clearly to his people an understanding of what they are trying to accomplish. He can keep them informed of problems and enlist their interest and support, whether it be in production, labor relations, or other matters. This not only improves motivation but also helps to reduce turnover and develop high *esprit de corps*.

J. C. Penney and Company decentralizes to a large extent to the manager of individual store units. By putting the store manager on his own, the company finds, decentralization gets more action at the right time.

It encourages the manager to bring more people into the act, to solicit their ideas and suggestions, and to encourage them to carry their full weight in day-to-day assignments. This makes the individual stores far more capable of independent action and also ensures that they will be more flexible and aggressive. It also motivates each store to make a better showing than similar stores in the company.

SUMMARY

Decentralization refers to the consistent and systematic delegation of authority to the levels where action takes place. Decentralization can occur in either a functional or a divisionalized form of organization, but it is greatly facilitated by the relative ease of establishing controls in the divisionalized type.

Decentralization can be effective only if it is balanced by an appropriate measure of centralization.

The central management authority of the company must make over-all decisions in planning, organizing, motivating, coordinating, and controlling if the decentralized operating units are to proceed with the necessary uniformity and coordination toward a common goal. Decentralization should be undertaken to ease the burden on top company executives, to facilitate diversification, to provide product and market emphasis, to encourage the development of managers, and to improve motivation.

CHAPTER 9 *Effective Decentralization*

"Decentralizing is like getting married," said one company president recently. "You take a lot on faith and try to work out the rest as you go along." There is undoubtedly a great deal of merit in this observation. However, just as certain fairly dependable guides to marriage can be established by observing and talking to happily married couples, we can also derive basic approaches to decentralization by study of companies which have decentralized successfully.

THE PROFIT CENTER CONCEPT

Company experience demonstrates that the most valid and useful concept of decentralization is profit center decentralization. This is the process of accompanying divisionalization with decentralization and establishing each divisionalized unit as an integrated, self-contained business within the management framework of the business as a whole. Each decentralized division is given its own management group, its own staff support, and is set up in business on a competitive basis. Each "profit center" is held accountable for the profit it earns and the loss it sustains. Adoption of the profit center concept puts teeth in decentralization. Instead of settling the burden of profitability on the shoulders of one or two top executives, it charges a large number of key managers with this obligation. It brings the profit maker closer to the point where profits are made. He knows immediately when operations get out of phase. And if his personal security is clearly at stake, he is likely to take vigorous action to remedy matters.

The profit center concept becomes a strong psychological spur to profitable action. The accountable manager is continually on the lookout for opportunities to cut costs, to seek additional sources of revenue, and to consider new ideas or suggestions for improvement. Companies decentralized on a profit center basis are characteristically more aggressive, show more initiative and ingenuity, and are more persistent in their search for profitable market opportunities than centralized organizations. This explains why, once an industry leader has decentralized effectively, its close competitors must follow suit or find themselves losing out. This is the law of the market place.

THE DECENTRALIZATION PATTERN

A certain amount of decentralization is consciously sought in almost every growing and diversifying company. However, a few, through long and persistent effort in systematic delegation of authority, have evolved an outstandingly successful pattern.

This pattern is graphically illustrated in the automobile industry. Since 1893, when Charles Duryea pioneered the automobile in America, over two thousand companies have been established in this field. Of this number, only a few were able to outfight and outthink competitors, maintain and expand markets, and develop the managers they needed for long-term profitability. The three that have been most successful demonstrate the need for decentralization and divisionalization as a concomitant of successful growth.

General Motors

For the first dozen years after its organization in 1908, General Motors was highly centralized within a functional structure. Most of the decisions were made by W. C. Durant, who put the company together. Mr. Durant was a merchandiser and promoter, and during the early years of its growth the company reflected his personality and preferences. The emphasis was on sales; organization and administration were haphazard.

In 1921, General Motors experienced a deficit of $38 million. Serious difficulties threatened the future of the company. It suffered from inadequate research and engineering facilities, unbalanced commitment of capital, and inadequate budgetary controls. There was little integration of the operations of the individual divisions. In 1921, under Alfred P. Sloan, Jr., General Motors centralized and integrated policy making and administration and provided for highly decentralized responsibility and operations. Mr. Sloan saw that centralization makes possible the economies that come from specialization and coordination, while decentralization develops initiative and flexibility and facilitates cooperative effort. The success of General Motors' philosophy is attested by its recovery from imminent failure and its rise to the largest and most profitable industrial organization in the country.

The pattern General Motors adopted can best be summed up in the words of Alfred P. Sloan, Jr. As he saw it, decentralization first requires divisionalization; that is, the company should be divided into "as many parts as can consistently be done." Mr. Sloan then advises:

> Place in charge of each part the most capable executive that can be found, develop a system of coordination so that each part may strengthen and support each other part; thus not only welding all parts together in the common interests of a joint enterprise, but importantly developing ability and initiative through the instrumentality of responsibility and ambition—developing men and giving them an opportunity to exercise their talents, both in their own interests as well as those of the business.

General Motors has divisionalized and decentralized on a profit center basis to secure the benefits of large-scale production while yet retaining the initiative and flexibility inherent in a small business. It finds that decentralization not only results in direct economic advantages but also gives more opportunity to individuals within the company to develop management ability and initiative.

General Motors has broken out thirty-five United States operating divisions and set each up much as if it were an independent business. The general manager of each division runs his own show. He designs, develops, manufactures, and markets his own products. He buys his own materials and component parts, either from other divisions of the company or from outside suppliers. He makes his choice of from whom he buys solely on the basis of where he can get the best product at the lowest price. Each division, in effect, is competing with every other company making similar products and with other divisions within the company itself. The general manager is accountable for the success or failure of his division. He and his people are rewarded in proportion to their accomplishment.

Each decentralized manager in General Motors manages as well as operates his own division. He is responsible for planning his own progress, for building his organization, coordinating his efforts, staffing his operation, and controlling his own results.

The division manager is not completely autonomous. His efforts are both limited and guided by a comprehensive system of centralized planning, coordination, and control. He manages within this over-all framework.

General Motors separates the activities involved in managing the company from those required to operate it. Policy making is the responsibility of two committees which report to the Board of Directors and are subcommittees of the Board. The Financial Policy Committee establishes financial policy for the company as a whole. The Operations Policy Committee, assisted by the Administration Committee, determines the over-all needs of the company in terms of its operations and develops policies for the guidance of the operating executives of the company.

Several policy groups meet regularly to consider and recommend policy formation in such areas as distribution, employee relations, manufacturing, engineering, personnel, and public relations.

Ford Motor Company

The second and equally dramatic example is found in Ford Motor Company. Ford was founded in 1903 on a capital of $28,000 by a mechanical genius who produced more and better automobiles at lower prices than had ever been seen in the world before. Henry Ford operated as the personal leader of a vast, sprawling industrial complex, centered in Dearborn. By 1914, Ford was selling 45 per cent of the motor vehicles in the country; by 1921, it accounted for 55 per cent of the market.

However, the company was highly centralized and remained so through the $5, eight-hour day, the Model T and Model A, almost to the time of Henry Ford's death in 1947. During these years, there were no financial or operating controls. The company knew where it stood only by its balances at the bank. Production facilities were unbalanced; there were constant bottlenecks; the company could engineer a superlative machine, but, because Mr. Ford's management scope was limited, so also was that of the company. As a result, Ford continued to manufacture automobiles of mechanical excellence but limited appeal while General Motors, earlier expert at management, grew up and around it.

Ford reached its crisis in 1947, when it had slipped almost to bankruptcy and was losing $9 million a month. However, under Henry Ford II and Ernest Breech, the company undertook a sweeping revision of its management concepts, including the establishment of profit center decentralization, and staged one of the most dramatic recoveries in business history. The company now ranks second only to General Motors in the automobile industry.

In Ford, profit center decentralization means that the company first divisionalized on a product basis; each division was given the management and physical tools and facilities it needed to operate as an integrated, self-contained business. Each division conducts its operations on a competitive basis; it orders its own materials, schedules its operations, and negotiates the sale of its finished products. It is accountable for the profit it earns or the loss it sustains.

Ford finds that profit center decentralization provides a strong incentive to divisional management to improve the efficiency of its operations. The division head, instead of merely being a production boss, is a manager in every sense of the word; actually, he operates in somewhat the same manner as the head of an independent business. This gives him the greatest possible encouragement to use every iota of management ability he can command.

Chrysler Corporation

Third of the automotive "Big Three," Chrysler's history reiterates the pattern already outlined. Founded in 1925, Chrysler has grown from a company with $85 million in assets and $137 million sales in 1925 to one with over $1.3 billion assets and $3.5 billion in sales. For many years, Chrysler led Ford. Before World War II, for instance, Chrysler had about 24 per cent of the market, Ford only 19 per cent; General Motors had about 47 per cent, and the smaller companies shared the balance. By 1950, a revitalized Ford, forging ahead with a divisionalized organization and decentralized management, had come from behind to take second place in the sales picture. Chrysler had outgrown the functional organization and the tight, centralized management that had served it so well in its early years under the personal direction of Walter P. Chrysler; as a result, it slipped slowly but steadily in the competitive race.

Chrysler, in its turn, has made a dramatic comeback. And it is significant that, once again, the vehicle is decentralization within a divisionalized structure. For Chrysler, the result has been improved sales and operations, better profit margins, and the ability to compete for top position once more.

Du Pont

The Du Pont Company is a classic example of effective profit center decentralization. Du Pont is organized on a product division basis; each of the ten operating departments functions much like an independent company. Each manufactures and sells its own group of products. They buy and sell among themselves, generally on the same terms quoted to outside concerns. Their products even compete with each other in the same markets.

The general manager of each of these profit centers is fully accountable for the company's investment in plants, laboratories, processes, and facilities assigned to him. He has authority to develop his own manufacturing processes and to buy his own raw materials. He staffs his department and is responsible for developing his own people. The department manager has practically complete command of all items which enter into his costs. He sets his own selling prices, in consultation with a vice president who acts as an adviser on major changes, or with the Executive Committee.

As a result of this ability to make independent decisions, each Du Pont department can compete with other companies in each of its many and varied markets. This independence of decision making is carried down to the lowest levels. Du Pont believes firmly that a person must be given authority commensurate with responsibility. It encourages and stimulates accountable managers to think and decide for themselves. As a matter of fact, the company pays a bonus to managers who are able to decentralize their own thinking and activity most effectively. This special premium goes to those who, through perseverance and persistence against opposition, both inside and outside the company, carry projects through to successful conclusions.

General Foods

The growth history of General Foods Corporation reinforces the fact that the large, extremely successful company was once small and had to overcome many difficult challenges in its climb to the top. General Foods also exemplifies the advantages of profit center decentralization. General Foods was formed in 1925 when the Postum Company acquired Jell-O and assumed the new corporate title. Up to 1929, the company expanded on a centralized, functional basis. Increase in sales volume was internal, through expansion of the company's original product lines, and external, through the acquisition of such other companies as Minute Tapioca, La France, Igleheart, Walter Baker, Franklin Baker, Maxwell House, and Certo.

There was good reason for centralization during this period. Because all the product lines were grocery specialties with high margins, the emphasis was on marketing. Competition in all lines was sharp. Centralization enabled the company to shift emphasis quickly, to marshal its forces when required to bolster a faltering product, and to make maximum use of an integrated sales force which could promote and service related product lines with economy and effectiveness.

However, by 1930 the company began to vary its basic product pattern. It acquired two new types of business in Birds Eye and Atlantic Gelatin. This diversification brought new kinds of problems into the business. To ensure sound, expeditious handling by executives who were thoroughly familiar with the new lines, the company set up Birds Eye and Atlantic Gelatin as product divisions under decentralized management.

The need for organizational separation and decentralization was further emphasized when it became obvious that Diamond Crystal Salt, which had been acquired in 1929, could not be treated as part of the basic product setup of the company. It had unique problems which differed from those of the regular grocery line. Diamond Crystal Salt was broken out of the functional organization and decentralized so that it could handle its own problems more effectively.

During World War II, General Foods found changes occurring in its business environment. Margins began to shrink, taxes took an increasing bite, competition was becoming sharper for each product in the company's line. To meet the challenge, General Foods broke out a number of additional product divisions and decentralized a great deal of authority to the management of each. This put each major product group on its own feet and let it concentrate exclusively on its own problems and opportunities. Each decentralized division had maximum motivation to advance its own profit objectives and, at the same time, those of the company as a whole.

Each of the twelve decentralized divisions in General Foods is treated as a profit center in itself; each is given the facilities it needs for production, sales, procurement, and other activities it requires to operate as a relatively autonomous business. Each product can move quickly and forcefully to maintain its position and meet every competitive threat at the time and in the place it first appears.

Over-all planning and control are maintained through a strong centralized management group. This includes central specialized staff departments for personnel administration, sales and customer services, advertising services, new products, research, public relations, headquarters administration, manufacturing and engineering, operations research, purchasing, traffic, controller, general counsel, secretary and treasurer.

HOW TO DECENTRALIZE

We can establish a definite sequence for accomplishing effective decentralization in the company. This includes the establishment of appropriate centralization, development of managers, provision for communication and coordination of the decentralized units, development of controls for the decentralized operations, and appropriate dispersion.

1. ESTABLISH APPROPRIATE CENTRALIZATION

The first step in decentralization is one of centralization. Provision needs to be made for a centralized management which becomes the nerve center of the enterprise. In the central headquarters, plans are formulated and communicated for the over-all guidance and direction of each part of the company, an adequate company organization structure is planned, major activities are coordinated, and control is exercised in terms of the plans originally developed.

Within such an administrative framework, individual operating components of the company can be established as profit centers and permitted considerable latitude of action. So long as all are proceeding in the same direction and operating under the same conditions, the more initiative and aggressiveness individual members of the team show, the greater will be the total result. Many companies that have decentralized without getting into administrative harness find the individual members of the team going in all directions at once, to the detriment of all involved.

The design of the administrative structure requires careful consideration of the needs of the company as a corporate entity and of the operating components as competitive units in their own markets. The greater the diversification of the company, the more need there is for a sound and balanced centralized management. A company with divisions operating in the electronics, aluminum, textile, lumber, steamship, steel, plastics, and machine tool industries obviously will find it more difficult to develop sound policies and controls which will be applicable to all its units than will a company operating entirely within the automobile or the food industries. Diversification requires more management. Internal stresses and divergences are greater, conflicting interests more prevalent, the uncertainties of the future multiplied. Without the strong cement of long-term planning, organization, coordination, and control, the diversified company is in danger of coming apart at the seams.

Because of its position within the organization structure, both central to and removed from the operating components, the centralized authority is best placed to make decisions which apply to all units of the company. It has the perspective, balance and objectivity necessary to determine the best course of action for all the units and the company as a whole.

Just as complete authority is rarely delegated, it is rarely centralized. Usually the centralized management group makes over-all decisions but delegates to successively lower levels the making of supplementary decisions necessary to implement over-all plans. Provision for centralized management is outlined below.

Centralization of Planning

The development of over-all objectives, policies, program, procedures, and budgets for the company should be centralized, even in highly decentralized companies. Centralized long-term planning provides a framework within which the operating components can develop sound short-term plans. This ensures continuity. By providing for consistency and uniformity, centralized planning also helps establish comparability in the performance standards that will later become a basis for controls.

Board of Directors. As representatives of their electors, the stockholders, the Board of Directors exercises authority for review and approval of the over-all company objectives, policies, programs, and budgets.

In the United States Rubber Company, the Board is responsible for farsighted planning and clarification of objectives. The Board of Directors in Nationwide Insurance reserves responsibility and authority for approving the objectives, principles, and practices governing the administration of the company's affairs. It also approves the annual budget for the company.

Chief Executive Officer. Whether president or chairman of the board, he is responsible for developing over-all plans for submission to the Board of Directors for approval. He is usually accountable for accomplishing the plans established by the Board.

In a large multiplant manufacturing company, the President, who is chief executive officer, is accountable for implementing the broad objectives and policies determined for the Company by the Board of Directors by establishing policies for all activities and, in cooperation with the Chairman of the Board, developing long-range plans for the accomplishment of established goals. He also directs the development of an annual operating program for the business, including capital expenditures, expenses, estimated sales, and margins. This is submitted to the Board of Directors for approval.

In Nationwide Insurance, the President is responsible for interpreting to the Board of Directors basic trends affecting the insurance industry and the possible effect of these trends on the company. He advises and assists the Board of Directors in the determination of sound objectives, policies, and programs which will merit and obtain support of policyholders and the public.

Central Specialized Staff Departments. These provide advice and service to the chief executive office and to the division managers and their staffs. Hence, the decisions made by the central specialized staff heads have to do primarily with the content of the recommendations and suggestions they forward to the chief executive in helping him to develop over-all plans related to their specialties. The specialized staff department heads also provide technical assistance in their specialties to line principals. For instance, the finance manager is best qualified, by experience and training, to advise the chief executive on finance objectives. The personnel manager can best advise on personnel objectives. Because specialized staff heads are largely responsible for shaping the content of objectives for their technical specialties, they are, at the same time, best qualified to help division and functional heads interpret technical objectives as they apply to their divisions and functions.

In Ford Motor Company, the Vice President–Finance is accountable for recommending to the Board of Directors, the President, and the Executive Vice President company policies, systems, standards, and procedures relating to finance and accounting, including general accounting, cost accounting, financial analysis, cash management, credit administration, and insurance.

Division General Managers. These men are the heads of the major accountability centers in the decentralized company. The division manager acts as chief executive for his own relatively autonomous unit within the framework of the company as a whole. In his position, the division manager represents the chief executive to his division and transmits the needs and reactions of his people to top management.

Because he has the best grasp of the problems confronting managers in the factory and the field, the division manager in the decentralized company provides valuable assistance to the chief executive in the formulation of over-all company objectives and corporate policy. He analyzes the need for changes in corporate objectives and policies and makes recommendations to the appropriate central staff agency and the chief executive officer.

Within the framework of over-all plans, the division manager develops objectives, policies, procedures, programs, and budgets for his own division. Calling upon his own line and staff managers for participation and assistance, he appraises opportunities within his division for expanding profitable volume, reducing costs, strengthening competitive position, and achieving other division objectives. He directs preparation of division profit plans and other financial plans and forecasts. According to the authority granted him, the division manager approves division plans for implementation or he submits them to his superior for approval. The division manager sees to it that over-all corporate plans and the plans of his own division are properly disseminated, interpreted, and complied with in his division.

In United States Rubber Company, the general managers of the eight highly decentralized product divisions have the responsibility of studying their own products, markets, and competitors thoroughly and systematically. They bring up recommendations and suggestions for changes in over-all objectives to the chief executive directly, or at various meetings at which the chief executive presides. The division general managers are accountable for reaching their own profit and operating objectives and for implementing over-all company plans to the extent that they apply to their divisions.

Chance Vought Aircraft has decentralized to a considerable extent within a functional organization structure. In this company, each department and section manager is given authority to formulate, define, clarify, and interpret long-term and immediate objectives, consistent with the over-all company objectives.

In Koppers Company, Inc., a decentralized division manager develops and recommends division objectives and prepares and recommends the division's programs in sales, costs, profits, investment, and so forth in a manner designed to attain his objectives. The division manager also establishes division sales, financial, manufacturing, and industrial relations policies to augment general company policies.

In Ford Motor Company, the general manager of a vehicle division plans, equips, and operates his divisional production facilities. He plans and directs sales, advertising, promotional, and service programs for the products he makes. He buys the parts and materials he needs, either inside or outside the company. Because of the economies possible in the use of interchangeable parts and standardized body chassis, authority for approval on product plans and production programs is centralized in the Central Office. The Division General Manager develops requirements covering the styling, performance, cost, and general mechanical characteristics of divisional products. He is assisted in this by the Central Engineering specialized staff, which creates, develops, and improves the style and mechanical engineering of the company's products to meet the vehicle division requirements. The division's product plans are recommended to the Central Office for consideration. The division manager develops production programs for the vehicles he will manufacture and forwards these for review by the central Scheduling Committee.

Division Specialized Staffs. These specialists provide advice and service on division matters to the division manager and to line and staff managers within the division. The division specialized staff department managers develop plans for the division manager for the handling of his specialty within the division.

In a decentralized company, division specialized staff generally should be accountable only to the division manager. The chief exception is in the case of the division controller or finance staff manager. In a number of decentralized and divisionalized companies, the division finance man is accountable to the central staff finance manager. That is, finance is centralized on a functional basis, while other staff departments are decentralized on a product or geographic basis. This is to ensure uniformity of accounting procedures and to provide an independent financial accounting for the division's activities.

Typical of the decentralized division finance staff activity is Ford Motor Company. Here the division controller reports directly to the general manager of the division. The division controller, working in conformance with company policies and procedures, develops and administers a program for the financial control of the operations of the division. This includes the establishment of adequate general and cost accounting procedures and systems, budgets, forecasts, interdivisional prices, and such other standards as may be used to measure financial performance. The division controller reports to management on the performance of the divisional operations as measured by financial standards.

The more highly centralized, functional relationship of finance is found in Johns-Manville Corporation. Here the controller of an operating division is accountable to the vice president for finance, central staff. The division controller is, in effect, a resident consultant. He acts as the adviser of the general manager of his division in respect to financial questions, provides him with financial service and assistance, and makes financial studies of operations on his own initiative. He establishes in his division methods for accounting prescribed by the central finance staff. The division controller examines product proposals and expresses his judgment concerning the effect of such proposals on gross profit. He examines price approvals and informs the general manager of any that, in his opinion, are not in the company's interest.

Other division specialized staff departments generally exercise advisory and service authority within the division. Columbia-Geneva Steel is a highly decentralized geographic division of United States Steel Corporation. In this division, the divisional director of purchases establishes and maintains purchasing methods and procedures for the division, in conformance with the over-all plans approved by United States Steel Corporation.

In Koppers Company, Inc., a product division industrial relations department is responsible for applying the company's personnel objectives and programs to divisional operations. The division Manager of Industrial Relations develops plans and policies for effective administration of divisional personnel matters. In general, he carries out the company's personnel program within the division, adapting its features to suit particular conditions within the division. The division Industrial Relations Manager maintains a working relationship with the central staff Industrial Relations Department to obtain maximum benefits of general developments and to assure maintenance of company policies and practices throughout the division.

Centralization of Organization

Authority for establishing the over-all company plan of organization must be centralized. In some decentralized companies, there is provision for participation to a relatively low level before long-term master plans of organization are finally approved. In other companies, the planning process for the company over-all is largely confined to the centralized executive group. Once established by the chief executive and the Board of Directors, authority for short-term implementation of the master organization plan is delegated to managers at lower levels. Typical centralization and subsequent delegations of authority for organization in decentralized companies is shown level by level below.

Board of Directors. Authority for review and approval of the company long-range organization plan should be reserved by the Board of

Directors. In the United States Rubber Company, for example, the Board has responsibility and authority to establish and maintain a sound plan of organization for the company. In Food Machinery and Chemical Corporation, the Executive Committee reviews and the Board of Directors approves the long-range plan of organization for the company and modifications or revisions of it.

Chief Executive Officer. The plan of organization for the company is drawn up and established by the chief executive officer in most decentralized companies. In some companies the chief executive has authority of final approval. In others, his approval is subject to review by the Board of Directors.

In Monsanto Chemical Company, which has a divisionalized and decentralized organization, the president is chief executive officer. In this company, the president is responsible for the implementation of the organization plan of the company and any of its components and changes therein. Subject to the concurrence of the Board of Directors, he directs changes in divisional general management positions. He has final authority to make changes in top management of staff departments.

The chief executive in Koppers Company, Inc., develops and adopts a sound general organization plan which will ensure proper coverage of all functions. He sees to it that adequate organization plans, procedures, and controls are employed by all units. In a food company, the president establishes the company plan of organization and authorizes changes therein. He directs the determination of the responsibilities and reporting relationships assigned to each position and authorizes the delegation and limitation of authority throughout the organization.

Central Specialized Staff Departments. The central staff department heads are, in general, delegated responsibility and authority for developing and establishing the plan of organization for their own departments within the framework of the over-all company plan. Where a specialized staff organization planning department exists, it provides advice and service to the chief executive, line, and other staff heads in developing their own and the company organization structure.

Division General Managers. These men develop organization plans for their divisions in consonance with the over-all company plan. The division manager has available the help and advice of centralized staff, his immediate superior, and his own staff departments. The division manager is responsible in most decentralized companies for explaining and interpreting the company and division plans of organization to his own people.

In Atlantic Refining Company, which has decentralized within a functional organization structure, the line department head is accountable for establishing and implementing a sound plan of organization for his assigned functions. In Food Machinery and Chemical Corporation, the division manager maintains a suitably qualified organization of sufficient size properly to execute all established long-range programs of the division. The division manager coordinates his organization with the over-all company organization plan.

In General Foods, the Division General Manager periodically reviews his division organization plan with the help of appropriate staff departments. If changes are necessary to improve efficiency or meet changing conditions, he makes the changes himself or recommends them to his immediate superior, the group operating officer, according to the authority delegated to him. He also sees to it that the plan of organization for his division is understood and observed and that corporate lines of organization are understood and followed by members of the division.

Division Specialized Staffs. These heads have authority to establish the organization plan for their own departments, in consonance with the over-all plan for the division as a whole, and to explain and interpret the division and company plan to their people. Where division organization planning staffs exist, they provide advice and service to the division managers and to line and staff heads in developing, interpreting, and establishing suitable organization structures in their own departments.

Centralization of Coordination

Decisions should be centralized which affect the over-all balance, unity, or timing of two or more of the operating components of the decentralized company. Where coordination is to be accomplished *within* the divisions, it should be decentralized to the division heads. The committee is a common device for achieving coordination. When the committee is used, it becomes an adjunct of the management principal accountable for the coordination.

Board of Directors. The Board is the top coordinating group in the company. All matters that cannot be reconciled at a lower level come before the Board for coordination. Usually the coordinating work of the Board is in part accomplished through various subcommittees.

Chief Executive Officer. Since the disparate activities of the company finally come together in the office of the chief executive, he usually has responsibility and authority for administrative coordination. For instance, in Koppers Company, Inc., the chief executive has responsibility and authority for coordinating the activities of all units of the organization. In particular, he ensures that the operating units receive adequate working advice, assistance, and service from staff units organized for that purpose.

The chief executive largely accomplishes coordination through use of personal staff, specialized staff, and committees. The personal staff of the chief executive consists of staff assistants and the executive vice president when the latter acts as a line assistant. Staff assistants largely accomplish the "leg work" of coordination. Acting for their chief, they consult with line and staff heads and with members of the Board, help to reconcile differences, and bring to a focus those points on which there is real divergence. For example, the assistants to the president may help him to coordinate the production and sales programs of the company by gathering basic data, study and analysis of the facts, review with appropriate line and staff agencies, and recommendation to the president for final action.

In Chance Vought Aircraft, Incorporated, the chief executive has a staff group that develops and coordinates operating plans for him. Among other duties, this group develops and coordinates the over-all production and experimental plans and schedules for design manufacturing programs covering engineering, tooling, materials, subcontract procurement, fabrication, assembly, and additional control operations. It provides the over-all coordination for the product programs to assist affected departments in meeting master plans and schedules.

In some companies, the executive vice president acts as line assistant to the chief executive. In this case he frequently is delegated responsibility for coordinating operating problems *for* the chief executive, thus relieving him of a good part of this burden. In other companies, the executive vice president acts as chief of staff, coordinating and reconciling the various and conflicting demands and referrals of the specialized staff departments before they reach the chief executive.

Specialized staff carries a great deal of the burden of coordination for the chief executive. In general, the specialized staff department coordinates matters in its specialty among line and staff divisions and functions. For example, in Nationwide Insurance, the Personnel Manager coordinates the uniform interpretation, understanding, and observance of all approved personnel policies, standards, and procedures, and government and other regulations affecting personnel and labor relations within the company.

In a food processing company, the Director of Purchasing assists the chief executive in coordination by proposing plans to ensure the uniform and effective performance of responsibilities for purchasing throughout the company. He also coordinates in his technical specialty by reviewing the performance of purchasing throughout the company.

The chief executive uses committees to help carry out his responsibilities in coordination. The operating or management committee of the chief executive is primarily a coordinating group. Membership usually consists of the principal line and staff department and division heads. This committee meets periodically to serve as a counseling, advisory, and coordinating group for the president. The committee considers and helps the chief executive to coordinate such matters as basic corporation objectives, major policies, programs for accomplishment of objectives, organization changes of company-wide scope, and other matters. It assists the chief executive, by expression of opinion, to coordinate the use and expenditure of funds for facilities, disposal of company property, and operating matters brought before it by the chief executive or brought to its attention by members of the committee or of other committees.

Division General Managers. Problems within the division are coordinated to a great extent by the general manager of the division. Only matters involving the interests of more than the division itself, or which are subject to policy decision at the top level, are referred to the chief executive. In most decentralized companies, the division general manager bears a major portion of the responsibility and authority for coordinating the efforts of members of his division and the central specialized staff departments. Where there are differences between central staff and members of his own organization, the division general manager attempts to coordinate and reconcile these himself. If satisfactory agreement cannot be reached at his level, he refers the matter for decision to his line superior, the chief executive officer.

Centralization of Motivation

Motivation is both the expression of a philosophy of management and the application of specific techniques of supervision and personnel administration. The philosophy of top management establishes the climate for motivation within the company. However expressed, this philosophy largely determines the type of supervision practiced and the scope and effectiveness of personnel administration. Some companies are notably *people-minded.* There is great consideration for employees as human beings, scrupulous attention to human relations, and a pervading feeling that people are the most important factor in company success. This climate *may* exist in one division or department of a decentralized company and not in others; however, the likelihood is that where it exists, climate favorable to motivation is general. It originates with the Board of Directors and percolates layer by layer to diffuse the entire organization.

Board of Directors. By its policy statements and its overt actions, the Board of Directors helps to encourage and stimulate high motivation in all employees. In the Carborundum Company, for example, the Board of Directors has thought through and enunciated the company's objectives and attitudes toward its people.

General Foods also has enunciated clear-cut and detailed policy statements designed to develop and encourage high motivation. In summing up its attitude toward its people, the General Foods Board of Directors says:

> The management of General Foods wants to make clear that, in addition to other responsibilities, each operating executive, manager and supervisor who directs the work of others will be held responsible for the whole-hearted and effective execution of the principles of personnel administration. We want, and need, the cooperation, interest, and loyalty of all employees. We want employees to be happy in their work relationships and well informed regarding the enterprise in which we are all engaged. We want this business to be conducted in an efficient manner and in a spirit of friendliness, to the mutual advantage of employees, management, stockholders, and consumers.

Chief Executive Officer. The chief executive officer in the decentralized company has responsibility and authority for implementing the policies of the Board of Directors with regard to people and for establishing programs and procedures in human relations and personnel administration. In a food company, the president directs the staffing of the organization with the quality and quantity of personnel required by the immediate and long-term needs of the business. He directs the establishment and maintenance of conditions conducive to the employment, retention, and development of superior personnel and the maintenance of good teamwork.

The chief executive in this company directs the development and administration of employee compensation and employee benefit plans and programs.

Central Specialized Staff Departments. The managers of specialized staff departments in decentralized companies are delegated responsibility and authority for motivation of their own subordinates and for applying and making use of company procedures and methods developed for this purpose. The personnel manager is delegated responsibility and authority for providing advice and service to the centralized top management in the development of objectives, policies, and administrative procedures designed to encourage motivation, and to division managers and their staffs for interpretation and application of these policies and procedures.

Division General Managers. They interpret and apply, within their own divisions, the policies and major procedures developed and enunciated by the chief executive. They also develop methods and procedures within their own divisions for motivation of employees.

Centralization of Controls

One aspect of effective decentralization is the reservation of authority for over-all controls to the centralized management group of the company. This is vital to the integrated character of the total effort of the company. Unless comprehensive controls are instituted and maintained, the operating and administrative integrity of the over-all enterprise is difficult to maintain.

Board of Directors. Just as the Board of Directors reserves authority for developing the major plans of the enterprise, it also reserves authority for checking on how well those plans are carried out. In United States Rubber Company, for example, the bylaws of the company provide that the business, affairs, and property of the company shall be both managed and controlled by the Board of Directors. The Board in U.S. Rubber delegates to its Executive Committee this management and control.

In Nationwide Insurance, the Board of Directors maintains administrative control of the operations and the financial affairs of the company. It reviews periodic reports and financial statements and appraises performance for conformity with authority objectives, programs, and budgets and instructs the president to take whatever corrective action it considers necessary.

Chief Executive Officer. The controls authorized by the Board of Directors are put into effect by the chief executive officer. In some cases, the Board centralizes in itself over-all financial controls and does not delegate these. In Du Pont, for example, the Treasurer and Secretary functions report directly to the Finance Committee of the Board of Directors.

The chief executive in a chemical company establishes standards and methods for appraising the company's effectiveness in meeting established objectives. He reviews performance and sees to it that corrective action is taken where needed. As part of his control responsibility, he keeps the Board of Directors fully informed on the condition and progress of the business and executes directives received from the Board for corrective measures.

In Koppers Company, Inc., the chief executive reports the progress of the company and its components to the Board of Directors, including its performance against programs and objectives for sales, profits, investment, and growth. He ensures that adequate organization plans, procedures, and controls are employed by each unit, to make possible the proper execution of their duties and attainment of their goals. As the final step in control the chief executive takes action to correct unsatisfactory conditions that may arise in any phase of operations and to order whatever action may be deemed necessary to accomplish approved objectives.

In Nationwide Insurance Company, the chief executive maintains administrative controls over the business as a whole. He reviews periodic statements and records which are basic to control. These include periodic reports, financial statements, and appraisals of performance for conformity with authorized objectives, programs, and budgets. When necessary, he effects whatever remedial action may be indicated.

Central Specialized Staff Departments. Each central staff department acts in an advisory and service capacity to exercise control. The staff assists and aids the chief executive in developing appropriate standards for performance, in measuring and reporting work in progress, and in analyzing results for its specialty as carried on by the line organization. The finance staff has responsibility and authority for developing for the chief executive a system of financial controls which includes the preparation of budgets, accounting for money spent, comparison of actual against budgeted expenditures, and reporting of results to appropriate line manager. Central staff departments also provide advice and service to division managers in developing division control systems in conformance with over-all company policy requirements.

In a few companies, the chief executive establishes a specialized staff department which is primarily concerned with controls as an administrative activity. In these cases, the control department concerns itself with developing controls for all kinds of work performed in the company.

Division General Managers. Within his own division, the general manager in the decentralized company establishes and maintains effective controls for his own operations. He uses his own personal and specialized staff to whatever extent is necessary to accomplish this. In most companies, he delegates responsibility and authority to his division specialized staff to inspect and review line operations involving their own specialties and to make appropriate recommendations for correction of discrepancies.

2. DEVELOP MANAGERS

A centralized company requires only a few highly qualified managers capable of making the important decisions that spell the difference between success and failure. In a decentralized organization, critical decisions have to be made at every accountability center. Companies that attempt decentralization without adequate preliminary preparation usually find their greatest shortage in managers capable of making effective management decisions.

Why should this be true? In the first place, under decentralization, managers no longer simply carry out the plans of others. They now are called upon to look ahead, to plan for themselves, to run a business within a business. This takes a higher order of skill. It requires people who have mastered the techniques of professional management, not simply of supervision.

Decentralization not only requires better managers, it demands more managers. Where five executives can manage a centralized company of 10,000 employees, decentralized operations, if carried to logical limits, may require up to 1,000 people with management skills. Decentralization provides more opportunity for more managers to make important decisions and to stand or fall by the results. This provides unlimited challenge and opportunity It also poses the problem of how to develop effective managers.

The factors basic to development of managers capable of handling delegated responsibility and authority have already been discussed in the chapter on delegation. The important consideration in training managers for decentralization, and one that is frequently overlooked, is that management is an art made up of identifiable skills. The usual training "programs" centered on classes and courses are rarely successful in imparting more than a smattering of the skills, knowledge, and attitudes required to *manage*. As companies such as Ford Motor Company, Du Pont, Food Machinery and Chemical, Armstrong Cork, Humble Oil & Refining Co., and Sears Roebuck have demonstrated, formal instructional methods must be reinforced by a general management attitude that encourages and vitalizes independent thinking, training of managers as developers of other managers, and a systematic and continuing process of counseling and appraisal on the job.

3. PROVIDE FOR COMMUNICATION AND COORDINATION

Managers operating with a great deal of autonomy tend to go their own way without too great regard for the needs of other units in the organization. The greater the decentralization, the more tendency there is to independence. This at once poses the problem of preserving the integrated, unified character of the company as a whole, while at the same time giving its component parts the greatest possible freedom of decision and action. In the decentralized company, this calls for special provision for communication and coordination. Decentralized managers need to know the thinking of both the centralized authority and other decentralized managers. They also must time and unify action they plan to take so that it meshes and integrates with that of other company units. Many administrative devices developed for decentralization also serve to improve and facilitate communication and coordination. Company programs of planning, organization, motivation, and control, are, at the same time, means of communication and coordination. However, most companies find it necessary to provide specifically for communication through use of group executive coordinating positions and of committees and other appropriate measures.

Group Executive Positions

Companies that decentralize on' a product or geographic division basis frequently find that, unless special organizational provision is made, the chief executive tends to develop an unwieldy span of supervision. In General Motors, for example, there are thirty-five United States operating divisions. Radio Corporation of America has fifteen. Other companies may run anywhere from ten to one hundred. Added to the normal span of central specialized staff, these numerous and complex subordinate units present a difficult problem in coordination and communication. The chief executive must keep informed of activities and problems in the decentralized divisions; he must make sure that the independence of action and authority he permits them to exercise does not jeopardize the integrity of the company as a whole. Many companies find that the intervention of a top coordinating position is an effective solution.

In General Motors, the operating divisions are divided into five groups of related product divisions. For example, the Car Divisions Group has the Buick, Cadillac, Chevrolet, Oldsmobile, and Pontiac Divisions. The Engine Group has the Allison Division, Cleveland Diesel Engine Division, Detroit Diesel Engine Division, Diesel Equipment Division, Electromotive Division, Euclid Division, Fabricast Division, and General Motors Diesel, Ltd. Each group reports to a group executive, who acts as adviser for and represents General Motors management to the divisional managers of his group. Through discussions, counsel, and advice, he directs and coordinates the activities of his group.

General Foods handles the problem similarly by setting up operating vice presidents for each group of related divisions. Each vice president is accountable for his own group of decentralized divisions.

In some companies, some of the product or geographic divisions are grouped, while others report direct. For example, in Radio Corporation of America, National Broadcasting Company reports separately to the President of RCA. The remaining fourteen product and service operational divisions and subsidiaries are grouped under a Senior Executive Vice President and three Executive Vice Presidents. Each of these executives is accountable for the profit performance of the divisions or subsidiaries assigned to him. They coordinate fully for the President.

The coordinating executive may have a staff, rather than a line role. He may coordinate only to the extent of advice and counsel, encouraging subordinate divisions to decide for themselves with the aid of his advice. 'If decision is required which cannot be made at the lower level, he aids in presenting the problem to top management for consideration.

In Standard Oil Company of California, for instance, there are many elements of the company which are geographically dispersed and which operate as subsidiary companies. To provide coordination, Standard of California has created a group of contact officers who are responsible for counseling the heads of operating companies on executive matters beyond their authority or which involve more than one major functional activity. The contact officers provide counsel and coordination. However, they have no authority to make decisions. Where indicated, they refer matters for decision to the Chairman of the Board, the President, or the Executive Committee.

These contact officers are effective without line authority largely because of the stature they hold in the company. Each has once been president or chairman of the board of a subsidiary company and is not only fully conversant with the full range of operating problems from personal experience but is also respected by line management because of his previous accomplishment in a line position within the company.

Committees

Coordination and communication may be effected through use of committees both at top and intermediate levels of the company. A management committee or operating committee reporting to the chief executive officer is commonly found. For example, in Ford Motor Company the Administration Committee is made up of the President and Chairman of the Board and the principal line and staff operating heads. This committee advises and consults with the president and board chairman and makes recommendations relating to the management or administration of the business affairs of the company. In bringing together the major operating and staff heads of the business, this committee provides for coordination of all activities and problems of common interest.

The Ford Committee System. Ford uses an integrated system of committees to provide for effective coordination of its decentralized operations and functions and to help avoid the overlap, duplication, and poor timing which can quickly result in increased costs and decreased efficiency.

The Manufacturing Committee coordinates the development of company manufacturing plans, policies, and standards applicable to the operating divisions. It reviews progress of the divisions toward established production programs and objectives for civilian products and coordinates action necessary to correct deficiencies which develop in the operation of these programs. This committee coordinates matters between divisions which concern the manufacture, delivery, or quality of component parts and assemblies for company products and resolves manufacturing difficulties in one division which may affect the performance of another division. The Manufacturing Committee also looks at promising developments of interest to the company in appropriate fields and at new or improved manufacturing processes and techniques and coordinates their application to company manufacturing operations.

The Industrial Relations Committee coordinates matters concerning personnel administration. It reviews and makes recommendations on company policies, procedures, and administration relating to employee procurement and training, wages and salaries, employee services and benefits, and labor relations and employee relations.

The Product Planning Committee passes upon proposals concerning areas of competition in which the company is to engage and the basic product, merchandising, and financial objectives of new model programs. It periodically reviews progress made by the Vehicle Divisions in the development of forward product plans, passes upon the styling and design of major product components, and approves prototypes of new models.

The Scheduling Committee establishes and coordinates the official production program of the company. It reviews and approves, or modifies, the proposed production programs of the Vehicle Divisions by product line and by body type, giving consideration to such factors as market demand, sales forecasts, production rates, retail deliveries, dealers' stocks, physical inventories, material availability and commitments, and the relationship of proposed programs to general financial and operating plans of the company.

The Foreign Operations Committee coordinates and considers matters relating to the foreign operations of the company. Through its subcommittee, the Foreign Exchange Committee, it considers the effect of foreign exchange restrictions and regulations on the company's overseas business and coordinates actions which can be taken to lessen the company's foreign exchange risks without unduly prejudicing sales programs and activities.

The Purchasing Committee coordinates proposed company policies relating to the over-all administration and conduct of interdivisional and outside purchasing activities and adopts such standard company-wide practices and procedures as are deemed necessary or desirable. It considers the advisability of negotiating patent license agreements or long-term purchase commitments with outside suppliers and determines general bases for negotiations. This committee determines those items for which total company requirements should be procured from an outside supplier on a coordinated basis by one or more selected purchasing activities. It also authorizes and coordinates the development and execution of special programs relating to purchasing, including those which pertain to company-supplier relations, purchase cost reduction, and the training of purchasing personnel. All these are of continuing importance to the company.

4. ESTABLISH ADEQUATE CONTROLS

The essence of decentralization is to give each local manager command of his own activity so far as can be done without jeopardizing the purpose and integrity of the enterprise as a whole. Since autonomous managers can be given a free rein only to the extent that the centralized authority can check on how well they are performing, a major problem in decentralization is that of establishing effective controls.

Every company, whether decentralized or not, makes use of some type of controls to evaluate its performance. But many companies which have decentralized find that the conventional methods of evaluating the business as a whole are not adequate. Profit center decentralization requires a control system that will assign costs fairly and indisputably to the accountability center that incurs them. This can sometimes become difficult if there is common use of production or sales facilities. It also requires careful handling in the allocation of general office administrative expense and the general selling expenses incurred on behalf of all the divisions.

Controls for profit center accounting should extend to managers of each profit center, including, as appropriate, foremen, superintendents and department heads, plant managers, division managers, central staff managers, and top management. Control should be based on appropriate standards. When budgets are used, the budget for a decentralized profit center is not an independent entity but should be an integral part of the over-all company profit objective.

Accountable managers at all levels should participate in budget formulation. Unless they understand and accept the yardstick by which they are measured, it is difficult to hold such managers accountable.

5. PROVIDE APPROPRIATE DISPERSION

It is much easier to operate a unit of the company as a profit center if it is cut loose physically. When facilities are separate and profit is figured as return on investment, the base can be figured directly with separate plants. It is easier to calculate the costs of engineering, maintenance, plant protection, janitor and cafeteria service, and other expenses in dispersed locations. Such expenses are lumped together or must be allocated on some arbitrary basis if facilities are shared. There are definite psychological advantages in dispersed operations. The decentralized manager in his own plant is literally "on his own." If he has his own facilities and equipment and is carrying on his own operations in his own plant, it is easier for him to consider himself a proprietor than if he is sharing floor space and manufacturing facilities with several other divisions.

There are many operating advantages in dispersed locations. It prevents the company from becoming a paramount influence in the economic life of the community. If the plant takes no more than 20 to 25 per cent of the labor force, there is no likelihood that a shutdown or strike or decline in business will seriously cripple the community as a whole, with attendant bad relations and poor publicity for the company and its products.

Dispersion enables the company to locate its plants close to its sources of supply and to its markets. It may effect material reduction in shipping costs or give the decentralized division a strategic advantage in serving its markets.

Small dispersed plants tend to promote motivation and to show better productivity than larger, integrated plants. This follows from our consideration of motivation, in which we found that cohesiveness is greatly facilitated in smaller groups.

Dispersion or physical separation of the headquarters building from the operating plants of the company can be of particular significance. When headquarters and plant share the same location, there is invariabiy a good deal of interference by central staff and top management people in the operation of the plant itself. One manufacturer of hardware attempted to decentralize without separating its main plant from central headquarters. As a result, the profit center management was continually harassed by orders and suggestions from the central staff and division management people, who had only to cross a small yard to enter the plant. Finally the complaints from the plant became so vigorous that the chief executive locked the doors of the office building entering on the plant yard. This was only mildly helpful, so, as a final step, the company built a new headquarters building in a city 20 miles away. This appreciably cut down the interference from the central group. Some companies have been so impressed with the need to separate plant and office facilities that they follow a rule of thumb of locating plants and headquarters offices at least ten miles apart.

SUMMARY

Profit center decentralization is best accomplished by first divisionalizing to form relatively independent organizational units and then giving the division managers the administrative tools they need for profit and loss accountability. This pattern is exemplified in the successful organization of such companies as General Motors, Ford, Chrysler, Du Pont, and General Foods.

Effective decentralization requires a balance of the necessary centralization of planning, organization, motivation, coordination, and control. Managers capable of undertaking the operation of the autonomous business units must be developed. Provision must also be made for coordination and communication between the profit centers, because this form of organization and management tends to make them insular and competitive. Also, effective decentralization requires adequate controls. Unless the central management group has a well-established system for measuring, recording, and reporting operating results, it is difficult to operate in profit center terms. Finally, appropriate dispersion of facilities is necessary.

CHAPTER 10 *Staff and Line Relationships*

The art and science of management organization is greatly complicated by misunderstanding of the proper role of line and staff. Of all
the difficult and sometimes intricate relationships that exist among managers, this is the most troublesome to define clearly and the least susceptible to rules and procedures. Many companies, frustrated in their
attempts to bring order to the confusion, studiously ignore the distinction. Others make a bold frontal assault, arbitrarily label certain functions line, others staff, establish a few ground rules to govern the in-
fighting, and hope for the best.

Consider the case of the president of a single-plant metal-fabricating
firm, who decided that manufacturing, sales, engineering, and finance
were the line departments in his company. He announced that the heads
of these functions would make final decisions on operating matters.
Within six months, the president found himself trying to arbitrate a series
of disputes between the finance vice president and the marketing manager over per diem allowances to field salesmen. He endured the pleas
of the personnel manager for support in the management appraisal
program, which the manufacturing vice president had refused to accept.
The climax occurred when the quality control manager reported that
the design specifications for a tight-fitting closure were off by almost
¼ inch and that a run of several thousand units had to be rejected.
Called on the carpet, both the engineering and the manufacturing vice
presidents blamed the other for the mistake. In desperation, the president called in a consulting firm. After organization analysis, the consultants were able to identify line and staff properly and to develop a
workable relationship among the various units of the company.

WHY DISTINCTION IS NECESSARY

Why is it necessary to distinguish between line and staff? What contribution does the establishment of a line-staff relationship make to

sound organization? Some authors feel that this distinction is quite unnecessary. Others believe that the terms have become so indefinite that it would be better to abandon them entirely. Many companies treat the line and staff designations as a means of distinguishing between productive and nonproductive effort in the company. Top executives often consider staff unnecessary "overhead" and fight doggedly to keep staff units off the payroll.

Much has been said to throw the concept of line and staff into question. However, upon analysis it is obvious that elements which do the work of "staff" must be provided if the growing enterprise is to accomplish its goals most efficiently and economically. People working together for a common goal must mesh their efforts so that they supplement and complement one another. This is possible only if each contributes his full share to the total effort. Line and staff relationships are established to guide people in the way they work together.

In practical situations, it is often necessary for people to overlap or even duplicate efforts if most effective teamwork is to take place. It may be necessary for one district sales manager, for example, to service a customer in another manager's territory because the first district manager cannot break a serviceman loose for the job. One manager may have to carry part of the load for another temporarily or to do something he overlooks. Relationships, in these cases, are not an inviolable "thou shalt not." Any sound relationship is established with full understanding that the over-all goal is the paramount consideration.

Formal definition of relationships is desirable only to the extent that it facilitates the informal activity that is prerequisite to good teamwork. Formal relationships help a man to realize when he *is* overstepping and clarify the normal role to which he should return. However, the formal relationship does not preclude a manager taking abnormal action if the exigencies of the situation require it.

The distinction between line and staff relationships is rigid and theoretical for conceptual purposes. Nevertheless, it should not be looked upon as an inflexible barrier or as an arbitrary classification. Different terms could as well be used to describe the relationship. We could say "supportive" or "auxiliary" or "service" in place of the term "staff." But we should not confuse an already difficult subject without clearly defining what we mean. If we are to treat organization in a professional manner, we must establish a defined, formal concept as our frame of reference.

The question is not whether staff really exists or whether it can be done away with. It is whether to attempt to define and clarify existing concepts of staff or to invent a completely new set of terms to describe the relationship. The first alternative seems the more practical.

Close examination of the growth history and method of operation of business enterprises will show that differentiation between line and staff roles is necessary to provide specialized, functional assistance to all managers, to ensure adequate checks and balances, and to maintain accountability for end results.

To Provide Specialized Assistance and Common Services

In modern business, the problems confronting the manager at all levels are so varied and complex he cannot possibly be master of them all himself. To *manage* effectively, the manager may have to know something of such subjects as budgetary controls, psychological testing, linear programing, input-output theory, motivation, operations research, and organization. He must keep abreast of new discoveries and concepts, new methods and systems in finance, personnel, engineering, marketing, and so forth.

This need runs from top to bottom of the organization. The president requires expert assistance in determining economic trends and their implications, in interpreting financial statements and reports, in setting long-term goals, and in making the important decisions that have application to the business as a whole.

The foreman needs help in locating people, in training and paying them, and in handling their complaints and grievances. He needs skilled technicians to help him set quality standards, schedule material, reduce costs, and perform many other activities.

This specialized assistance can be provided best by highly trained and experienced internal consultants, capable of counseling and advising individual managers on their complex and important operating problems; in other words, by agencies which have a staff relationship to the organization as a whole.

Staff can be a means of actual dollar savings by performing specialized work for a number of units rather than by having this work carried out individually by each organization unit. It is obviously inefficient and wasteful, for example, to have each production section recruit and interview its own employees or purchase its own supplies and materials. According to J. K. Louden, Vice President and General Manager, Commercial Division, York Corporation, subsidiary of Borg-Warner Corp., "It is neither practical nor desirable for each line executive, such as a foreman, to have his own independent staff group. Therefore, plant and company-wide functions must be created to perform that work for him to the degree he requires it and in accordance with established company policy." [1]

---

[1] J. K. Louden, "Line and Staff—Their Roles in the Organization Structure," *Advanced Management*, vol. 14, no. 2, p. 81, June, 1949.

Improved service results from the greater technical skill of staff and its ability to concentrate its entire resources upon one specialized area or problem. For example, the marketing vice president of one chemical products company with a growing volume in chemical specialties found himself so immersed in the day-to-day marketing problems that he could not guide and coordinate his staff sales promotion, advertising, market research, and sales training functions properly. Several new proprietary and ethical products with great long-term potential were being lost under the immediate demands of the dominant chemical lines. The sales managers in the field concentrated on the more profitable standard line and gave only incidental attention to the new products. The marketing vice president needed some means of bringing independent, aggressive, and sharply focused attention to the long-term needs of the new product lines. He secured this by creating two product manager positions, which were given responsibility for providing advice and service in the development of plans for market penetration and expansion, analysis of competitive practices, coordination and stimulation of sales, training of salesmen, preparation of sales forecasts to guide the manufacturing function in its planning and scheduling, and contacts with key accounts and related matters.

To Maintain Adequate Checks and Balances

Sound administration requires that a system of countervailing forces be set up in the organization so that authority delegated to individuals and groups will constantly be kept within prescribed bounds by counterbalancing authority. Effective control in particular requires appropriate checks and balances of this kind.[2] Managers who perform work should not also be required to evaluate their own performance. To secure proper perspective and objectivity, the manager needs control assistance from organizational agencies that are not directly accountable for operating results.

Planning and doing should also be separated to some extent. In planning, the manager can profit by the participation of his direct subordinates, but this participation will be colored by self-interest. If he wants objectivity and perspective, the manager needs assistance from organizational agencies that are not directly tied in with operations.

To illustrate: The marketing vice president is accountable for identifying and locating customers for products of the company and persuading them to buy those products. He delegates to the sales manager the

[2] Robert W. Porter aptly states that the system of checks and balances requires that "each force or activity throughout the organization is opposed by a counterforce which operates as a check and thereby sets up a balance of forces. Through the balance of forces the energies of each activity are regulated." *Design for Industrial Co-ordination,* Harper & Brothers, New York, 1941, p. 69.

actual work of selling. In managing his function, the marketing vice president plans, organizes, coordinates, motivates, and controls the total marketing effort, while the sales manager manages the work of the field sales crews. Both need assistance in planning the work to be done and in checking performance. This help should come from people other than those who are carrying out the work because those accountable for end results will inevitably slant their participation to their own personal interests.

Staff can provide an objective viewpoint in the solution or handling of specialized problems common to many departments. For example, the marketing department is usually inclined to be liberal in recommending credit policies because its performance is measured in terms of the total amount of product it sells. A staff credit department brings an objective viewpoint to the development of credit policies because it is concerned with maintaining the greatest possible volume of business with the smallest possible credit loss. Again, every manager wants to give the people reporting to him salary increases as frequently as he can find justification, to help maintain morale and improve productivity. A staff wage and salary function in the personnel department can provide objective counsel and assistance in the development of policies and procedures that will ensure fair and productive allocation of the company's wage and salary expense.

To Maintain Accountability

The line-staff relationship is not only a device for bringing to the manager's aid specialized and objective assistance; it does this while *maintaining the integrity of positions that have accountability for end results.* This is important. Successful operation in modern business is dependent upon the effective cooperation of people with different skills working together for a common purpose. Under most circumstances, people working together can do so in a team spirit. Each member of the group contributes from his experience and knowledge and cooperates with the other members to attain their common ends. However, to ensure planned, systematic, and coordinated action, the organization must anticipate those circumstances when cooperation does not take place easily—when people are new, when there are personality clashes, when there is disagreement. In these cases, a sound organization will identify the *individuals* who are accountable for end results. And it will also ensure that these individuals can exercise the authority necessary to attain those results. Our present concepts of control and decentralization require that no matter how effective the cooperation, an *individual manager* must be accountable. The staff-line relationship makes this identification possible.

DIFFERENTIATION IN OTHER FIELDS

The line-staff relationship is not peculiar to business and industry. Whenever work becomes so technical or complicated that one person cannot possibly be master of all its aspects, there arises the need to pool and coordinate the skills of two or more people to get the job done. And when several people work together, there is the need to identify individuals who are accountable for end results.

Staff and Line in Medicine. On the surgical team, the surgeon does the surgery. However, continuing discoveries in pharmacology and physiology, in physics and mechanics, preclude the surgeon alone remaining master of all the apparatus and procedures that should be utilized in the welfare of the patient.

Other expert workers aid the surgeon—the resident and the surgical nurse, who help him with surgery; the anesthesiologist, radiologist, and pathologist, who do work that is not surgery but is closely related to it and indispensable to the success of' the total effort. Although the terminology is rarely used in medicine, the surgeon and anesthesiologist work in a line and staff relationship on the surgical team.[3] The anesthesiologist is responsible for providing advice and service to the surgeon in determining the operability of the patient and the choice of anesthetic and advising in the diagnosis and treatment of shock. Complete cooperation between the surgeon and anesthesiologist is necessary for efficient operative care of the patient. Each is primarily concerned, not with the sanctity of his role, but with the welfare of the patient on the operating table. When an emergency arises or when action is to be taken, there is no need to identify roles or relationships. Each member of the team has been schooled and drilled in his part so that he plays it perfectly. The important point is that these roles and relationships must be identified if they are to be taught the members of the team.

Staff and Line in Football. Staff and line relationships exist in much the same fashion in team sports, such as football. On the football team, each player has a "formal" or defined part to play in carrying the ball forward. This standard relationship requires the quarterback to call the signals, the halfback to carry the ball, the tackles to take out the opposing linemen. However, once the action gets under way, there may be a rapid interchange of roles and relationships. The end carries the ball on some plays, the back plugs the line, the lineman pulls out and

---

[3] See Warren H. Cole, M.D., and Max Sadove, M.D., "The Need for Complete Co-operation between Surgeon and Anesthesiologist," *Journal of the American Medical Association,* vol. 162, no. 5, Sept. 29, 1956, pp. 437–441, for an excellent discussion of this line-staff relationship between the surgeon and anesthesiologist.

blocks. These interchanges and shifts are not disruptive of team effort because each knows his normal or "formal" role and relationship and promptly returns to it after he has made his contribution. One reason practise and "skull sessions" are so important to a successful football team is to help the players learn their roles and relationships until they do become automatic. When teamwork becomes instinctive, there is little need to differentiate between "ball carrying," "pass receiving," and "blocking" roles. But these concepts are necessary if we are to train people to play football, to play the same kind of football at different times and places and with different players, and if we are to think in the abstract about football as a means of refining and advancing our methods of playing the game.

MINIMIZING NEED FOR DISTINCTION

In some companies, there is little attempt to differentiate between line and staff and yet good working relationships exist. The reason for this apparent inconsistency lies in the type of social groupings that have developed. Characteristically we find this situation in old, well-established, and stable organizations, where small administrative groups predominate. There is low turnover and promotion is predominantly from within. Where these conditions prevail, members of management have opportunity to develop a high degree of group cohesiveness through sharing of experience and personal interaction.

In these cohesive groups, there is less need to establish unitary accountability, that is, to identify accountable *individuals*. Consequently, there is less need to differentiate between staff and line roles because the members tend to work together most effectively as a team to accomplish their common goals, with sharing and interchange of responsibilities and authorities and less insistence upon maintenance of formal relationships. Under these circumstances, if turnover is nominal, newcomers quickly take on the habit patterns and attitudes of their companions.[4]

DIFFICULTIES IN IDENTIFICATION

There are many reasons for misunderstanding and difficulty in identification of the line-staff role. Many managers find it difficult to decide what is line and what is staff and what relationship should exist between

[4] See Seymour Lieberman, "The Relationship between Attitudes and Role: A Natural Field Experiment," University of Michigan, Survey Research Center, Ann Arbor, Mich., 1954, for an illustration of attitude and role change.

them because they have been misled by one or another of the current myths that have sprung up concerning the staff role.[5]

Difficulty in identification of staff frequently arises because of confusion of staff as a distinct type of organization, failure to identify authority limitations, and faulty classification.

Confusion with Organization Type

Line and staff is often considered a distinct and identifiable type of organization. The assumption is that some organizations are wholly line, others completely staff, while still others are a composite. This is erroneous. Every business enterprise of any size has both line and staff. The pure line organization is almost never found in business. Staff units have no purpose if there is no line organization.

Failure to Identify Authority Limitations

Many and various are the categories of staff recognized in the literature. A casual review will find mention not only of functional, service, and auxiliary staff groups, but also of operative and nonoperative, administrative and supervisory, technical and nontechnical. This multiplicity is in itself bewildering.

Further confusion is caused by failure to establish a logical and consistent basis for classifying those functions which are predominantly staff. For example, it is commonly assumed that finance, manufacturing, and sales are always line, never staff. As a matter of fact, finance is almost always staff. Manufacturing and sales, under certain conditions, may also be predominantly staff in their relationships. And functions commonly regarded as staff, such as purchasing, engineering, research, and transportation, may at times properly be classified as line. Further misunderstanding is caused by confusing the different types of staff. For example, in many instances the term "staff" is reserved for personal staff positions, while specialized staff is classified as a "service" group. In few instances is distinction drawn between line and staff assistants.

LINE AND STAFF DEFINED

Differentiation between line and staff is the assignment of roles. At any time two or more people work together, the distinction is a means

[5] Robert C. Sampson lists four such myths in *The Staff Role in Management,* Harper & Brothers, New York, 1955, pp. 41–42. 1. Staff are those who do the knowing-thinking-planning. Line are those who do the work. 2. A staff man cannot issue orders to a line officer. 3. Staff prescribes method. Line decides when the act shall be performed. 4. What is specialized, aside from major operations, is staff. He points to the mistaken interpretation of staff in each case.

of determining who makes decisions directly related to the attainment of end results and who provides advice and service in making those decisions. Line refers to those positions and elements of the organization which have responsibility and authority and are accountable for accomplishment of primary objectives. Staff elements are those which have responsibility and authority for providing advice and service to the line in the attainment of objectives.

THE LINE RELATIONSHIP

We have defined line elements as those which have responsibility and authority for direct accomplishment of primary objectives. Line managers have a clearly defined role to play in the organization, which requires understanding of the nature of line authority and of the line relationship.

Line Authority

Managers identified as line are not subject to command by staff positions. The line manager, on the other hand, does not have *authority over* staff but must give consideration to staff suggestions. The decisive factor in the authority limitations of the relationship is that, in case of disagreement, the line manager has the right to make final operating decisions. The only exception to this occurs when specific

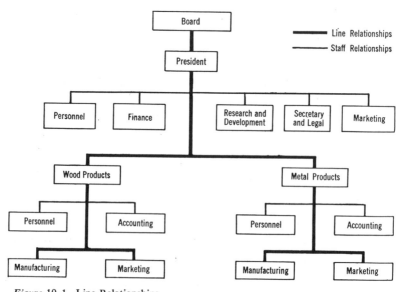

Figure 10–1. Line Relationships

delegation is made by the common line principal or when company policy is paramount.

In a pharmaceutical company manufacturing antitoxin, for example, the staff quality control manager, acting as the agent of the line principal, is delegated specific authority to reject lots in which he finds contamination. If effective teamwork is to be preserved, it is important that the authority delegated in this fashion be clearly limited to specific acts and that all concerned understand and appreciate the reasons for it.

The line within the company is the relationship that identifies and connects people working toward a common goal. This relationship may be looked upon as a chain of command, of communication, and of accountability (Figure 10–1).

The Line as a Chain of Command

A command relationship exists between each superior and subordinate. This arises from the process of delegation. In accepting the entrustment of part of his superior's responsibility and authority, the subordinate at the same time obligates himself to obey his commands. The superior is always in a "line" relationship, the subordinate in a "staff" to his principal. In every business organization, we can identify one series of delegations and redelegations which extends from the point at which basic objectives or end results are accomplished back to the Board of Directors and stockholders of the company. This is the primary chain of command. There are also secondary chains of command within each organization component that has its own established objectives.

Mooney and Reiley point out that it is "essential to the concept of organization that there be a formal process through which . . . coordinating authority operates from the top throughout the entire organized body." They identify this as the "scalar principle" and define it as the relationship which exists between superior and subordinate. This scalar chain enables the topmost coordinating authority to exert his influence through the entire organization.[6]

The Line as a Chain of Communication

The line can also be regarded as a means of communication between members of the organization. Coordination, delegation, and in fact the entire process of management are dependent upon communication. Establishment of the line relationship is the development of a channel through which communication can proceed most effectively.

Chester I. Barnard considers the line primarily a line of communication. Communication is necessary if the purpose of the organization is

[6] James D. Mooney and Alan C. Reiley, *The Principles of Organization,* Harper & Brothers, New York, 1939, pp. 14–15.

to be established and instructions for action are to be transmitted. Mr. Barnard describes several controlling factors which determine the character of this system of communication. Among these, he points out that the line should be clearly established and that every member of the organization should be tied into the system of communication by having someone to report to and others who report to him. To facilitate its use, this line of communication should be kept as short as possible.[7]

The Line as a Carrier of Accountability

Identification of the line elements within the organization is a means of establishing what positions and functions are accountable for end results and hence must be permitted to make operating decisions with respect to those results if the integrity of the work in progress is to be maintained.

We have seen that accountability is effective only if it is unitary. Modern business is organized, coordinated, and controlled in terms of individual managers who can be given clearly defined work and held to account for doing it properly. If we hold two or more people accountable for the same responsibility and authority, the obligation of each becomes diffuse and indefinite.

The line is a line of accountability. Each management position in this line assumes and retains accountability for end results, even though the work involved in discharging this accountability is not performed until the operating levels of the company are reached.

Consider, for example, a West Coast multiplant company which is organized to manufacture and sell electronic and mechanical products. In this company, the stockholders delegate to the Board of Directors responsibility and authority for management and operation of the enterprise.

The Board approves over-all plans and organization and passes on matters of over-all coordination, motivation, and control for the corporation. It performs certain operating work. The Board remains accountable to the stockholders for manufacture and sale of the company's products, but it serves as a carrier of accountability in that it delegates this responsibility and authority almost completely to the president.

The president, in turn, reserves and carries out responsibility and authority for developing detailed objectives, policies, programs, and budgets that will serve to guide the company in its operation. Since all the disparate activities of the company come to a focus only at his

[7] Chester I. Barnard, *The Functions of the Executive,* Harvard University Press, Cambridge, Mass., 1938. See especially pp. 106–111 and 175–181.

level, he devotes a large share of his time to coordination. The president appraises, counsels, and coaches his immediate subordinate officers, establishes sound communications, gives directions, and concerns himself with other aspects of motivation. He exercises control by reviewing company progress against approved plans and taking steps to correct unsatisfactory conditions which have arisen. He also performs a certain amount of operating work, such as contact with the public and with major suppliers and customers. The president acts as a carrier of accountability for the manufacture and sale of the company's products, in that he delegates the actual performance almost completely to the vice presidents of manufacturing and sales, respectively.

Each of these line principals in turn reserves responsibility and authority for managing and acts as a carrier of accountability for the manufacture and sale, respectively, of the company products. This process continues down through the various levels of the manufacturing and sales functions until the products are finally manufactured and sold to customers.

This process is common to every company. It is shown schematically in Figure 10–2, page 210. Note that each management position acts as a carrier of accountability for the actual accomplishment of the company objectives (manufacturing and sales, in this case). At the point where the product is manufactured and sold, the work is operating in nature, so that the terminal positions have the least management content.

Company Examples. A primary line of accountability can be traced in every soundly organized company. Nationwide Insurance Company, for example, identifies as line officers those who direct operations and are finally accountable for securing end results in conformity with approved objectives, policies, and standards. In Nationwide Insurance, the President is the principal line executive. From him, the line chain goes to the Vice President–Operations, Vice Presidents–Zone Managers, regional managers, and, in turn, to their subordinate department heads.

Armco Steel Corporation identifies line management as all members of supervision who are part of the direct line formed by the delegation of responsibility and authority from the highest executive through succeeding levels of supervision to the people producing and marketing the products of the company.

Objections to the Concept of Unitary Accountability. We must note at this point the objections of some researchers in the social sciences to the concept of unitary accountability. The point of view here is that group cohesiveness and unity of effort, which are prerequisite to high motivation, are threatened if one person is held accountable for the results of the group. This objection is based on the concept of the authoritarian, production-oriented supervisor. It fails to take into ac-

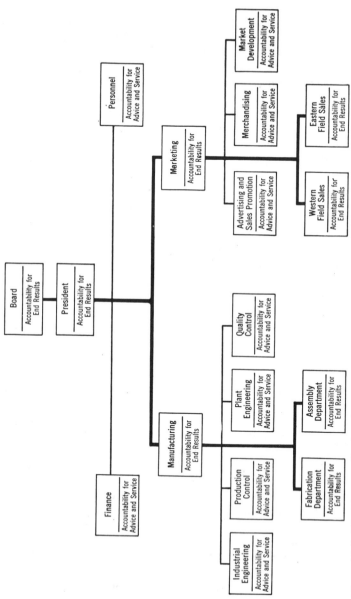

Figure 10–2. The Line as a Carrier of Accountability

count the true nature of the management process. A manager organizes for coordination and motivation. If he is accountable, he provides for participation, communication, and personal interaction, the raw materials of motivation. If unitary accountability is not identified, the typical situation in an unstructured group, the members of the group go through a laborious and frustrating period of trial and error in reaching compromise group agreement or in selecting an informal leader. Neither alternative is acceptable in the rigorous competition of the market place. Management of modern business is based upon accountability. Management accountability always must include the development of motivation.

WHAT FUNCTIONS ARE LINE?

For organization purposes, it is necessary to identify those functions which have a predominantly line relationship. Managers from these functions are assigned a line role and are expected to conform to it under normal circumstances.

Single Functions as Line

In some companies, a single function, such as manufacturing, sales, or design may be line. Manufacturing alone may be line when sale or disposition of the output of the company is assured by contract or by marketing through a manufacturer's agent. For example, a company manufacturing cartons on long-term contract for a food company has a guaranteed sale at current market quotations. Since competition sets the price, the company's primary emphasis is on manufacturing to contract specifications at lowest possible cost.

C. H. Masland & Sons, a manufacturer of rugs and carpets, operated with manufacturing alone as a line function until 1953. For eighty-seven years, Masland sold through a sales agent. It had no sales force of its own and maintained a staff sales function for liaison with the sales agent. However, Masland found it difficult to establish corporate and brand identity with dealers and the public. As its sales volume grew, it felt that it could afford and could get even better sales penetration if it had its own people selling Masland carpets exclusively. This led to establishment of a nationwide marketing organization that has already brought promising results.

A manufacturer's agent is essentially a sales organization. For example, a large Chicago sales agency is organized to sell cosmetic, drug, and food products to retailers, jobbers, chains, and department stores. It maintains warehouses and display rooms. Sales alone is line in this company.

Manufacturing and Sales

In the great majority of manufacturing companies, both manufacturing and sales are line. The basic objective of the Alan Wood Steel Company, for example, is to produce and sell at a profit steel and related products of maximum value to the company's customers. The line functions in this company are production and sales. The Carborundum Company is organized to manufacture and sell abrasives, super refractories, electrical components, reactor materials, and other specified products. Manufacturing and sales are the line functions.

Purchasing

In retail establishments, buying or purchasing may account for as much of the company profit as selling. As a result, buying or procurement and sales are often recognized as line functions. In a large department store, buying, a line function, procures merchandise, maintains stocks and assortments, and delivers merchandise to the selling floor. The sales function, which is also line, sells the merchandise and handles customer service.

Research

Research is a primary activity of the business in some companies. For example, more than half the products sold by a chemical company may not have existed ten years ago. The company can compete successfully only if it replaces products as quickly as they become obsolete. Research and development, therefore, may be a line function, together with production and marketing.

In E. I. du Pont de Nemours & Company, production, sales, and research are the line functions in each of the industrial departments, or product divisions. Research has the same status as production and sales.

Other Line Functions

A wide variety of other functions may be line. An integrated oil company is typically organized to find oil, bring it out of the ground, refine it to salable products, operate its own transportation facilities, and market its products. In this instance we would expect to find exploration, producing, refining, transportation, and marketing line functions.

For instance, the Creole Petroleum Corporation has the objectives of finding, producing, and refining crude oil, and the transporting and marketing of crude oil and petroleum products. These objectives represent the line functions in Creole, namely, exploration, production, transportation, refining, and marketing. The Geological Department explores for crude oil and other hydrocarbons. The Production Department is responsible for the production, recovery, and conservation of hydrocarbons and the transportation of crude oil by pipeline. The marine transportation of crude oil and products, exclusive of export liftings, is the responsibility of the Marine Department. The Refining Department develops and carries out refining programs. The Marketing Department promotes and distributes in Venezuela petroleum products and related specialties and accessories. The Export Sales Department in New York is responsible for the sale of crude oil and products entering export markets.

To operate as a going entity, an aircraft company must design and engineer, manufacture and sell its own aircraft, and provide such services as modification and test flight. We would expect to find these functions identified as line in such a company. This is usually the case. In Chance Vought Aircraft Company, for instance, the line departments are Engineering, Manufacturing, and Sales and Service.

Many other combinations are possible. For example, in Rubel & Company, New York decorative accessories firm, design and sales are line. Rubel acts as sales organization for some thirty independent factories but has no factories of its own. Rubel also designs and sells the well-known line of art and decorative accessories designed by Fred Press. Thus, design is a line function within the firm, together with sales.

Functions Rarely Found as Line

Certain functions are rarely found as line. Personnel is invariably staff because few companies are organized for the primary purpose of performing personnel work. The exceptions here might be an agency which handles employment, compensation, and other personnel matters for client companies or a consulting firm which offers a personnel service. The National Industrial Conference Board and the American Management Association both have line personnel divisions which create the end product of the organization: research studies, reports, conferences, seminars, and so forth.

Finance is often mistakenly classified as line. Upon analysis, however, it will be clear that the finance function and its components exist primarily for advisory and service purposes. An exceptional instance, in which finance is clearly a line function, occurs in an accounting and tax service firm in Philadelphia, which provides bookkeeping, accounting, and tax services to retail stores and small firms.

Public relations usually has a primary staff relationship. Here, again, however, exceptions may be found. In the public relations consulting firm of Maurice Feldman, Public Relations Counselors, New York City, for instance, public relations is the primary line function, because the organization exists to provide this service to clients.

LINE IN STAFF DEPARTMENTS

A secondary or internal line can be traced in each of the staff departments of the company. Here accountability for the objectives or end results of the function is carried from the head of the function to the lowest operating level. For example, the personnel department (Figure 10–3) has the objective of providing advice and service to other elements of the company in making most effective use of human resources. In a steel company, the personnel department has an internal line extending from the personnel manager to the people recruiting and interviewing, handling job evaluation, leading training conferences, and participating in the grievance procedure. This is as truly a line as that which extends from the manufacturing manager to the production supervisor. In this personnel department, there is also a personnel research section. This provides advice and service to the four line units and is staff to the internal line of the specialized staff personnel department.

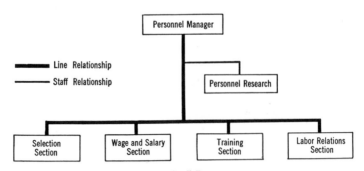

Figure 10-3. Internal Line, Personnel Staff Department

LINE IN FUNCTIONAL AND DIVISIONALIZED ORGANIZATIONS

In the functional organization structure, the line can be traced from the Board of Directors through those functional departments that are directly accountable for accomplishing the objectives of the company. The accountable head of each line function has authority and responsibility for his function throughout the entire company. Thus, in a multiplant company, the line manufacturing departments in each plant are extensions of the headquarters manufacturing function.

In divisionalized structures, the product or geographic divisions are the major line components. Within each division, the line then continues through the functional groupings which represent the primary activities of the division. The line functions may differ in different operating divisions of the same company. For example, a multiplant manufacturing company organized on a product division basis has one division which makes highly complex electronic assemblies. These products may quickly be made obsolete by technological innovations introduced by competitors. To stay in business, this division has to put as much stress on research, engineering, and development as on manufacturing and sales. As a result, the line functions in the division are a combined research, engineering, and development department, plus manufacturing and sales. In the other product divisions of this same company, farm and garden tools and equipment, ladders, and painting equipment are manufactured. The line functions in each of these divisions are manufacturing and sales.

THE STAFF RELATIONSHIP

The manager who has more work than he can handle needs help. As we have seen, his best means of sharing his burden is to delegate both responsibility and authority to line subordinates. There are many advantages in getting as much assistance as he can from this source. It enables him to delegate some of his authority and responsibility on matters of detail and routine and thus relieve himself of all but initiation and final decision on the *management* aspect of his work.

To the extent that his line subordinates help him, they will understand and be sympathetic to his point of view. Also, because they are close to operating problems, their assistance is likely to be practical and realistic.[8]

However, we are also confronted with the limitations and deficiencies of human beings. It is virtually impossible for line subordinates to perform their own work effectively and at the same time provide objective, expert advice and service to their principals. At some point it becomes necessary to secure help from other than line subordinates. This gives rise to the staff relationship.

---

[8] There is great motivational potential in this type of participation. As Maison Haire of the University of California says, "It is very difficult to overemphasize the importance of participating from a psychological point of view. Time after time, in industrial studies, research workers have come back to participation as a basic principle by which a subordinate may be given an opportunity to develop, his morale may be improved, and his skills and abilities may be maximally and productively utilized." *Psychology in Management,* McGraw-Hill Book Company, Inc., New York, 1956, p. 63.

Definition of Staff

Staff refers to those organization components that exist primarily for the purpose of providing advice and service to other units. As we have seen, every position has a staff relationship at times, in the sense that it provides advice and service. For example, the line manufacturing department helps the personnel department to determine training needs and to develop a training program in cost control; the sales department provides advice and service to manufacturing in preparing a sales forecast; the president advises and counsels the finance vice president on his performance; every subordinate provides advice and service to his superior.

For practical purposes, while it is important to recognize the sometimes transitory nature of the staff relationship, it is convenient to identify as *staff* those positions and units which have a predominantly advisory and service relationship to the line, and to other staff departments.

Sources of Assistance

In securing help, the manager has two choices. He can create a staff position that will serve only himself and will not be available to other units. This is *personal staff*. Or he can create staff positions that will be available to all line and staff positions that require assistance. This is *specialized staff*. Because personal staff is limited to the service of one principal, it can attend to a great variety of duties. Specialized staff, which may service a dozen or more different functions and divisions, cannot be skilled in all areas in which these groups require help; therefore, each specialized staff department specializes in one kind of assistance, such as accounting, engineering, production control, purchasing, personnel, and so forth.

PERSONAL STAFF

Personal staff may be defined as those assistant positions which provide advice and service to one manager in helping him to carry out his reserved responsibilities. Personal staff characteristically serves one principal only. The responsibility, authority, and accountability of the assistant are those of his principal. Personal staff is made up of staff assistants and line assistants.

Staff Assistants

Staff assistants (Figure 10–4) are commonly referred to as assistants to, executive assistants, administrative assistants, and special assistants. The staff assistant is employed when the principal requires help in a limited portion of his reserved responsibilities. In United Air Lines, the staff assistant assists his superior in the management of specific phases of the organization element in which he is employed. In a chemical company, the staff assistant normally represents his superior in matters of administrative detail. He is an interlocutor in the sense that he transmits his supervisor's instructions, not his own. He may observe for his superior, but he does not supervise.

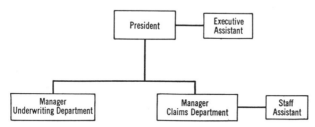

Figure 10–4. Staff Assistants

Staff assistants may vary in capacity from inexperienced trainees to executives of vice presidential rank. Since titles are used rather indiscriminately, a uniform nomenclature, such as that outlined below, will help clarify staff assistant positions:

Assistant to and Staff Assistant. These titles are used to designate assistants who are not restricted to one specific portion of the principal's work but are used on almost any part of his reserved responsibility as occasion requires. They may undertake special assignments and pursue such duties as the principal may direct.

Executive Assistants. This title is applied to staff assistants and assistants to who assist the chief executive officer of the company.

Special Assistants. These men aid their principal by providing specialized advice or service primarily in one kind of work, for example, legal, medical, finance, taxes, economic forecasting, management development, speech writing, organization. In effect, the special assistant is a specialized staff position restricted to the advice and service of one executive.

Administrative Assistants. These persons are limited to work of a minor administrative nature. They may help their principal by routing mail, meeting and entertaining visitors, providing office services, answering inquiries, assembling records, and so forth.

Line Assistants

The line assistant (Figure 10–5, page 218) is known by such titles as the "assistant manager," "assistant director," and so forth. He has two identifying characteristics: (1) He helps his principal with the full range of his reserved responsibilities; and (2) he assumes authority and responsibility for his superior and acts in his stead when the latter is absent.

In Continental Can Company, the line assistant assists his superior in the over-all management of the function and acts for him in his absence. Boeing Airplane Company uses the line assistant to provide as-

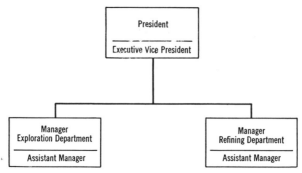

Figure 10–5. Line Assistants

sistance to his principal in the performance of any duties of his position. The line assistant in Armstrong Cork Company acts fully for his principal when the latter is absent or not available. When his superior is present, the line assistant helps him in the performance of his responsibilities.

The line assistant is used in several ways. In some companies he serves as an alter ego, that is, he *acts for* his principal in specific areas; in other cases, he assumes a team relationship, that is, he *acts with* his principal in the broad scope of his job. In still other instances, the line assistant is delegated clear-cut packages of authority and responsibility; he acts much as a subordinate manager.

Alter Ego. The line assistant may assume specified portions of his principal's job and carry these out for him, even while the principal is on the job. For example, it is not uncommon for the executive vice president, acting as line assistant, to serve as the first contact point for staff heads before they go to the chief executive. In this case, the executive vice president bears the brunt of screening and integrating many of the requests and demands of staff before they reach his chief. However, the staff head has the privilege of going directly to the chief executive and by-passing the line assistant if he so desires.

The line assistant may act as his principal's agent by traveling to sales and district offices, plants, and vendors' facilities. He may maintain contacts and relationships, for his chief, with specified customers, prospects, and even competitors. In many cases he will make confidential studies or conduct surveys in the field.

Team Basis. The manager and his line assistant may act as a team, one working with the other to carry the full weight of the principal's responsibilities between them. The manager remains accountable for the job as a whole, but he and the assistant manager share the day-to-day activities, each taking those parts of the job for which he is best suited. Thus, if the principal is strongly oriented toward people, he may select an aide who is an excellent technician and analyst. If a top executive is weak in finance, or marketing, or some other part of his responsibilities, he may prefer an assistant who will both compensate for his weakness and help him to acquire the knowledge and understanding he needs. This arrangement works well only if the personalities involved mesh effectively, if each has confidence in the other, and if there is free and constant interchange of information.

Subordinate Manager. In some cases, the line assistant is delegated a separate package of responsibility and authority and made accountable for it. This may go so far as to have the line assistant assume authority for certain subordinate functions. For example, in one multiplant consumer products company, two assistant managers report to the sales manager. One assistant has the sales promotion and advertising sections reporting to him. The other supervises a continuing project in market analysis. Both act for the sales manager in their responsibilities and make independent decisions with respect to their work. The sales manager finds this arrangement leaves him free to spend a good deal of time on the road with his sales crews.

This use of the line assistant does not fit the requirements of the position. In practice, it results in confusion between the status of the assistant and other subordinate managers. There is question as to the utility of a general assistant who is not free and available to help his principal perform his reserved managerial responsibilities but actually assumes direct operating responsibilities, presumably *for* his chief, but often to the confusion of other subordinates.

DANGERS IN USE OF PERSONAL STAFF

Personal staff positions are widely accepted. It is the rare company that does not have at least a sprinkling of assistants throughout the organization. Some companies, however, consider assistant positions of dubious value and are taking steps to eliminate them as largely as possible. Many others are scrutinizing personal staff positions with renewed care. General Electric Company, for example, does not use assistants. When a manager's job in General Electric gets too big for one person, it is reorganized into additional positions, each with its own authority, responsibility, and accountability.

There are good reasons for this critical appraisal. To his dismay, many an executive is finding that the assistants who have proliferated on his management roster account for a disproportionate share both of office space and of the administrative payroll. As a result, from small corporation to large, there has been eager search for a yardstick that will enable the company to determine how many and what kinds of personal staff it really needs.

It is clear that a great many assistant positions can be eliminated with advantage to the assistant and gain to the company. Often the assistant does not have a clear-cut, meaningful job but becomes an organizational ambiguity. He is assigned work that can be more effectively performed by other agencies. He provides artificial support for managers who lack competency and he tends to mask organizational deficiencies. The assistant is often asked to play a role that is poorly defined, that is contradictory, and that he may find impossible to fulfill satisfactorily.

As a case in point, one company president became alarmed at the disproportionate increase of general administrative expense. A count of the kind and number of salaries that were being funneled into the cost reports showed a density of two assistants for every ten managerial positions. The president instigated a thorough investigation. His findings were revealing. For one thing, an assistant had become a mark of prestige. A section head promoted to department manager automatically rated an assistant. In some cases, the assistant in turn had acquired his own personal staff. The company management development program encouraged the process. Every manager who aspired to move ahead was impressed with the need to develop a capable replacement. This gave quasi-official sanction to a great many assistants who were "in training" or "being broadened" or "getting over-all perspective on management problems."

There are several potential dangers in the use of personal staff. These include the tendency of the manager with assistants to reserve detail and routine for his own performance, the possibility of overlap and duplication in the work of personal staff and of line subordinates, the tendency of the manager with assistants to neglect his subordinates, personal friction between line subordinates and personal staff, and the use of the assistant as a crutch.

Reservation of Detail and Routine

The manager with personal staff always has the temptation to reserve for his own performance routine and administrative detail which might be performed effectively at levels lower in the organization and which could better be delegated as a package to an accountable position. In one company, for instance, a busy division manager maintained two administrative assistants and a line assistant. He parceled out to them, more or less indiscriminately, the task of arranging travel and hotel reservations, handling the details of his many talks and public appearances, opening and routing correspondence, relaying messages, entertaining visitors, and writing speeches.

When organization analysis was undertaken in the company, it showed that most of the minor administrative work could be handled by the division manager's secretary, who normally had little to do, and the staff traffic department. The work of entertaining visitors and speech writing was assigned to the public relations department, which soon demonstrated it had the specialized resources to do an even better job than had the assistants.

In another instance, a division manager with two assistants made lists of the work he was having his aides perform and sent these to his line subordinates and to specialized staff heads in his division, with a note asking, "Should this work be assigned to your department?" He was amazed to find that at least one, and in some cases, up to three of the managers he contacted believed they should be doing one or more parts of the assistants' work.

When the principal does reserve more authority and responsibility than is necessary because he has an assistant, several undesirable results are likely to follow. The assistant may be delegated—or assume—authority of his own. This gives rise to difficulty because the assistant and his superior may issue conflicting instructions or line subordinates may have trouble deciding to whom to go with a specific problem. Again, receiving instructions from a staff assistant who is obviously junior to them in age, experience, and pay does not sit well with many capable line heads and there may be a good deal of subterranean, but nevertheless effective, resistance.

In addition, there is the possibility of creating "crown princes" who will commandeer the line of promotion and make it impossible for other aspirants to receive consideration for the top spot. In other cases, the assistant is used to observe and report occurrences in the company or plant to his boss. This gives rise to uncomplimentary remarks about the assistant and resentment against the boss.

Neglect of Line Subordinates

To the extent that he assigns work to and confides in his assistant, the manager runs the risk of neglecting the legitimate needs and aspirations of his line assistants. One advertising manager, for example, in a New York multiplant chemical company was much disturbed and complained bitterly because the sales vice president had just called him in and told him he was hiring a new advertising agency. "He talked it over with those two assistants of his for more than a month, but he never brought me into the act," the advertising man said. "The agency people knew what was going on, and so did I and everybody else in the shop. I had to pretend I was being consulted but that didn't fool anybody."

When ignored in such fashion, the line subordinate loses interest and motivation and becomes resentful. At the same time, the executive is handicapping himself by using his second team instead of his first string in making important management decisions.

Use as a Crutch

One of the greatest dangers in the use of assistants is the tendency to use the aide as a crutch to overcome the deficiencies of unsound organization or to compensate for lack of managerial ability on the part of the principal.[9] It is difficult to argue that a crutch should be taken away if it is really needed. However, when a crutch *is* provided, the true purpose of the assistant should be acknowledged, a systematic investigation of the underlying weakness undertaken, and attempts made to rectify it.

There is frequent argument that no one man is capable of fulfilling all the exacting requirements of a management job; therefore, a manager needs assistants to provide him with technical help and advice. This assumption is built upon a misunderstanding. A manager should be given the job of *managing*. He should be given every opportunity to identify his weaknesses in *management* skills and to overcome them. He should not be encouraged to camouflage his deficiencies with capable assistants. If a manager really needs technical assistance, this can best be provided through specialized staff. It is both more realistic and more economical to create even a one-man specialized staff position that will service *all* the organization rather than a personal staff post that is restricted to one principal.

The only exception to this conclusion is the case of the chief executive officer. The pressures of modern business undoubtedly make more demands upon the president than he can handle himself. He often needs personal staff. However, even in this event there are other possibilities which should first be explored, as will be described later.

---

[9] Business practice amply seconds the observation of Lao-tzū: "When a man has not the strength to do what he is required to do, then he tries to deceive; when a man cannot cope with a situation, he tries to cover it up." *The Wisdom of Lao-tzū,* Modern Library, New York, 1948, p. 270. The writings of this Chinese sage have many lessons for modern managers.

WHEN IS USE OF PERSONAL STAFF JUSTIFIED?

There is one situation in which use of personal staff is probably justified. If the manager is absent from his job for a large part of the time, as in traveling or because of attendance at committee meetings or conferences, there is plausible need for a line assistant to cover home base for him while he is away. However, here again there are obvious dangers. Men of the caliber needed to take over the boss's job temporarily probably have the ability and aggressiveness to play the leading role themselves. As a result, they may find the part of the stand-in onerous and either become impatient and frustrated or leave the company for the bigger job they are capable of handling in their own right.

There are other means of covering the principal's position if he is away. These offer even more advantages than use of assistants. The best approach is for the manager to build up a strong subordinate organization so that he can delegate to one of his section heads the responsibility and authority of running the function while he is absent. This provides an unequaled opportunity for the subordinate manager to shoulder, even if temporarily, the full burden of the top spot. Assumption of real authority serves, as nothing else, to prove a man under fire and to help him gain experience and breadth for a step up the ladder. The delegation of temporary assignment to the top job should be rotated among the full complement of immediate subordinate managers. This will give each an opportunity to broaden himself and enable him to bring back to his job an appreciation and understanding of the problems confronting his chief.

SUMMARY

Distinction between staff and line is necessary to establish accountability when several different groups are working toward the same end results. Assignment of a staff role to a person or department limits it to provision of advice and service. In this role, staff can provide specialized skills to the organization.

The "line" refers to those elements which are accountable for primary objectives. A line exists in staff as well as line departments.

There are two categories of staff, personal and specialized. Personal staff consists of line assistants and staff assistants, who provide advice and service to one principal in helping him to perform his reserved responsibilities. Specialized staff provides advice and service in one kind of work, such as finance or personnel, to the organization at large.

Use of personal staff may result in the reservation of unnecessary detail and routine by the accountable manager, which, in turn, frequently leads to failure to delegate meaningful and important work to line subordinates. This can be detrimental to the entire organization.

CHAPTER 11 *Specialized Staff*

Specialized staff consists of those elements of the organization which provide advice and service to the line and to other staff units. Specialized staff has three characteristics: (1) It is limited to provision of advice and service and has no authority over other elements; (2) it is available to all departments and divisions, both line and staff; and (3) it provides advice and service in specialized areas of work.

As we have seen, every manager in the company is accountable for all aspects of his job. However, the operating manager is immersed in day-to-day problems. He has little time for research and study, for attending conferences and seminars, so that he can keep up with the newest thinking. He tends to rely upon tested methods and to resist change. This is human nature. But the company that wants to grow and expand must think ahead of today. No matter how large or diversified it becomes, it must match or better its competitors, not only in production, engineering, and marketing but also in its methods of selecting and training personnel, of financing its activities, of purchasing, and of management planning and control. It needs to organize not only to accomplish primary objectives in its products and markets but also in the kinds of management and functional work it does. These are the areas in which specialized staff has its proper place.

WHAT AUTHORITY FOR SPECIALIZED STAFF?

There is much disagreement over the limitation of specialized staff to advisory and service authority. Many believe that since the staff man knows most about his specialty, he should have the right to enforce his knowledge upon other units. Staff managers frequently see their job as that of determining objectives and policies for their functions, preparing programs, and seeing to it that these are carried out properly in the line departments. Some staff managers feel they should

224

have authority to inspect and correct work in the field to be sure a good job is being done in their specialties.

The dilemma of staff is pictured in the remark of a quality control manager: "If substandard product gets shipped and our costs for customer returns and re-work go up as a result, the vice president always calls me in and lays down the law. But if my inspectors get into an argument with the foreman because a lot going through is not meeting specifications to their satisfaction, they can't shut down the line. If we're to be held accountable for quality, we need more authority."

In another case, the training manager of a large Pennsylvania chemical by-product plant instituted a new training program. He was perturbed because attendance at training classes was poor. "I've designed these courses to develop management skills," he said, "and our managers need development. Plenty of it. But I rarely get as high as 40% attendance. If the company is laying out money for training, I feel I should have some command of attendance."

In some cases, the president of the company is the source of the difficulty because he fails to recognize and establish a workable relationship. In a textile company, the president delegated to the controller responsibility and authority "to decide and enforce policies and programs for operating budgets." The controller took this as his charter. He sent out a letter to accountable managers, detailing a procedure for preparation of budget estimates, together with a deadline for completion. After he had reviewed and analyzed the budget estimates he received, he visited the department heads and gave instructions for the amendments and reductions he believed desirable. A storm of protest arose that quickly filtered through to the president. At the next management committee meeting, the president announced he had given the controller authority to establish budgets and that he intended to back him to the hilt. The president had his way. However, to this day the controller is an unpopular individual and the company suffers from "poor relationships" between the line and the controller's department.

Taylor's Solution

Many solutions have been offered to this problem. Frederick W. Taylor felt it almost impossible to get in one man the combination of brains, education, technical knowledge, and other qualities necessary to handle all the requirements of an operating job. Therefore, he proposed that the conventional type of organization be abandoned and what he called "functional management" adopted in its stead. Under this arrangement, every production worker would have eight bosses, each of whom would give orders in his functional specialty. The worker would get separate orders from gang bosses, speed bosses, inspectors, repair bosses, the order or work and route clerk, instruction card clerk, time and cost clerk, and the shop disciplinarian.[1]

Delegation of line authority to functional heads in this fashion places primary emphasis upon the work to be done. This is what Taylor meant in his principle that "the work of each man in the management should be confined to the performance of a single leading function."[2]

This concept has not worked out in practice. The foreman reporting to eight bosses finds himself in an impossible quandary. Experience has shown that one man must be held accountable for the total result to be accomplished on a job. He should have all the technical and specialized help he needs, but he cannot divide his authority with the staff that helps him and still maintain the integrity of his position or his work.

Functional Authority

A more recent development of the functional management concept is that of functional staff authority. This provides for delegation of authority to the staff man to make final decisions with respect to his functional interests. For example, the industrial engineer has authority over production foremen in cost reduction; the safety engineer can issue independent instructions for correction of unsafe operating conditions; the personnel manager hires and places employees in those jobs where he thinks they best fit. In theory, this is an acceptable solution. However, if the manager concerned is to be held accountable for profit and loss, he cannot be made to assume accountability unless he has command of all the elements that go to make it up. This is the major weakness of delegating to specialized staff command authority over line, even in specialized functional areas.

Advisory and Service Authority

Companies with sound and harmonious line-staff relationships restrict staff to advisory and service authority. Staff has the right to counsel, advise, assist, and recommend to line. It can do things *for* line. But it has no authority *over* line. As R. E. Gillmor, formerly Vice President, Sperry Corp., puts it,

Staff positions providing auxiliary services are made responsible through single lines of responsibility for giving advice or assistance wherever or whenever required by any part of the organization. By this concept the auxiliary or staff service has a status similar to that of a law firm, consulting engineer, or other independent advisory agency. The departments utilizing staff services become their clients and are free to use their services or not

---

[1] Frederick Winslow Taylor, *Shop Management,* Harper & Brothers, New York, 1911, pp. 96–106.
[2] *Ibid.,* p. 99.

as they see fit. Recommendations of staff services which are approved by executives become the decisions and directives of those executives.[3]

Specialized staff should not be delegated decision making or "command" authority over line. It should be delegated responsibility and authority and should be held accountable only for the provision of advice and service to the various elements of the organization.

Advisory Authority

This is the right to provide advice, counsel, assistance, guidance, and recommendations. Advice may be given with respect to any or all of the aspects of planning, organization, coordination, motivation, control, and operations in each of the specialized, functional areas for which staff agencies are provided.

Service Authority

This is the power or right *to do things for* other organization agencies, both staff and line. It is implicit in the staff role that, to the extent that it is more economical or efficient for it to do so, the staff agency may perform specified work for other agencies. For example, production control schedules production for the production superintendent and foreman, the sales promotion specialist arranges store displays for the sales supervisor, the personnel manager interviews and screens applicants for accounting jobs for the finance manager.

In some cases specialized staff acts as an agent for the line principal in conveying his wishes with respect to specified action, just as may personal staff. For example, in preparing a consolidated balance sheet for the company as a whole, the accountant may require use of a standard chart of accounts and standard methods of collecting, recording, and reporting costs. However, the accountant does not insist that this be done because he wants it done that way. He is reporting to the managers concerned the desires of the chief executive, who has already made policy decisions to cover this requirement.

THE JOHNS-MANVILLE INTERPRETATION

The role of specialized staff with relation to the line operating organization is well described by Johns-Manville Company in its organization manual, as follows:

The relationship [between the staff specialist and the operating man] does not rest upon authority of one man over another. . . . The specialist interprets and explains policies to the operating man, and makes suggestions

[3] R. E. Gillmor, *A Practical Manual of Organization*, Funk & Wagnalls Company, New York, 1948, p. 14.

that he thinks will be helpful, because his duty to the president requires him to do so. He does not expect the operating man to put his ideas into practice because *he* says so; in fact, he does not *expect* the operating man to do anything; it is the president who expects the operating man to make proper use of the specialist's ideas because he, the president, has declared them to be worthy. . . .

Indeed, these ideas of the specialist are not his own ideas. They may have been his own originally, but they are not his when he expresses them to an operating man. They are the ideas of the president because, whether expressly or by implication, the president has approved them and adopted them. Even if they are details which the president has not specifically considered, they are still the president's ideas in the sense that they are the specialist's best judgment as to what the president would say if he were speaking. If the specialist uses his own judgment, it is not to say what he thinks should be done, but what he thinks the president would want done. . . .

The operating man receives such expressions in the same sense. He accredits them as the president's views because they are spoken by the man who is in the best position to know the president's views. They carry great weight with him, not because uttered by the specialist, but because they are the president's. He puts them into practice because his duty to the president requires him to do so.

The relationship is best termed a consultative one. It is no more than consultative because neither consultant can compel the other. It should be close, because it focuses the highest intelligence upon the company's operating problems. The specialist should seek to supplement, to bolster, and to encourage the operating man in his activities related to the specialist's field. The operating man should seek the advice and suggestion of the specialist as the best-informed man in that field.

THE STAFF ROLE IN DU PONT

E. I. du Pont de Nemours & Company provides staff groups of highly trained specialists at the top management level and within the product divisions to serve management and the entire company in their specialized fields. At the corporate level, there are thirteen staff or auxiliary departments, which provide special services and talents in advertising, legal, engineering, research, foreign relations, and other activities.

The Employee Relations Department in Du Pont, for example, provides advice and service to the company as a whole in personnel matters. It assists the president and the executive committee in the development of general personnel policies and works with the product divisions in the interpretation and application of these policies to operating problems. For instance, the company has a policy of developing understanding of the needs and interests of employees, of helping employees to understand the company and its management, and of treating each employee as an individual. Each product division in Du Pont handles the application of this policy to its own circumstances. However, it has the constant aid and assistance of specialists from the Employee Relations Department in this application.

Staff groups are also located within the product divisions and plants of Du Pont, to provide personnel, accounting, process, engineering, sales development, and related services to operating management. The company is firmly convinced that if a man is given a job, he must be equipped with full authority to handle it and that to give him less would dilute his accountability. Consequently, the company places full authority for decision with the line manager and limits the staff functions to advisory and service activities.

OTHER COMPANY INTERPRETATIONS

An advisory and service role for specialized staff is advocated by most companies that have thought through this problem. In some cases, companies have abandoned the use of staff designations for a time but have finally come back to the need for interpretation and establishment of the staff role and education of managers in effective staff-line teamwork. There is an increasing trend for companies to spell out the line-staff relationship in company organization manuals, training manuals, and by other means. Interpretations of the advisory and service role of staff by several leading companies are outlined below.

Ford Motor Company

Ford assigns an advisory role to specialized staff. In Ford, the staff is responsible for formulating or advising on plans and policies, outlining procedures, analyzing information, and advising the executives they serve as to courses of action which they believe should be taken. The specialized staff in Ford is primarily responsible for studying, investigating, and planning for Ford operations and serving operating management.

Armco Steel Corporation

Armco sees the role of specialized staff as that of furnishing line managers with specialized assistance and counsel. In Armco the staff determines needs and formulates controls for line management; it gives opinions upon proposed plans and policies; it keeps line management informed of significant developments and carries out functions requiring specialized knowledge and experience. Although staff provides assistance and counsel in these activities in Armco, line management is still held accountable. For example, the safety department is charged with establishing and promoting Armco standards of accident prevention, plant cleanliness and order, and fire prevention and control. However, the safety department is not held accountable for the safety of crews, for plant cleanup, or for the cause of fires. These are exclusively the accountability of line management.

American Enka Corporation

In this company, the auxiliary role of specialized staff is emphasized. Staff acts primarily in an advisory capacity in American Enka. It gathers information and develops plans, procedures, and programs which it recommends to accountable line managers.

The staff official in American Enka coordinates plans and proposals among staff and line managers so that the final plan or proposal will be fully developed and concurred in by all concerned before being submitted to the line principal for approval. A staff official has no authority in his own right to issue instructions to line personnel. Where circumstances warrant, however, such authority may be delegated for a particular assignment. The provision is made here that even when he exercises this authority, it must be in the name of his line principal.

Standard Oil Company of California

Specialized staff in Standard of California is made up of experts in the functional areas of the company's activities. They advise management and recommend policies in their areas for his approval. Staff then follows through, aiding the operating units in the interpretation of policy and in its application through the development of appropriate programs, procedures, and methods. In Standard of California, the line operating head, *not* specialized staff, is accountable for application of the advice which he receives. The line head is never subject to the orders, supervision, or control of the staff head.

General Foods

Specialized staff activities have evolved over a period of many years in General Foods. In this company, specialized staff assists top management in the development of company policies in its specialized areas. It provides top management and other line and staff managers with advice, counsel, and services. General Foods specialized staff is made up of highly qualified specialists who have broad experience, special skills, and time to research and study functional areas of importance to the company. They bring to operating problems a fresh viewpoint and complete objectivity which contribute to sound decisions, to the advantage of all elements of the organization.

DEFINITIONS OF STAFF ADVICE AND SERVICE

As we have seen, each specialized staff function is delegated responsibility and authority and assumes accountability for providing advice and service in its functional specialty to all levels of management. In providing advice, specialized staff counsels, advises, consults, and recommends. In furnishing service, specialized staff *does things* in its specialized area for other units because they do not have the specialized ability, the time, or the objectivity to do it for themselves. The responsibility, authority, and accountability of specialized staff are outlined below in terms of the advice and service it renders.

Staff Advice and Service in Planning

Specialized staff is of great value in assisting managers in planning activities. Humble Oil & Refining Company, for example, trains members of its management group to discuss plans with specialized staff during the developmental stages, so as to take advantage of every assistance the staff is able to provide. William H. Newman suggests that

. . . one of the best ways to regard staff assistants and staff divisions is as extensions of the thinking capacity of the executives they serve. They do planning work that the executive might do himself if he had the time. In order to secure an integration of planning . . . the findings and recommendations from the staff typically flow through the executive who is authorized to make the final decision.[4]

Planning advice and service by staff usually encompasses objectives, policies, programs, procedures, and budgets.

Development of Objectives and Policies

Specialized staff has clearly delineated *responsibilities* in providing advice and service in the formulation and interpretation of objectives and policies in its area of functional specialization. As we have seen, at the top management level, the Board of Directors and the chief executive have responsibility for determining objectives and policies for all aspects of the business, including not only over-all goals and policies but also those that relate specifically to such functional areas as finance, personnel, purchasing, and so forth. In most instances, however, neither the chief executive nor the Board has the time or the specialized training to study and investigate these areas to the extent necessary for effective

[4] William H. Newman, *Administrative Action,* Prentice-Hall, Inc., Englewood Cliffs, N.J., 1951, p. 97. This work contains an excellent analysis and discussion of management and administrative action.

planning. Accordingly, responsibility for studying the company's requirements in functional areas and for preparing and forwarding recommendations is delegated to the specialized staff department. The chief executive reviews the recommendations of his staff, integrates them with the sometimes conflicting demands and suggestions of other functional heads, assesses the whole in terms of the long-range objectives of the company, and either arrives at a decision himself or makes appropriate recommendation to the Board of Directors.

Specialized staff has *authority* to consult with managers at all levels to ascertain their needs and desires with respect to objectives and policies in the functional area concerned. Staff authority is limited to providing advice and recommendations for the accountable line superior and to preparing statements of objectives and policies for top management consideration if requested.

In assisting with preparation of objectives and policies, specialized staff is *accountable* for securing full participation and expression of line and staff managers as to scope and content of objectives and policies. Staff is accountable for reconciling so far as possible its own views and those of other managers and of bringing irreconcilable differences to the attention of the accountable line superior.

Interpretation of Objectives and Policies

After objectives and policies in specialized areas have been determined by top management, the specialized staff is *responsible* for providing advice and service in interpreting them to all levels of management. Jones & Laughlin Steel Corporation points out that, since specialized staff participates in objective and policy formulation in the first place, it is best equipped to explain these plans to other managers.

In interpreting plans, specialized staff has *authority* to explain to line and staff managers the purpose, intention, and meaning of top management objectives and policies in its functional area. It is *accountable* for accurate explanation and interpretation and for developing understanding of top management's intentions and desires.

Programs

The specialized staff manager is *responsible* for developing programs for installation and operation of his functional specialty for approval of his superior. Specialized staff may be delegated requisite *authority* for observing and analyzing operating conditions and for discussing problems with personnel to whose activities the program will apply. It is *accountable* for securing the participation and cooperation of line and staff managers. The staff man reconciles the technical requirements of his specialty with the expressed needs and desires of the managers concerned. Where there is disagreement, he refers it to the common line superior.

Procedures

Development of procedures is a *responsibility* of specialized staff. The staff has *authority* to study operations and consult with the personnel to whom the procedures will apply, within limits set by the accountable manager. If the procedures apply to two or more organization components, final authority for procedures is vested in the line manager accountable for all units involved. The staff man has authority for preparation of detailed statements of procedure in his functional specialty for approval of the accountable manager. *Accountability* of the staff man in developing procedures is limited to the technical adequacy of the procedures prescribed and the participation and cooperation of the personnel who will use them. It also includes referral of irreconcilable differences to the accountable manager.

Budgets

The staff manager is *responsible* for providing advice and service to line and staff managers in the preparation of budgets for activities involving his specialized function. He is also responsible for preparing budgets for his own function. His *authority* in budget preparation is limited to studying and analyzing, upon request of managers concerned, their needs as to his functional specialty and appropriate budget requests. He has *authority* to question and consult with the personnel who will be doing the work for which the budget request is being made within limits prescribed by the accountable manager. The specialized staff man is *accountable* only for the technical adequacy of his recommendations within limits prescribed by the accountable manager.

Company Examples

Specific examples of the role of specialized staff in planning are found in the finance function of Kimberly-Clark Corporation and the industrial relations function of Blaw-Knox Company.

Kimberly-Clark Corporation. In this company, the Vice President–Finance is accountable to the President for directing the Corporation's affairs in the areas of corporate finance, reports to regulatory bodies and lenders, changes in corporate financial structure, cash management, independent audits, taxes, credits, purchase or sale of investments and of equities in other companies, employee stock sales and options, contributions to Retirement Trust, financial and pension analyses, land, and insurance.

He formulates and recommends to the President corporate objectives, policies, and programs concerning his area of responsibility. He explains to his associates and deputies those which are authorized. He explains and interprets Finance Division objectives, policies, and programs. He directs the management and performance of division programs and provides advice, counsel, and services in his area of responsibility to the corporation's subsidiary and associate companies. Although his advice is used by members of such companies as the basis for decision, their resultant actions are their personal responsibility for which they are accountable to their respective principals.

Blaw-Knox Company. Among his other responsibilities, the Vice President–Industrial Relations Department of Blaw-Knox Company has these specific planning duties:

1. To develop and recommend industrial relations objectives and policies which will make for an efficient and cooperative employee group.

2. To keep informed of developments in industrial relations policies and practices in fields in which the company is engaged, to the end that company practices may include such developments as seem advisable.

3. To supervise the development of procedures and methods for installing and maintaining industrial relations programs at all applicable locations. To review, revise, and approve procedures and plans developed within the department and to assist in their execution.

4. To supervise the development of and recommend plans for the company's labor relations work and to supply advice, assistance, service, and information on those matters to the company's operating units.

5. To review continuously the company's industrial relations objectives and programs in order to measure the progress being made in their application and the results secured. To recommend changes which will strengthen the company's position in the industrial relations field.

Staff Advice and Service in Organizing

Specialized staff functional groups have *responsibility* for counseling with the line departments and with similar specialized staff departments or units on organization of their specialized activities in the plants and divisions of the company. Their *authority* is limited to advice and service only and their *accountability* to the technical quality of the advice and service they provide.

As we shall see in our discussion of changing the organization, there is a growing trend to the organization of a central organization planning department, which provides advice and service to all components on organization matters, including study and identification of the work performed, definition of responsibility and authority, and establishment of relationships. Many companies are organizing such groups and find them of great value in maintaining a well-balanced organization structure.

Staff Advice and Service in Coordination

Specialized staff has *responsibility* for assisting the chief executive and functional and divisional heads in the coordination of activities that concern his functional specialty. The staff manager keeps line and staff managers informed on matters of importance that develop in his area of specialization. He also coordinates activities of his own function with those of other organization components. *Accountability* of staff is limited to communication of information, securing participation, and reporting disagreements to the accountable line superior.

In some companies, specialized staff positions are created to encourage and facilitate coordination among all units of the organization in matters of common interest. A management development coordinator may act primarily to help balance and unify activities designed to train managers, a product planning staff may be concerned primarily with coordinating the efforts of such diverse groups as manufacturing, engineering, research, and marketing in the development of new products for the company. Illustrative is the administrative production planning staff in Columbia-Geneva Steel Division, United States Steel Corporation, which provides coordinating advice and service.

Columbia-Geneva Steel Division, United States Steel Corporation. The administrative production planning staff in Columbia-Geneva Steel as part of its work provides advice and service in the development of a coordinated sales and production program for the division. In developing this program, the sales department in Columbia-Geneva Steel first forecasts maximum possible sales without regard to plant capacities. The administrative production planning staff then reviews and modifies the sales forecast in the light of steel supply, plant capacities, and so forth. The operating department recommends changes in view of expected mill repairs, crew availability, and other local operating conditions, after which the administrative production planning staff combines the sales and operating proposals. The resulting proposal is reviewed in detail by the coordinating committee, which recommends a program for executive committee action. The accounting department forecasts net profit in terms of this program by product, plant, and for the division as a whole; the administrative production planning staff supplements the recommended program with a forecast of net profits. The completed recommendation is reviewed by the executive committee, which decides upon the final program. Decision of the executive committee is translated into production budgets, sales quotas, and raw materials requirements by the administrative production planning staff. Detailed plans are finally issued by the sales, operating, and purchasing departments, as a guide to the entire organization.

Staff Advice and Service in Motivation

Motivation is largely a matter of leadership; consequently, the *responsibility* of specialized staff managers is limited to motivation of the people who report to them, except for the personnel specialized staff function. Specialized staff managers may also have responsibility in recommending appropriate measures to improve motivation of people working in their specialized area in the plants and divisions. For example, the engineering or research manager might provide advice as to the best means for effective utilization of engineering or research talent in the operating departments. All specialized staff heads have some responsibility in recommending or screening personnel in their specialty who are being recruited or transferred to other units of the company.

Authority of specialized staff for motivation is limited to advice and service. Each staff manager, however, is accountable for motivation of people reporting to him. *Accountability* is limited to the technical quality of the suggestions or recommendations made.

In most companies the personnel department provides advice and service to all units in motivating employees. It should be noted, however, that responsibility and authority for selecting, compensating, training, and developing people and performing other activities inherent in motivation is the accountability of the line and staff managers to whom these people report. It is the function of the personnel department to provide the line organization and other staff departments with the advice and service they need to do this job, but the personnel staff itself is not accountable for selecting, compensating, training, or motivating employees.

Staff Advice and Service in Controls

Staff has *responsibility* in several of the activities involved in management control. The specialized staff department assists in the development of *performance standards* for its specialized function by helping to establish objectives, policies, programs, procedures, and budgets, which are in themselves yardsticks for performance. It also helps develop other objective criteria as circumstances warrant. Staff may aid in the *measurement* or determination and recording of the degree of performance. For example, the accounting department records and reports money spent, the personnel department measures and reports turnover and absenteeism, the quality control manager maintains continuous checks on the quality of products. Analysis and *evaluation* of the control information secured may be undertaken by staff for its specialized area. The purpose of evaluation is to compare actual performance with the standards established. For instance, the safety director analyzes plant safety in terms of safety standards. The controller compares actual expenses with those budgeted. The wage and salary manager evaluates wages and salaries being paid against the ranges established. Evaluation leads to determination of need for *corrective action* designed to rectify undesirable conditions and bring variations and discrepancies back into line.

Staff *authority* in control is limited to advice and service. Staff may offer recommendations as to appropriate corrective action, but the prosecution of that action is always the prerogative of the accountable line manager.

Specialized Staff Management Departments

Some companies have organized specialized staff departments which provide advice and service, not in functional areas but in the processes of management. Typically, such departments specialize in the techniques and methods of planning, organization, coordination, and control. Usually they report to the chief executive or to the division or plant manager whom they serve. Two outstanding examples are the Economic Controls group in United Air Lines and the Administration Department of Kaiser Aluminum & Chemical Corporation.

United Air Lines. In United Air Lines, the Economic Controls Administration Department secures from all major departments of the company estimates, projections, forecasts, and plans and from these develops company-wide master plans which serve as performance standards for company operations. These cover traffic and service patterns, aircraft, ground facilities, personnel, market and financial projections, and forecasts. These master plans are recommended to the president for approval. The staff department then develops operating controls involving such techniques as methods analysis, standards setting and application, forms and control analysis, job analysis and specifications and job evaluation, regulations, organization control, and quality control. Financial controls are also developed, including total sales quotas, personnel budgets, operating expense budgets, and capital expenditure budgets.

When the Economic Controls Administration in United Air Lines detects inconsistencies or noncompliance with accepted programs, standards, methods, and procedures related to economic controls, it recommends corrective action to the departments concerned. The Economic Controls specialized staff is also available to provide assistance and consultation to any element of the company on economic control matters.

Kaiser Aluminum & Chemical Corporation. An Administrative Department has been organized by Kaiser Aluminum & Chemical Corporation in several of its plants. This staff group has the objective of relieving the plant manager of as many of his administrative, organizational, and analytical duties as possible.

This specialized staff group assists the plant manager by developing and presenting future goals and programs and by formulating all policies guiding the management of the plant. It plans the plant organization and the assignment of functional authority, responsibility, and duties. This group prepares budgets, with those concerned, to serve as a base to which executive thinking and planning can be related and from which variations can be measured as conditions change. It establishes, maintains, and improves uniform plant standards for material and manpower utilization, equipment operation, and administrative practices.

The Administrative Department assists with the assimilation, analysis, and evaluation of data, the reasons for and significance of actual versus desired performance, and the effective presentation of the results to those concerned. It also aids in the standardization or centralization of administrative duties and services which affect all departments in the plant.

VARIATIONS IN ADVICE AND SERVICE

In defining the work of staff elements, we should note that while specialized staff provides advice and service to all levels of management, there is a difference in the help they offer different levels of the organization, just as there is a difference in the management work performed by the foreman and the chief executive. We can characterize this difference most accurately by saying that specialized staff mostly provides advice and relatively little service to top management levels. To lower management, most of its help is in the way of service, little in the way of advice. What we are saying, in effect, is that specialized staff does a considerable amount of specialized and technical operating work *for* lower management levels. Since top management is mostly concerned with management, little with actually operating, we find, as we would expect, that specialized staff at top levels is also mostly advisory.

In the production departments, for example, the industrial engineer plans process and machine layout for the superintendent, the production control staff specialist makes up a master schedule from the sales forecast, the training specialist teaches foremen the techniques of job instruction. At the top management level, however, the central staff manufacturing manager spends most of his time advising the chief executive on over-all manufacturing objectives, policies, and procedures, advising division heads on administrative implementation of these plans, and advising division and plant staff on technical implementation at the operating level.

The work performed by central staff, division staff, and plant or operating staff groups differs. Top staff concerns itself with plans, coordination, and control of company concern. Division specialized staff concentrates its efforts on accurate interpretation and explanation of company plans and on assistance to division management in the formulation of division plans. Plant staff is primarily concerned with helping operating line management perform in terms of the guiding principles and goals laid down by division management. As we have seen, the latitude of decision making delegated to each level within the limits of overall objectives and policies largely determines the extent of decentralization (Figure 11–1).

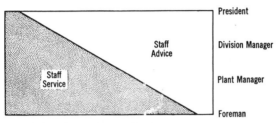

Figure 11–1. Variations in Advice and Service

SERVICE, AUXILIARY, AND FUNCTIONAL DEPARTMENTS

Some authorities and companies attempt to differentiate among functional, service, auxiliary, technical, and specialized staff. Service departments are assumed to be different from line and staff departments because they do work different from either. Auxiliary departments are identified as those which are neither line nor staff but which perform specialized functions assisting in line jobs. Functional departments are said to resemble staff departments, in that they are assigned specialized functions. Functional departments also have authority over their own specialized work, wherever it may be performed in the company.

In terms of the concepts outlined, functional, service, technical, and auxiliary departments can all be identified as specialized staff groups. The essential difference lies in the amounts of advice and service rendered at different levels. Distinction in terms of functional, service, auxiliary, and technical departments is purely semantic. All have similar responsibilities; the differences are in degree, not in kind.

ROLE OF CORPORATE AND DIVISION STAFFS

In the small, functional company with combined plant and headquarters facilities, one group of staff functions serves all units. As the company grows, dispersed plants may be constructed, or the organization may be divisionalized. Each plant and division usually establishes certain specialized staff functions of its own, such as personnel, accounting, and purchasing, duplicating to some extent the functional staffs first established in the central office. In some cases, the company continues to grow by building or acquiring plants additional to the first unit. In this case, each plant has its own staff facilities. The question now is: What role does corporate staff play with relation to division and plant staffs? (See Figure 11–2.)

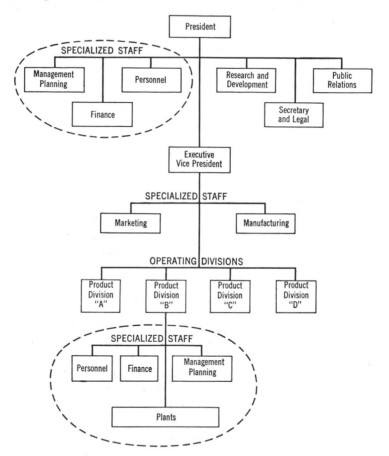

Figure 11–2. Corporate and Division Staffs

Corporate Staff

Specialized staff functions in the company headquarters serve to advise and assist top management in the *over-all* planning, organization, coordination, motivation, and control of work in their specialized areas. Because corporate staff must serve as eyes, ears, and brain for top management, it should include all the major areas of work which require top management attention. Corporate staff functions should also be organized when work has to be performed in the individual divisions or plants which, although essentially operational, can be done more effectively or economically at a central point for the company as a whole.

For example, the seven operating divisions of one pharmaceutical company buy great quantities of bottles, chemicals, medicinals, and other materials. These could be purchased individually by each division. However, the company finds it much more economical and effective to contract for the entire output of certain sources of supply at very favorable prices through a corporate purchasing office.

Product division and plant heads make use of corporate staff when it can provide more or better consultative services than is available within their own staff groups. Division managers also use corporate staff to evaluate the technical competence of their own staffs.

By means of the policies, programs, and administrative procedures which it prepares and recommends for top management approval, corporate staff prescribes and guides the manner in which its specialized work will be carried on throughout the company. Since this work has a direct effect on the efficiency and profitability of operations, corporate staff must take the lead in developing and maintaining sound working relationships at all levels.

Division and Plant Specialized Staffs

Staff work should take place as close as possible to the point at which action occurs. This is particularly true of repetitive and routine work directly related to operations. The more levels staff is removed from operations, the less readily available it will be and the less realistic its advice. Staff specialists close to the scene can best solve problems in quality and cost, personnel selection and training, engineering and marketing. To the extent that corporate staff takes over these functions, the less effective it will be in the broad-gauge and creative role it should fulfill.

Where Should Division Staffs Report?

Most divisionalized companies must face up to the problem of whether division staffs are to report to the accountable plant or division manager or to the corporate staff at headquarters. The answer depends largely upon the extent and type of decentralization within the company and the nature of the staff function.[5]

---

[5] Holden, Fish, and Smith suggest that in assignment of staff, if the effort of the staff group is to be devoted primarily to the interests of one branch or division of the company, it should be made accountable to the divisional executive concerned.

There are several advantages in having specialized staff in the plants or divisions report to corporate headquarters staff. For one thing, this ensures the highest degree of technical competence, because the corporate staff will have authority to select, train, transfer, and direct division or plant staff groups. Central direction will also ensure that each staff group is carrying out company policies and procedures in its specialty in a standardized and uniform manner. This can result in greater effectiveness and economy in the operation of company-wide programs and related activities.

The primary disadvantage of line direction of plant and division staff by headquarters staff executives is the weakening of authority and accountability of plant and division managers. To the extent that he lacks command of his specialized staff, the local manager cannot be held to account for results to be accomplished through the services provided by those staffs. The division manager cannot be held accountable for the effectiveness of his training program if it is directed from central staff, nor can the director of marketing be held to account for market penetration if his advertising and sales promotion programs are not within his command.

This is particularly true if the division or plant manager is to be measured in terms of profit or loss. He must then have command of the elements of expense that go to make up costs. This invariably includes the cost of the specialized staff that serves him.

DEVELOPING SOUND LINE-STAFF RELATIONSHIPS

The relationship between specialized staff and the line organization can have a profound effect on the over-all operation and profitability of the company. The larger and more complex the company becomes and the more top management leans upon specialized staff groups to complete the work leading to final decision making, the more pervasive and important the staff role becomes. This growing stature is inevitably threatening to the line organization and promises increasing personal and jurisdictional disputes unless a workable basic relationship is evolved.

Difficulties

There are many difficulties in the establishment of line-staff teamwork. One is misunderstanding of the staff role by many managers. They look

---

If the staff agency "is to serve two or more divisions impartially, it should report to general management either directly or in combination with other closely related staff functions." Paul E. Holden, Lounsbury S. Fish, and Hubert L. Smith, *Top-Management Organization and Control,* McGraw-Hill Book Company, Inc., New York, 1948, p. 37.

Specialized Staff   243

upon staff as "academic" or "ivory tower," no matter what its qualifications.[6]

One result of this misunderstanding is that line managers tend to call upon staff only in emergencies, or after a situation has so far deteriorated that even the most expert consultation can do little to retrieve it. This reluctance to use staff may arise from the natural suspicion by the line manager of the "expert" who constantly threatens his position and status; it may be due in part to the staff man's lack of tact or his eagerness to take credit.

This attitude on the part of line makes the staff man, in turn, feel insecure. To establish a niche for himself, he tends to appropriate and exercise as much authority and responsibility as he can. In the process, he often takes over work that can only be performed properly by line or lets himself be maneuvered into a position where he makes line decisions and is held to line accountability. Both positions are in contradiction to his proper role and are essentially untenable.

The situation is further complicated by rivalry between staff and line managers. The line manager wants to demonstrate that he can "do it on his own." The staff man wants a share of the credit if results are good and he is constantly striving to place himself in a position where he can say "I told you so" if the project goes to pieces. The relationship that exists under these circumstances is based on fear. The staff manager fears that the line will manage to dispense with his services and his job. Line fears that the staff man will rob him of credit and build up the staff role at the expense of his own.

There are other reasons for difficulty. Frequently companies try to build staff by drawing expert operating people from the line departments. In many cases the operating man does not have the special skills needed for staff work. He may not have the patience or ability to search out and analyze data and construct alternatives. He may not be able to divorce himself from implementation of the plan he has helped develop. Again, it is often difficult for the operating man to get out of the habit of operating, to limit himself to advice and counsel while others perform what he considers the most interesting part of the work. When this situation arises, staff tends to exercise authority it does not have. This invariably gives rise to friction and antagonism.

[6] As Hugh J. Phillips, Jr., Director of Organization Planning, United States Steel Company, puts it: "The line executive, concerned with the everyday problems of satisfying customers or meeting production schedules, may think of staff men as a group of brain-trusters who make life more complicated for him and provide precious little help. He may consider them theoretical specialists who know only part of the problem. They are always planning changes which interfere with established routines. They don't have to meet schedules." From "Making Effective Use of Staff," a talk given before the 365th Meeting of the National Industrial Conference Board, Atlanta, Ga., Mar. 22, 1956.

The net toll to the company of such misunderstanding is loss of efficiency, unnecessary expense, and jeopardy to effective teamwork. While the solution to the problem will vary in detail from company to company, there are certain fundamentals which apply to all situations.

Acceptance of Staff Advice

Line-staff roles are based on the development of conditions most conducive to giving and receiving advice. As a prerequisite to establishment of sound relationships, it is necessary to understand the conditions which govern the willingness of the line manager to accept advice and other conditions which may alter the character of the information he receives from staff.

Both line and staff can operate more freely and effectively if they understand the forces which influence their opposite numbers. It is paradoxical, but true, that the staff man does not necessarily do his best job when he offers the most valid and logically reasoned data.[7]

He is most useful when he offers data the line manager will accept because it most nearly conforms to the conditions imposed upon its acceptance. This does not gainsay the possibility of persuasion, but persuasion is a condition of acceptance and must be understood by the staff specialist as such. His task is to understand the reasons why the logical and technically best solution often will not prevail and in terms of this understanding to so modify it that it will be acceptable and useful. At the same time, he must lay the groundwork for subsequent acceptance of the solution he believes best suited.[8]

At best, the staff manager is in an anomalous position. His reputation and usefulness depend upon his ability to give unadorned, uncolored advice based on an objective and dispassionate analysis of all the factors that enter into a situation. The line manager's work is to make the final

[7] In this connection, John L. McCaffrey, President, International Harvester Company, remarks, "There is another fact about the specialist which is a problem to him and therefore to the organization. It arises from the fact he knows more about his specialty than his superiors or anyone else in the business. This situation frequently arises: a problem comes up related to his special field. He produces a solution which is entirely satisfactory from the standpoint of good practice in his specialty. But then the higher management won't buy it. They do something else instead. This can happen either because the specialist has failed to explain and sell his solution adequately, or because he did not take into account other factors of the· problem which lie outside his special field. . . . Such a situation can occur either because top management knows more than he does or because it knows less. In either case . . . his advice has been disregarded and his judgment overruled." John L. McCaffrey, "What Corporation Presidents Think about at Night," *Fortune,* September, 1953.

[8] See Lyman Bryson, "Notes on a Theory of Advice," *Political Science Quarterly,* September, 1951, vol. 66, pp. 321–339, for an exposition of the factors underlying the acceptance of advice.

decision. He instinctively resists any obvious coloration of the advice he receives that he thinks is designed to influence his decision.[9]

The paradox is that, in reality, many line managers *want* to be influenced. It is impossible for the principal to be informed about all the technical subjects for which he is accountable. However, he has neither the time nor the inclination to acquire the information he needs to understand the issues put before him. Often he wants to have his mind made up for him. He will look for evidence that is overwhelmingly in favor of one of the several alternatives present. He will welcome the ready-made decision which is technically sound, yet which he feels will be accepted and put to use.

If this kind of solution is not presented to him, the principal may confer endlessly with associates and his staff. If asked, he will say that he is trying to get all the facts. Actually, he is shopping around looking for the compromise which will best satisfy—or at least lull—his sense of what he knows to be technically best, and at the same time which has promise of being accepted by the people to whom it applies.

The psychological factors involved in decision making point strongly to the value of participation and the need for the staff man to develop skill and patience in consultation. Developing and understanding these factors, and delineating and clarifying the part that line and staff are to play in an effective relationship, are the responsibility of the accountable executive with jurisdiction over both line and specialized staff positions.

Using Staff in Problem Solving

How can line make most effective use of staff? Since staff is primarily an advisory and assisting agency, it follows that staff can be of greatest utility in helping line to solve line problems, that is, problems directly connected with successful accomplishment of the end results of the business.

Problem solving follows a definite sequence. First comes the need to identify the problem, to spell out its nature and exact dimensions. Then a body of facts having to do with the problem must be gathered. On the basis of these facts, it is possible to analyze the problem as stated and to derive a set of alternative solutions. The final step is selection of the best solution among these alternatives and putting it into effect.

[9] On the basis of an extensive survey, Norman H. Martin and John Howard Sims conclude, "The able executive is cautious about how he seeks and receives advice. He takes counsel only when he himself desires it. His decisions must be made in terms of his own grasp of the situation, taking into account the views of others when he thinks it necessary. To act otherwise is to be subject, not to advice, but to pressure; to act otherwise too often produces vacillation and inconsistency." Norman H. Martin and John Howard Sims, "Thinking Ahead; Power Tactics," *Harvard Business Review,* November–December, 1956, vol. 34, no. 6, p. 28.

Staff can be of value in each of these steps. It can help to identify line operating problems. The line organization is usually well acquainted with the symptoms of problems; however, because it is continually beset with operating detail, the line frequently cannot bring to bear the resources necessary to identify the true nature of its problems.

The sales manager of one small company manufacturing household tools and implements was very much interested in broadening and expanding the product line. He continually encouraged his salesmen to send him suggestions and recommendations for product improvement. Soon he was almost embarrassed by the wealth of suggestions that flowed in upon him. Because he had neither the time nor the facilities to study and analyze their possibilities, he sent most of them to the head of the manufacturing department, who, in turn, forwarded the best to the president. The president conscientiously reviewed the ideas and in turn forwarded those he felt had most promise to the sales manager. This circle continued for over a year. Finally the president turned the problem over to his administrative planning specialized staff manager. After study and investigation, the staff man pointed out that the company was continually losing position in its industry; that its best chance for profits lay in capitalizing on the higher margins possible in product innovation and not in fighting for constantly decreasing income available through sale of standard and highly competitive lines. He showed that the leading firm in the industry had committed almost 2 per cent of its net sales to new product development and that the only way to compete was to meet its challenge in research as well as marketing.

As a result of this suggestion, the president organized a staff product planning group reporting directly to himself. He delegated to it responsibility for collecting new product ideas from sales, manufacturing, and engineering, conducting tests and surveys to determine market potential, and coordinating the activities necessary to put the most promising of the new products into distribution channels as quickly as possible.

If it is to identify problems, staff must have access to operating reports, attend operating meetings, and be in position to study and observe operating situations. If the safety supervisor is to be of maximum service, for example, he must have authority and must be encouraged to inspect plant operations regularly and to consult freely with plant supervision. If the training director is to develop useful training programs, he needs to spend a great deal of time in the plant and field so that he can help identify the problem areas that require most attention.

Frequently staff is handicapped because it is called in after a situation has deteriorated to such a stage that only emergency action can save it. Remedial activities at this point are at best expensive and often are foredoomed to failure.

Provision of Qualified People

Staff specialists can operate effectively only if they have technical competence and sufficient background to fully understand the general nature of the problems with which they deal. Provision of qualified staff is partly a matter of selection, partly a matter of training. Because he is primarily concerned with problem solving, the candidate selected for staff work should have the mental equipment necessary to do his job effectively. The staff specialist should also have a good knowledge of the company and its operating problems so that he can place staff problems in their proper over-all relationship to the business as a whole. Many staff men fail, not because of technical inadequacy, but because of inability to establish a proper perspective as to the importance of their own speciality.

One of the best ways to secure the necessary breadth of experience is to see to it that staff people have line operating experience at some point in their careers and that line managers are given every opportunity to serve in staff roles. As Dr. Joseph M. Trickett, Professor of Management, Santa Clara University, points out, lack of such experience can be a serious weakness in the development of fully effective executives.[10]

A BASIC LINE-STAFF RELATIONSHIP

The roles of line and staff tend to be worked out fortuitously in the company. Most commonly, the relationship established is a reflection of the personal strengths and weaknesses of the line and staff principals involved. This approach is usually unsatisfactory. A logical and integrated relationship has been developed by companies such as Atlantic Refining, Ford Motor Company, General Foods, Nationwide Insurance, Du Pont, and many others. The characteristics of such a relationship may be summarized as follows:

1. Those functions and divisions of the company which are designated as line are accountable for accomplishing the basic objectives of the enterprise and must be delegated authority for final decision in the attainment of end results.

2. Staff functions are created for the purpose of providing advice and service to the line and other staff units in performing specialized work. Both line and staff are delegated authority to carry out their responsibilities. Both make decisions. However, the authority they exercise and the decisions they make differ as to kind and degree. Staff authority is

---

[10] See Joseph M. Trickett, "Are We Selecting the Right Men for Management?" *Alumni Bulletin* of the Graduate School of Business, Stanford University, XVII, November, 1947, pp. 6–9.

advisory and service in nature. Staff has no authority *over* line or othei staff functions except by express delegation from the accountable manager concerned. Such delegated authority is limited to specific activities authorized by the line principal and is exercised only in the name of the line principal.

3. Staff should offer its advice and service where it believes it is needed and without being specifically invited. It is not necessary for staff to wait to be called: It should keep itself informed about the problems confronting the line, think ahead, make constructive plans, and help the line solve its difficult operating problems.

4. Line should give serious consideration to all offers of advice and service tendered by staff functions. Line heads should use staff in matters where it possesses more information or knowledge than is available within their own units. Where there is doubt, the sole criterion for acceptance of the advice should be whether it is in the company's best interest to do so.

5. Line managers have authority to accept, reject, or modify the advice or service proffered by staff. The only exception is in those cases where top line management, as a matter of policy, has decided that specified staff advice or services will be used by all company units. This decision is binding for all groups at all levels.

6. In cases of disagreement, both line and staff must have the right of appeal to higher line authority. However, when the exigencies of the operating situation so require, this right of appeal should not be permitted to supersede line's authority to make immediate decisions.

The rules outlined above will provide a sound basis for harmonious working relationships between line and staff. While variations and modifications will always be occasioned by the personalities involved and the immediate operating situation, it will serve as a useful pattern for executives concerned with making use of all available resources in developing maximum productivity and teamwork.

SUMMARY

Specialized staff should be limited to authority and responsibility to advise, counsel, and guide other elements of the organization and to do things for other managers because they do not have the time, skill, or experience to do them for themselves.

Staff advice and service should be available to managers to help them do an effective job in the specialized aspects of planning, organization, motivating, coordinating, and controlling work; and, where occasion requires, to do this work for them. Specialized staff can also provide managers with valuable assistance in performing their operating work.

Effective relationships between line and staff are often difficult to establish. To overcome this, staff should understand the conditions underlying the acceptance of advice. A basic line-staff relationship requires that line be accorded primary accountability for operating results, while staff advises and helps to secure those results. Staff must have the option of offering advice when it is needed, and line should give such offers serious consideration. The option of refusing the advice and service proffered must lie with line; however, both should have the right of appeal to the common line superior.

CHAPTER 12 *Top Management Organization*

Leadership of the modern corporation is the most difficult and demanding task in the entire management hierarchy. If not diverted, the full weight of decision making, direction, and coordination of the business tends to be drawn to the top. This burden and its attendant problems generally fall squarely upon the chief executive. In a company of any size, it is humanly impossible for one individual to do justice to the multitudinous and complex demands of both managing and operating the business; many a company has crippled itself in making this demand upon its top officer, or, alternatively, has permitted him to kill himself in the attempt.

Although we are primarily concerned with the organization of the chief executive's job,[1] we shall first indicate the place of the stockholders, the Board of Directors and Board Chairman, and their role in the management of the corporation.

STOCKHOLDERS AND BOARD

The ownership of the corporation is vested in the stockholders, who provide the funds for plants, tools, equipment, and facilities. Since it is impractical and inconvenient for the stockholders themselves, as a group, to run the enterprise, they select a small group of individuals, the Board of Directors, to exercise trusteeship and act for them in the direction of the company's affairs.

Board of Directors

The Board concerns itself with review and decision upon matters of major importance to the company's success. The Board reserves responsibility and authority for deciding long-term objectives, policies, pro-

---

[1] The chief executive is usually the president of the company and will be so referred to here. It should be noted that the Chairman of the Board is sometimes chief executive officer.

grams, and budgets that apply to the company as a whole; it approves the over-all company organization and exercises control through review of over-all financial and operating results.

The Board elects the officers of the company. This is one of its most important single activities, for in so doing it largely determines the administrative success of the enterprise. The Board is empowered to establish whatever controls it considers necessary to safeguard the interests of the stockholders.

Since the Board exercises trusteeship for the capital furnished by the stockholders, it also reserves authority for commitment of significant amounts of capital funds. It is not only the province of the Board to authorize the borrowing of money to finance company operations; it also authorizes capital expenditures and the disposal of assets.

The operating work of the Board is relatively limited. It includes the establishment and revision of company bylaws and the declaration of stock dividends.

Chairman of the Board

The Board Chairman normally acts to give leadership to the Board and its activities. He presides at meetings of the Board and acts to facilitate and expedite its deliberations. The Chairman can be of great assistance to the president by advising and counseling him and working with him to develop plans and proposals for presentation to the Board.

CHIEF EXECUTIVE

Sound organization of the top executive function has particular implications for the company as a whole. Leadership of the enterprise must originate here, and the philosophy, attitudes, and reactions of the president tend to establish a climate for the entire organization. Several problems have special pertinence to the arrangement of the president's job. These have to do with the organizational placement of the position itself, the evolutionary needs of the business, and administrative factors.

Organizational Placement

The position of president is normally accountable only to the Board of Directors and is organizationally located above all other organizational elements. As a result, only the president can handle problems involving two or more subordinate units with perspective and objectivity. Unless special provision is made for coordination at lower levels, all management and operating problems of consequence come to focus in this position. Again, the top position is the link for the three "publics" upon which the corporation and its work constantly impinge: its employees, its stockholders, and the public at large.

The president is the transition point between the trusteeship exercised by the Board of Directors and the active management of the company. As a member of the Board, he is a direct representative of the share-holders, and since he is supervisor of the operating elements of the company, he is best placed to protect the interests of the stockholders by prudent and profitable use of the company's funds and property. At the same time, because of his supervisory position, he has an obligation to the managers and employees of the business to represent their interests by use of his personal authority and representation to the Board. Finally, the organizational placement of the president gives him unique advantages in representing and speaking for the company to public agencies, such as the government, educational groups, other companies, and the community.

Evolutionary Needs of the Business

Organization of top management must meet the evolutionary requirements of the growing business.

Many companies, in engineering widespread organization changes which involve redistribution of major responsibilities, creation of new staff groups, and rearrangement of the line divisions of the company, make little or no provision for accompanying changes in the top management function. However, such changes are necessary to parallel the evolutionary shift from centralization to decentralization and from functionalization to divisionalization.

In the small, young company, the initial organization of top management is commonly represented by a single position, the presidency, in which one man performs the work of both managing and operating the enterprise as a whole. Because the president exercises so much independent authority, he tends to tailor his position to his individual personality requirements, often to the neglect of the real needs of the enterprise. Again, because the pattern for the possible alternatives is not correctly identified, attempts to reorganize the top management function to meet the changing demands of the business may be haphazard. Several reorganizations may take place before a satisfactory combination is found. Much of this fumbling is unnecessary and can be avoided if the alternative basic patterns are correctly identified.

Administrative Factors

The nature and type of the problems that reach the top level must be considered. When the flow of problems is largely operational in nature, when detail and routine filter through, the top executive will either have to handle them himself, provide personal assistants who will do the work for him, or correct the organizational and administrative deficiencies that exist.

Frequent emergencies may make inordinate demands upon the time of the top man. Often these are related to the type of business and cannot be anticipated. Fluctuations in the price of materials, need to reconsider inventory policies, union demands and attendant threat of stoppages and strikes, a competitor's introduction of a radically new product line, these and other problems of major importance may come up unexpectedly and require his personal attention.

The pressures generated by emergencies and problems that rise to the top depend largely upon what and how the president delegates. Since he has greater command of the resources of the company than any other manager, theoretically, at least, it is possible for him to delegate most completely. The kind and amount of work he delegates depends upon the extent that he insists upon operating, rather than managing. While he must perform a certain amount of operating work himself because of provisions of the bylaws, the need to maintain firsthand acquaintance with operating conditions, and the requirements of his position, he has available or can create personal and specialized staff and subordinate line positions to take over responsibility and authority for operating problems and to assist him in the detail and routine of his management activities.

The administrative practices of the company have a direct influence on the organization of the chief executive function. Comprehensive, carefully formulated and interpreted objectives and policies can provide direction and furnish answers to many problems and questions that would otherwise be referred to the top man for decision. Budgets are useful in defining limits within which each manager and function must operate. Properly established, the budgetary system provides automatic answers to the question: "How much can I spend and for what?"

Organization can be a recurring problem to the chief executive, particularly if the structure is built around personalities and each transfer or position vacancy requires a corollary realignment of the organization. Consistent planning *ahead* of present needs through use of a master plan of organization and phased-in interim plans can be of great value in minimizing this.

The control system is an important factor. If routine detail is screened from the chief executive and he controls in terms of exceptions, there will be less demand upon his time and energy. If the control system requires corrective action of accountable subordinate managers first and involves the chief executive only to the extent of correcting lack of such action or of noting the action taken and its results, it can help ease the burden on the top position.

WHAT KIND OF ORGANIZATION?

Determination of the type of organization best suited to the needs of the chief executive can best be made in consideration of the work expected of him. The basic pattern of this work falls into three categories:

1. *Over-all Management.* Initiation and final decision with respect to the planning, organizing, motivating, coordinating, and controlling of the work of the enterprise

2. *Over-all Operations.* Implementing the plans, organization, controls established, and providing motivation and coordination to subordinate elements

3. *Relationships.* Representing the company to employees, stockholders, and the public

The nature of this work in itself makes inordinate demand upon the president because of the variety of personal skills and aptitudes it requires. Much of the work is analytical, contemplative, and creative. Looking to the future, assessing its potential for the company, weighing the available alternatives calls not only for judgment but also for vision and imagination.

At the same time, in handling operating problems, the president must make immediate decisions that are practical and workable in terms of the situation as it exists today. This calls for a reorientation of his viewpoint to judgment based on what *will work,* in terms of what resources the company can now bring to bear on the problem, not *what can be made to work* in terms of what resources can be developed. It is rare, indeed, to find combined in one person the personality traits, aptitudes, and interests that enable him to fill both these roles effectively. If we add to this the fact that in conducting his relationships the president must have facility in communication, human understanding and compassion, and persuasive ability of the first order, we find the potential difficulty in staffing the position greatly multiplied.

A Top Executive Function

The best answer in organizing the top management job is to look upon it not as an individual position but as a grouping of work which must be performed at the apex of the organizational pyramid because it cannot be carried out effectively at lower levels. On occasion, this function may consist of only one position, to be filled by one executive; however, in most cases two, three, or more positions for the function must be provided.

Organization of the top executive function calls for answer to the questions: What work must be done? How can it best be grouped for effective performance? The best answer lies in grouping separate and identifiable packages of work and establishing these as positions for which individual executives can be held fully accountable. This is preferable to extensive use of assistants, which tends to push some of the work to one side but does not clearly separate it. The four major alternatives in organization of the top executive function are: (1) the chief executive alone; (2) division between chief executive and chief operating officer; (3) division between chief executive, chief operating officer, and chief staff officer; and (4) group organization of the top executive function.

CHIEF EXECUTIVE ALONE

When the company is small and in its early growth stage, the top executive function usually contains only one position, that of chief executive. For the young company, and particularly one with an outstanding individual at its head, this may be the best possible organization, because it enables him to exercise personal leadership most effectively and, literally, lift the whole enterprise through his personal genius. The chief executive in this position may be identified as the president, chairman of the board *and* president, and other variations. The position reports to the Board of Directors and the major functional and divisional unit heads report directly to it. If there is an executive vice president, he serves as a line assistant. The chief executive position, standing alone, may be shown as in Figure 12–1.

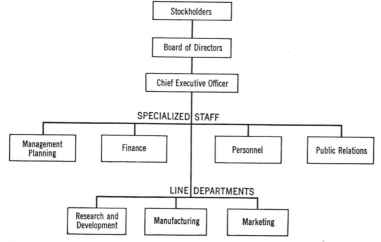

Figure 12–1. Chief Executive Alone (Illustrative Grouping)

Operating in this fashion, the chief executive reserves for his own performance responsibility and authority for both the over-all management and operation of the company. There are several advantages to this arrangement. First, it provides direct access to the top by the operating heads and it ensures that the chief executive will have close personal knowledge of every problem of any consequence. To the extent that he has unusual assets in mentality or experience, the president can invest these directly in operating situations for the benefit of the company and its operations.

Because there are no intervening layers between the top man and his subordinates, all have personal access to the chief executive. This enables each to plead his case with maximum emphasis. Unfortunately, this often means that the best talker and not the best solution wins out; also, the very fact that the chief executive is available means that he is not screened from the detail and routine that might better be handled at a lower level.

The first cost, at least, of one-man leadership is lowest. The immediate salary expense is at a minimum and, theoretically at least, there is top return for the salary dollar expended. However, first costs for the most important position in the organization are not particularly indicative. We must also take into consideration the corollary expense which arises from the use of personal staff, the additional man-hours consumed in committee meetings, and the wear and tear on the chief executive himself.

Disadvantages

When he tries to be top manager, top operator, and top public relations representative himself, the president finds himself so immersed in day-to-day operating problems, coordination and reconciliation between line and staff heads, and outside contacts that he cannot fulfill all roles satisfactorily. Since the pressure of operating problems is most immediate and insistent, the president, when holding the function as chief executive alone, tends to put most time and effort on operations and often relegates to the background the over-all management problems of the business.

Another major disadvantage of one-man leadership is that it fails to provide for succession to the top. Subordinates remain highly specialized in their own functional areas and do not have opportunity to face problems and make decisions involving all aspects of the business.

As the pressures on the president's job build up, he tends to create personal staff positions to help him perform his work. This spreads the responsibility but it does not solve the basic problem, that of splitting the duties involved. Personal staff aligned with the chief executive in this grouping includes the executive vice president as line assistant and the use of staff assistants of various kinds.

Executive Vice President as Line Assistant

The president can extend his capacity to handle the work of his position by appointing an executive vice president who will act as a line assistant to him. In this case, the executive vice president assists the president in over-all planning, organization, coordination, motivation, and control. He handles much of the detail or directs appropriate line and staff subordinates of the president in the collection and presentation of recommendations preliminary to decision making. The executive vice president acts for the president when he is absent, except in those matters which the bylaws require the president to handle personally.

The executive vice president may take over specified parts of the president's job and perform them for him. For example, he may work with the personnel head on contract negotiation, with marketing, production, and research on new product development. He may make speeches and public appearances for the president.

This arrangement has the advantages and disadvantages already noted for line assistants. On balance, it provides the president with an aide who can be of great assistance to him in carrying out his responsibilities. The advantage of this grouping can be retained, however, and its disadvantages largely minimized by making a clear-cut division of the duties of the chief executive and delegating part of these to the executive vice president as chief operating officer, as later described.

Staff Assistants

More so than for any other position, there is a tendency for the chief executive to create staff assistant positions to help him carry out his responsibilities. These assistants may perform detail and routine work for the president that he might otherwise attempt to perform himself. There is no intrinsic fault in this delegation; the difficulty is that the assisant is likely to take over work that could be done more effectively or economically by an accountable subordinate agency. The better alternative is for the chief executive to split the total responsibilities devolving upon him so that he can delegate responsibility and authority for performance to others. The first such split to be considered is that between the chief executive and the chief operating officer.

CHIEF EXECUTIVE—CHIEF OPERATING OFFICER

The most efficient and workable organization of the top management function is division of the total responsibilities between a chief executive

and a chief operating officer. This takes into account the basic requirements of the two major kinds of top management work and helps to
eliminate the staffing predicament that usually results. Instead of looking for a good planner who can also operate, or a good operator who
can also plan, or asking the incumbent to become schizophrenic to this
extent, we can now make a clear-cut assignment (Figure 12–2).

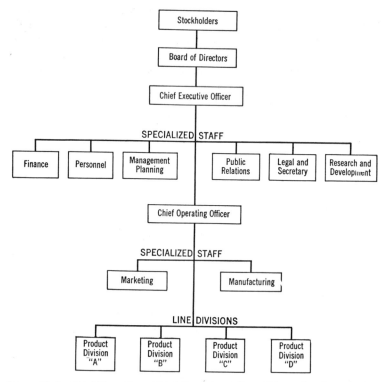

Figure 12–2. Chief Executive—Chief Operating Officer (Illustrative Grouping)

Variations in Title

In this alternative, the chief executive is usually known as the president, as in Bigelow-Sanford Carpet Company and the Pennsylvania Railroad Company. The chief operating officer titles vary. He is known as
the Executive Vice President in Bigelow-Sanford and Vice President in
Pennsylvania Railroad. Other combinations are found. In Jones and
Laughlin Steel, Lockheed Aircraft, and Johns-Manville, the Board
Chairman and President, respectively, fill the roles of chief executive

and chief operating officer; in Thompson Products, it is the Chairman of the Board of Directors and the President and General Manager.

Responsibilities of Chief Executive

In this grouping, the chief executive concerns himself primarily with initiation and final decision on matters of planning, organization, motivation, coordination, and control. His operating work consists of those duties specified by the Board and the company bylaws, such as executing legal instruments, presiding at Board meetings, and so forth. Both the chief executive and chief operating officer should participate in representing the company to its employees and the public.

The chief executive devotes much of his attention to the long-term aspects of the company's business. He handles only exceptional matters that come up in day-to-day operations. All work directly concerned with operations, that is, the line activities of the business, is delegated to the chief operating officer.

Under this arrangement, the chief executive is freed to study and assess economic growth and development. He evaluates the needs of the company in broadening and expanding the products and services it offers and initiates studies involving possible mergers, acquisitions, and innovations. He develops objectives in all major aspects of the company's business for the approval of the Board of Directors. The chief executive reviews and authorizes major policies and programs that have impact on the company as a whole. He authorizes capital expenditure and operating budgets for the company and establishes a control system that will alert him and require his action only when accomplishment falls short of plan or when emergencies occur. He maintains control through review of a few key operating and financial reports and frequent personal contact with his subordinates.

The chief executive concerns himself with the long-term organizational needs of the company. He sees to it that adequate programs are undertaken and implemented for effective motivation of employees and for development of managerial reserves.

Chief Operating Officer

The chief executive delegates to the chief operating officer responsibility and authority for the operation of the business and holds him accountable for operating results. The authority of the chief operating officer should be limited to development and recommendation of objectives and policies for the operating divisions or line functions of the company. Objectives and over-all policies should be authorized by the Board, on the recommendation of the chief executive. For example, the Board establishes specific objectives for increasing sales volume; the

Board and the chief executive decide what new products will be manufactured, what general marketing strategy will be followed, what capital commitments will be made, how funds will be secured. This provides a framework within which the chief operating officer can be made accountable for day-to-day operating decisions. Thus, while the chief executive and the Board of Directors will decide what new products are to be manufactured and marketed, once the general characteristics of the product are established, the chief operating officer can make final decision concerning the exact specifications for the product and the models and sizes. The chief executive would decide whether a complete product line was to be discontinued, but the chief operating officer would give final approval to proposed modifications and improvements in the existing product line.

Specialized Staff

Both the chief executive and chief operating officer should be provided with the staff agencies they need to operate most effectively. The chief executive should have reporting directly to him those agencies most intimately related to the work he reserves for himself: usually Finance, Research, Management Planning, Personnel, Legal, and Public Relations. The staff functions most closely related to operations then report to the chief operating officer. These would differ with the nature of the company, its operations, problems, growth stage, diversification, and so forth. However, functions such as Purchasing, Traffic, and Engineering are often best placed in this reporting relationship. Both staff groups are freely available to both chief executive and chief operating officer for advice and service.

Staff agencies assist the chief executive and chief operating officer by performing much of the work involved in accumulation, study, and review of pertinent data, observation of operating conditions, consultation with staff and line heads to secure their participation, survey of practices in other companies, and so forth. It is important for these staff components also to be available to the heads of the major functions and divisions for advice and service.

In addition to specialized staff functional groups, one or more specialized staff administrative groups in Management Planning or Administrative Management should also be provided. This will make available to the chief executive the same type of assistance he would secure from personal staff. Since this assistance is used by other elements of the organization, higher salaries and hence more experienced and capable staff people will be justified, than would be the case if assistants were used.

Specialized staff administrative units have many advantages over personal staff. They are likely to be more practical and operations-oriented; they should earn the confidence of subordinate managers more completely because they also are required to provide advice and service to them. Acting in this liaison capacity, specialized staff can be of great value in communicating *downward* the philosophies and methods of approach which the chief executive espouses. At the same time, it is strategically placed to communicate *upward* the attitudes, reactions, suggestions, and recommendations of his subordinates.

In the absence of the chief executive, the chief operating officer assumes the top position. He may either hold down both positions, or he may ask one of the division or staff heads to assume the chief operating officer position for the interim, thus creating a valuable opportunity for training and orienting his subordinates to the problems of the chief operating officer position. This kind of temporary assignment can also be carried to lower levels in the organization if desired.

Advantages

Dividing the top function between the chief executive and chief operating officer positions has many positive benefits. First, it divides the total burden. Because the chief executive has delegated authority and responsibility for operations, he can hold the chief operating officer accountable and can separate himself from the details and routine of day-to-day operations.

This organizational arrangement also separates over-all planning and control from execution of plans. Checks and balances are exercised as a function of the structure; that is, plans are established and results are evaluated by agencies different from those that actually perform the work.

This arrangement makes both the chief operating officer and the chief executive more readily accessible to their direct subordinates, because each has fewer subordinates than would otherwise be the case. Also, because the chief operating officer is given real accountability, he is receiving the best possible grooming for the top spot.

The chief disadvantage of this grouping is the possibility that it will screen off the chief executive from the operating line heads. This can be a serious disadvantage if there are differences of opinion between the chief operating officer and the operating heads who report to him. The best alternative here is to make the chief executive freely available to subordinate line heads on matters which they feel should be carried to him. Being accessible does not mean that the operating heads report *to* the chief executive; definitive action should only be taken *through* and with participation of the chief operating officer. Since close teamwork and the ability to interchange quickly on their respective assignments is a prerequisite for effective operation, it is quite probable that this accessibility will be arrived at harmoniously if the arrangement works at all.

Alternative Groupings

Many variations on this basic grouping pattern are found. With the president acting as chief executive, the operating responsibilities may be divided between two or even more chief operating officers. Thus, in Ford Motor Company, the president is chief executive, with the key central staff groups reporting directly to him. Operations are divided between two Executive Vice Presidents, who are both chief operating officers. One heads up the car and truck divisions, one the basic manufacturing divisions.

The Chairman of the Board acts as chief executive officer in Carrier Corporation. He has reporting to him the finance, legal, planning, public relations, integration and acquisition, and personal staff groupings. The operating divisions and related staff groupings report to two chief operating officers, the president and senior vice president.

The New York Central Railroad Company makes a basic division between the chief executive and chief operating officer in the positions of president and vice president–operations. The president, as chief executive, has all the staff groupings reporting to him. The vice president–operations is accountable for the operation of the four geographic divisions into which the railroad is divided and has the general managers of these divisions reporting directly to him.

CHIEF EXECUTIVE—CHIEF OPERATING OFFICER— CHIEF STAFF OFFICER

As company growth continues and the burden placed upon the chief executive and chief operating officer increases, the major staff departments may be grouped together and made to report to a chief staff officer (Figure 12–3).

This organizational arrangement provides for a three-way alignment, which requires the chief executive to supervise only two other positions. Usually, however, this span is increased by special reporting relationships which are set up because of operating or personality factors in the company. When so organized, the chief staff officer may go under a variety of titles, such as Administrative Vice President, Executive Vice President–Staff, and Corporate Staff Officer. In some cases, only a portion of the specialized staff groups report to the chief staff officer, the balance reporting to the chief executive. This is particularly true of the finance and research and development staff. In other instances, two or

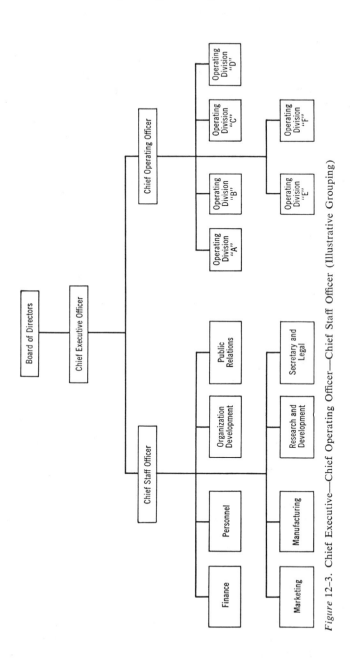

Figure 12–3. Chief Executive—Chief Operating Officer—Chief Staff Officer (Illustrative Grouping)

even more chief staff officers act to coordinate staff activities; for example, one may have finance and related groupings reporting to him, another the technical, and a third the relationships groupings.

This grouping has certain advantages. It frees the chief executive from the need for reconciling and evaluating the various and conflicting points of view presented by individual staff officers. It is to be expected that each staff head, highly expert in his own field and thoroughly convinced of its importance, will present his viewpoint with as much skill and vigor as he can bring to bear. The full brunt of these repeated onslaughts can be temporized by screening them through a chief staff officer position.

Full integration of staff advice and service is assured if one man devotes his full attention to the task. Advice and service to subordinate elements of the organization are in no wise impaired because each staff unit is still fully accessible to line and other staff units.

Creation of a chief staff officer position helps provide for succession to the chief executive position. Experience in this job will give the incumbent opportunity to understand and evaluate the problems and needs of all the staff functions and to develop means of maximizing their value to the chief executive while making least demand upon him.

This arrangement provides balance in that it consolidates all advisory and service work under one major head and all operating work under another. In arriving at a major decision, the chief executive can thus secure the assistance he requires by calling upon only two individuals.

There are objections to this arrangement which should be given serious consideration. Most importantly, it tends to block the individual specialized staff heads from the chief executive. There is a well-based school of thought which feels that, to be effective, a specialized functional head should have the opportunity to present his case at the point where the decision is actually made.

Also, this grouping tends to screen from the chief executive the agencies which should be closest to him if he is to do his work of planning for the company's forward progress. Another disadvantage is that it adds salary expense. The chief staff officer must be comparable in ability, experience, and salary to the chief operating officer. To the small company especially, this may be a significant item.

EXECUTIVE GROUP

An alternative form of organization of the chief executive function which is applicable in special circumstances is that of vesting the chief executive function in a Board of Directors, or Committees of the Board. In this case, the Board, as a group or through its committees, establishes policy and makes decisions on those matters which cannot be settled at lower levels. An outstanding proponent of this approach is the Du Pont Company (see Figure 12–4).

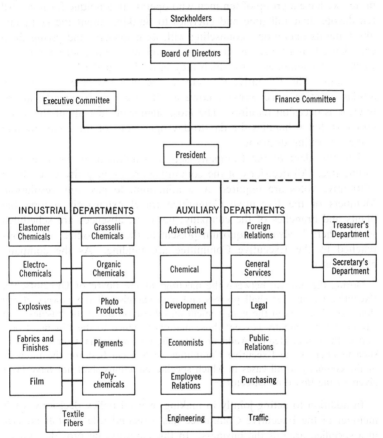

Figure 12–4. Administrative Organization, E. I. du Pont de Nemours & Company

Du Pont

The Du Pont organization of the chief executive function depends upon a Board of thirty members. Nearly half of these are top executives currently active in administration of the business. Most of the others are retired top executives who contribute as elder statesmen. The Board meets monthly.

The Board of Directors of Du Pont, in effect, runs the company on a day-to-day basis by delegating to two major and two minor committees responsibility and authority that would otherwise be exercised by a chief executive.

The Finance Committee and the Executive Committee are the key groups in the Du Pont top management system. In the Executive Committee we have a group of ten men who operate in a unique fashion. All ten devote their full time and energies to thinking about the company, observing its operations, counseling with its managers, and giving them experienced assistance in planning, organizing, and coordinating the work of its components, to which they have delegated responsibility for operations. The Executive Committee's regular schedule calls for an all-day meeting once weekly; however, it meets as frequently in the interim as occasion requires. The most significant fact about this committee is that it handles the day-to-day operations of the company and makes operating decisions.

The President of the Company acts as Chairman of the Executive Committee. All decisions of the committee are by majority vote. Four affirmative votes are required, as a minimum, to pass any resolution Members of the Executive Committee travel extensively among the plants and branches of the company; however, absences are scheduled so that there is always a quorum present at the head office. Decisions reached by the Executive Committee are binding. As the company bylaws put it,

During the interval between the meetings of the Board of Directors, the Executive Committee shall possess and may exercise all the powers of the Board of Directors in the management and direction of all the business and affairs of the company (except those matters assigned to the Finance Committee, the Committee on Audit or to the Bonus and Salary Committee), in such manner as the Executive Committee shall deem best for the interests of the company in all cases in which specific directions shall not have been given by the Board of Directors.[2]

In addition to acting jointly in making over-all policy decisions, each member of the Executive Committee has a second role as staff adviser in a specified area of the business. In this capacity, he provides advice to operating department and staff division heads who have problems with which they require assistance, or who need help in interpreting or applying company policies to their own operations. Executive Committee members serve as advisers in production, sales, research and development, engineering, personnel, purchasing, traffic and general services, and so forth.

Responsibility and authority for operations are delegated to the eleven operating departments. The ten men of the Executive Committee, acting

[2] By-Laws of E. I. du Pont de Nemours and Company, July 20, 1953. as amended, June 21, 1954, pp. 8–9.

as a group, supervise the activities of the operating departments. Department general managers refer to the Executive Committee those decisions not encompassed by their own wide authority. They may do this in person or by report, frequently after consulting a committee member on his second role of staff adviser in the area involved.

The Executive Committee considers the long-term and current needs of the company. It may request the operating departments and staff divisions to forecast and identify these needs and to develop plans to meet them, or it may review and coordinate proposals initiated and advanced from the operating groups. For example, if an operating department general manager wishes to add a new product to his line, he presents his proposal, together with a request for capital to finance the undertaking, to the Executive Committee. The Executive Committee will study the proposal to determine whether it fits the company's overall plans for expansion and diversification and whether it has sufficient potential for profit to warrant the investment required. Decisions involving substantial investment must be approved by the Finance Committee.

Once the request is approved, the department general manager is given full authority to construct the facilities he requires, purchase equipment and materials, and obtain the necessary personnel. He manufactures and sells the new product line, and he is rewarded in terms of the results he accomplishes.

The Finance Committee of the Board of Directors is the other major group that shares the responsibility and authority of the chief executive function in Du Pont. This committee has charge of all the financial affairs of the company and exercises the authority of the Board of Directors in financial matters. It is made up of eight members. The Treasurer, who is chief financial and accounting officer, reports directly to the Finance Committee.

There are two smaller committees of the Board. The Committee on Bonus and Salary consists of five members, none of whom is eligible for bonus. The Committee determines the salaries of the Chairman of the Board, the members of the other committees of the Board, and the vice presidents. It also determines all payments to be made under the company's bonus plan. The Committee on Audit is made up of three directors who are no longer active in the direct management of the company. It selects an independent firm of public accountants who audit the company's financial records, procedures, and statements. It reviews and acts upon all reports of the auditors.

Taken as a whole, these committees bring to bear on the over-all problems of the company a highly skilled group who are thoroughly schooled in Du Pont philosophy and practice. From long operating experience in the departments and divisions of the company, these men have a firsthand knowledge of the problems they discuss and the needs for which they plan. They are selected to balance one another's specialized skills and interests, so that the complete range of matters of concern to the company are constantly under scrutiny.

No one group is the law unto itself. The work and results of the operating department are under continuing scrutiny by the Executive Committee. Expenditures above a specified amount approved by the Executive Committee are, in turn, approved by the Finance Committee. The Treasurer, who collects, accounts for, and handles funds, reports to the Finance Committee. Audit of these financial transactions is arranged for by yet another independent agency. The salaries and bonuses to be paid to the managers handling these affairs in turn are determined by a fourth agency separate from these others. As a final step in this pattern of checks and balances, the work of each committee is periodically reviewed by the Board of Directors itself.

Advantages

The team or group organization of the top management function has several important advantages. Because it brings to bear on every important problem the combined talents and experience of several highly selected executives, it ensures better balanced, more effective decisions. Top level problems in the modern large business have so many ramifications and impinge on so many related areas that the top executive responsibility becomes exceedingly complex. In the large company it is literally impossible for one individual to fill it properly. When several people study and deliberate on each critical problem, there is more assurance that every facet will be thoroughly explored and weighed in terms of the interests of the company as a whole. Once divorced from operating responsibilities, the members of the top executive group individually can devote more of their time to study and *thinking* about the needs and the future of the company as a whole. Because of its character, group organization helps spread the burden. More effort and time are devoted to each problem; however, the effort and time required of each individual in the executive group is decreased.

Group organization of the top executive function makes the top decision-making group more accessible to subordinate managers. Each member of the group can act as adviser and counselor in one area of management to all operating and staff heads. The operating executive with a problem in plant location, for example, can secure ready audience with the member of the executive group who is contact officer in this area. If the problem has ramifications in other areas, additional top-flight brains can be brought to bear on it. And, finally, if policy decision is required, the matter can quickly be brought before the entire group.

Negative Factors

In spite of its advantages, group organization of the chief executive function is not to be undertaken without consideration of several factors which influence its success. To begin with, the group organization is more expensive. Salary, pension, and other compensation obligations are multiplied. Office, clerical, and other overhead expenses are also greater. The volume of business of the company must be sufficient to warrant this additional cost.

If this type of organization is to succeed, qualifications and personalities of the members of the team become of extreme importance. Each member of the group must be able to work harmoniously with the others but with great independence of thought and expression. Once the group decision is made, it is vital that it be wholeheartedly endorsed and supported by each executive officer. This calls for real maturity, a willingness to sacrifice self-interest for the greater good of the total effort, and humility.

By its nature, the executive group must develop from within. The individual members must be selected for their intelligence and demonstrated ability. They must have the respect of the executives of the company and a sharp awareness of their problems and the personal assets and liabilities they bring to bear in solving those problems. All this means that the members of the chief executive group will, characteristically, have come up through the company and will have had intensive experience in a number of its functions or divisions. People of the caliber described, willing and capable of assuming the responsibilities involved, are rare in any company. Usually there is difficulty in finding one chief executive, let alone a group of this caliber. If group organization of the chief executive function is to be adopted, it will be successful only when the staffing problem has been anticipated. This usually will mean early identification of promising people, planned transfers and developmental opportunities to enable them to develop ability and judgment, and a method of compensation that will help hold this outstanding talent within the company, rather than forcing it to leave for adequate reward.

Once adopted, the group organization of the chief executive function presents two potential dangers. For one, decision making may be slowed. The need to get a group together and to discuss all relevant factors can be time-consuming. If emergency action is required, this delay may be dangerous. This danger is largely overcome in practice by scheduling a group meeting once each day, so that any matter is ensured prompt consideration. Again, quorum requirements are set so that less than the full group can act, almost within the hour, with its decisions subject to review by the group and the Board.

Diffusion of accountability is a further danger. If the group decides, who is to be held accountable for mistakes or for specific actions? The answer here is that the executive group, acting as it does *for* the Board of Directors and subject to the review of the Board, is accountable *as a group* just as the full Board is accountable as a group to the stockholders.

SUMMARY

Top management consists of stockholders, Board of Directors, and chief executive function. The chief executive has a complex and difficult role, involving over-all management of the enterprise, over-all operations, and public relationships. This work can be organized by creating one position, the chief executive, to be accountable for all activities. Assistants are created as required.

However, the better method, except in the very small company, is to split the function into two or more positions, those of the chief executive and chief operating officer. The chief executive is responsible for over-all planning, organizing, motivating, coordinating, and controlling. The chief operating officer is delegated responsibility for the line operations. Each executive has reporting to him the appropriate special staff agencies.

A further elaboration is an additional split to form a chief staff officer position. Here all staff positions report to one executive. Thus, the chief executive has only two people reporting to him. Various modifications of these basic groups are used successfully in many well-organized companies.

A fourth arrangement of the top executive function is use of a group of executives. As established in Du Pont, it is a very successful adaptation. However, special circumstances attendant upon its use include the availability of a large group of exceptionally able men, who have worked together long enough to form a highly cohesive group.

PART THREE

Dynamics of Organization

CHAPTER 13 *Changing the Organization Structure*

In the preceding chapters, we have largely discussed the concepts and tools of organization. However, the organization we have described is not an end in itself. Organization, properly designed, can help improve teamwork and productivity by providing a framework within which people can work together most effectively. But we must relate the people to the design. In many cases, the organization structure which has technical excellence is, for practical purposes, quite useless because it is not fitted to the needs of the people it is designed to serve. It is a lifeless pattern.

We are now concerned with putting the tools of organization to work. How do you go about changing the existing organization in terms of people? What specific steps should be followed to ensure that change takes place with least disruption to the operation of the company?

In practice, organization change has no clear-cut beginning or end. A business changes in many respects every day of its existence. The forces dictating change may be temporary—personnel transfers and promotions, fluctuations in the production cycle, or seasonal variations in customer requirements. Pressure for change may also be potent and irreversible. There may be purchases or mergers of the business itself or introduction of a new product line. Changes in public taste and demand may occur, bringing need for new technologies and a means of entering and exploiting new markets. Death and retirements may lead to changes in the ownership or direction of the business.

Borg-Warner decides to go into air conditioning and buys York Corporation. The International Telephone and Telegraph Corporation buys the Capehart-Farnsworth and Coolerator companies to get into the home appliance business, and, a few years later, sells the radio, phonograph, and home TV portions, retaining the large research and development activity as the Farnsworth Electronics division of the corporation. United States Envelope Company has to locate and build many new plants. It finds it necessary to add to its existing organization a function devoted to the problems of plant location.

Changes such as these occur continually in every company. Each demands a balanced, informed judgment as to how best to undertake the organization modification necessary to accommodate the change itself.

STAFFING FOR ORGANIZATION CHANGE

Who is to make decisions and who is to do the work of implementing organization changes? As we have seen, responsibility for initiating and making final decision on the over-all company organization must be reserved by the Board of Directors and the chief executive officer. At division, department, and lower levels, each manager is accountable for implementing the over-all company plan as it applies to his unit and for design of a structure within this framework fitted to the needs of his operation.

Organization is a technical and highly demanding activity, requiring special skills and abilities. The development of sound organization demands understanding and perspective as to the total needs of the company—its markets and products, its past and its future.

This function is best performed by a specialized staff group reporting directly to the chief executive, or as part of an administrative management staff grouping reporting to the chief executive. Other alternatives are personal staff, outside consultants, and committees. In many cases, combinations of one or more of these will fit the company's needs.

Organization Planning Specialized Staff

The organization planning staff group should be available to study the over-all needs of the company in organization, to analyze the existing organization, to suggest modifications and improvements to accountable managers. As an important part of its activity, the organization function should conduct research in organization to discover new or improved methods of organization. It should inform and teach managers the principles of organization adopted by the company and help develop their abilities to review and improve their own organizations. A statement of the purpose and responsibilities of the organization function follows:

ORGANIZATION FUNCTION

PURPOSE

To provide advice and service in the development of organization plans and controls and in coordinating organization matters. To assist in the interpretation and implementation of organization plans and controls as requested by accountable managers.

RESPONSIBILITIES

A. *Planning*
   1. Participate in the development of corporate and organization objectives and policies and make appropriate recommendation to the president.
   2. Design and propose, with the participation of accountable managers, a plan of organization to provide maximum operating effectiveness and economy for the company and its components over the short and long term.
   3. Conduct research in organization to develop new and progressive thinking and plans for the company with respect to its organization problems.
   4. Undertake organization studies and analyses of the company and its components and develop programs and schedules for accountable managers in installing and implementing organization changes.
   5. Propose procedures for ensuring conformity with the approved plan of organization throughout the company.
   6. Develop and propose, and counsel with accountable managers, on budgets for organization planning purposes.

B. *Organizing*
   1. Develop with participation of subordinates a balanced and effective plan of organization for his own function, consonant with the over-all company plan, and implement it on a continuing basis.
   2. Define the responsibility, authority, and accountability of his subordinates.
   3. Delegate to subordinates all responsibility and authority except that which he is specifically required to reserve for his own performance.
   4. Establish effective relationships among all positions in his function and with other functions and agencies of the company.

C. *Motivating*
   1. Select qualified people for his department and place them in positions where they can perform most effectively in terms of their experience and abilities.
   2. Provide for communication and participation of his subordinates in matters of concern and interest to them.
   3. Ensure equitable compensation for his subordinates in consonance with company wage and salary policy and procedure.
   4. Develop his people to their maximum potential by regular and consistent appraisal, counseling, coaching, and training.
   5. Carefully investigate and report to the personnel department the cause of all discharges and terminations in his department.

D. *Coordinating*
   1. Consult with other line and staff heads to ensure balanced prog-

ress of the work of his department in harmony with over-all company programs and schedules.

2. Offer the services of his department, as indicated, to help unify and integrate, by organizational means, the work of other functions and departments.

3. Act for the president, as directed, in coordinating organization matters by personal contact, committee meetings, or other means.

E. *Controlling*

1. Develop and propose standards for organization.

2. Maintain the master charts for organization as directed by the president.

3. Provide for the preparation, distribution, and maintenance of the organization manual and for recording and reporting organization changes.

4. Observe compliance with approved plans of organization in all components of the company. Discuss deviations with accountable managers and, as necessary, with the president.

5. Study and analyze the operation of the company organization and recommend to accountable managers such revisions as may be necessary and desirable in the interests of the continuity and profitability of the company.

F. *Operating*

1. Teach, inform, communicate, explain, and interpret to all company personnel matters related to organization.

2. Attend meetings and conferences, both inside and outside the company, and discuss organization matters with recognized authorities to remain abreast of the newest developments in his specialty.

3. Speak for the company in organization matters to outside agencies after coordination, as required, with the president and the public relations department.

Specialized staff organization planning departments are found in an increasing number of companies. Typical is that found in Ford Motor Company.

Ford Motor Company. In Ford, the central staff organization department advises and assists in the organizational development of the company toward approved objectives. It develops and recommends organization standards, principles, and relationships for application through the company. When required, it prepares organizational studies of company activities, including recommendations on management and administrative problems and on the assignment of general functions and responsibilities. It reviews and advises on proposed organizational plans or changes down to and including the section level in the central offices of the company and to the departmental level in the divisions. The organization department assists in resolving any organizational differences between company units. It prepares and publishes the Ford Motor

Company organization manual, reviews and advises on division organization manuals, and coordinates the release of information on company organization.

Reporting Relationships

The organization planning function should, preferably, report directly to the chief executive. This is particularly important when the company is undergoing major organization changes or must constantly study its organization to keep ahead of the demands made by diversification.

This reporting relationship is found in companies such as Jones & Laughlin Steel Corporation, International Business Machines, Ford Motor Company, Creole Petroleum Corp., Pillsbury Mills, Celanese Corporation of America, Kaiser Aluminum & Chemical Corporation, Chrysler Corporation, KLM Royal Dutch Air Lines, and many others.

In some companies, this direct reporting relationship is maintained but the organization planning function is grouped with other management advisory services. This is the case in American Enka, where it is part of the Management Services Department; United Air Lines, in Economic Controls; and Koppers Company, in the Control Section.

Organization planning may also be grouped with personnel. In this case, it is important that the personnel head be skilled in organization techniques and capable of providing advice and counsel in terms of the total requirements of the company, not simply the personnel aspects. Since planning and staffing the organization are so closely allied, the organization planning department may be grouped with management development and made the organization development function, reporting directly to the chief executive.

Personal Staff

The chief executive frequently makes use of an executive assistant or an assistant to in effecting the reorganization. This brings the process of organization survey and analysis under his personal direction and ensures that he will be informed constantly of important developments. At the same time, however, it mitigates against frank expression of organization needs by subordinate managers because the assistant must speak for and represent the person of the chief executive only. It also tends to withhold from the organization as a whole the potential value of the staff man as an internal consultant, because he is, by definition, not fully accessible to provide advice and service to subordinate elements.

In practice, it often turns out that the term "assistant" is a misnomer when applied to organization staff. The staff man responsible for providing advice and service on organization often builds a department of his own devoted to organization matters. When the title "Assistant to the President" is maintained under these circumstances, most often it is to lend status and importance to the work of reorganization.

Outside Consultants

Consultants can be of great assistance in formulation and installation of the plan of organization. Consultants should be used in place of internal staff agencies only when full use can be made of the special advantages they offer. The two chief assets the consultant can bring to the company are specialized skill and experience, and objectivity.

By virtue of special training, study, or research, the consultant may have acquired knowledge, techniques, and skills that are not available within the company. Particularly if he has studied and worked with other companies with similar problems or in the same industry, he can make a unique contribution. Familiarity of the consultant with organization approaches tried in other enterprises can result in substantial economies in time and effort.

A large metal products firm that manufactured special design and close-tolerance components for the aircraft and electronic industries had a constant problem in scheduling and coordinating work between engineering and manufacturing and meshing it with purchasing and research to meet customer requirements for design changes and modifications and also to honor delivery promises. A consultant, called in on the problem, was able to apply a concept of organizing material planning and control that he had worked out in similar assignments with other companies and to effect a satisfactory solution in short order.

The consultant should work closely with company personnel to familiarize them with his techniques and approach. Otherwise, he carries his specialized skills with him when he leaves and the company is overly dependent upon him for implementing the organization plan.

Objectivity in examining and analyzing the company and its problems is a further advantage of the consultant. Since he has no personal stake in the changes he advocates, except with respect to their practicality and technical excellence, he can look upon the organization and its people in terms of facts and not emotions and make recommendations predicated upon the over-all welfare of the enterprise. If personnel changes are indicated and management is unwilling to shoulder the responsibility, the consultant is often made a convenient scapegoat.

Many companies use consultants to effect major reorganizations, such as change from a functional to a divisionalized structure. Preferably, an internal organization staff should be also created at this time and groomed to pick up the work after the consultant leaves.

Use of consultants is also indicated for organization audits. A biennial review of the total organization by a competent outside professional will usually reveal many opportunities for tightening up the organization or anticipating difficulties which escape inside staff because of their proximity to the problems and the people involved.

Committees

Committees can be used effectively in providing advice and recommendations to the chief executive on over-all company organization changes. They are also valuable in coordinating organization changes among all managers directly concerned. When so used, the committee should be limited to advisory authority only. It should be under the leadership of a capable chairman and should be provided with whatever data-gathering agencies it needs so that it does not waste its time in collecting information.

Cluett, Peabody & Co. This company made extensive use of an organization committee in effecting a major reorganization that extended over a period of some eight years, involving change from a centralized, functional organization to a divisionalized organization decentralized on a profit center basis. Cluett, Peabody decided to make use of a committee to study the problem and make recommendations to the president. However, it found it desirable to leaven the personal interest of the committee members in the proposed changes by introducing an outside consultant who worked closely with the group.

The organization planning committee was given three responsibilities: (1) to crystallize the company's long-range goals, (2) to study the company's organization structure to determine its suitability in terms of helping the company attain these goals, and (3) to help plan any needed changes in the organization structure that should logically take place. After a year's work, the committee developed the over-all plan for the change-over and drew up the program and schedule for its installation.

Carrier Corporation. In effecting divisionalization and decentralization, Carrier decided that it would undertake the reorganization itself but that it would employ an outside consultant to guide and criticize the approach and the plans it developed.

An organization planning committee, made up of the top officers of the company, was first appointed in 1952. It was given the assignment of developing a basic plan of organization to fit the long-term needs of the company. This group met with the consultant, developing an over-all philosophy of organization and agreeing on principles and the approach to be followed.

The committee recommended that Carrier's product lines be grouped into three separate families and that three product divisions be formed. Organization charts were prepared through the department level at this point. After review and reconciliation by the entire officer group of the company, the recommendations and organization charts were presented to all major department heads.

After this review, the department heads were divided into four committees, each with its own chairman and an adviser from the officer group. These committees were given responsibility for reviewing the organization proposals that had been developed and criticizing their applicability to their departments. The findings of these committees were reported back to the officer committee. When the master plan was finally evolved, it incorporated the thinking of all accountable managers and had every assurance of support.

Once the master plan was prepared, Carrier dissolved the original committees and organized a new committee, the Senior Organization Committee, giving it the responsibility for developing the plans for installing the approved organization. At this point, company management appointed the heads for the product divisions in the new structure. These division heads recommended appointment of their major department heads.

The major department heads for each division, in turn, were organized into subcommittees of the Senior Organization Committee. Each subcommittee coordinated the selection of subordinate managers for its department. As new subordinate managers were appointed, they became members of the subcommittee and helped in its work.

Most of the burden of putting the plan into effect was borne by these subcommittees, made up of managers who were closest to the activities affected. They prepared the final organization charts and position descriptions for their groups and selected the people to staff their new organization units. They determined space requirements for the change-over and formulated plans for the transfer of departmental operations. The total process required a little over eighteen months. The plan was put into effect in November, 1953, with a minimum of disruption and confusion.

STEPS IN ORGANIZATION CHANGE

A definite sequence of activity should be followed in changing the organization. This applies equally to the over-all company structure and to units and components within the company. This sequence anticipates major administrative requirements prerequisite to effective change. It provides a constant organization goal toward which change proceeds and it makes full provision for the people in the organization.

Effective organization change is dependent upon certain planning steps which must be undertaken first. This includes the formulation of objectives, policies, and other plans which will specify the work that the organization is to accomplish. If objectives and plans already exist, they should be carefully reviewed as a basis for determining the appropriate organization structure.

Once we have clearly identified what we expect the organization to accomplish, we analyze and evaluate the existing organization structure to determine its adequacy for the company's long-term needs. We then prepare an ideal or master organization plan which becomes the pattern for guiding all interim changes. To reach this goal, we develop a series of phase plans, which enable us to advance toward our organizational objective with minimum disruption of operations and full utilization of the people now in the company. These steps can be outlined in the following sequence:

1. Develop objectives and other plans
2. Analyze the existing organization
3. Prepare an ideal plan
4. Try out the plan
5. Prepare phase plans
6. Establish uniform nomenclature
7. Overcome resistance to change

DEVELOP OBJECTIVES AND OTHER PLANS

As we have seen, all work done in the organization must be pointed to the accomplishment of predetermined objectives, policies, and programs. If work does not contribute to the implementation of objectives and plans already established, it is not necessary and should not be performed. This is true also of each element of the organization. Each section, department, and division should have clearly defined objectives and other plans which are part of, and consonant with, the total objectives and plans of the organization. Each such unit should perform only that work necessary to reach objectives.

No company is static. Its goals may change for many reasons. For each such change, there should be a concomitant modification of the organization structure. Unfortunately, this is not always the case. Many a company—and its divisions or functions—has followed the easier course. Instead of changing the basic structure to meet long-term needs, it has simply reapportioned duties among the people in the organization. The invariable result is a jerry-built structure, with a function tacked on here and a department added there but with no underlying and progressive movement toward a balanced, integrated plan.

To illustrate: During the early years of a hardware distributing chain in the Middle West, the president created the job of finance manager to make a position and an impressive title for his son-in-law. The treasurer reported directly to the president. A controller was also appointed, also reporting to the president. As time went on, the son-in-law wished to create a job and a title for *his* son. Accordingly, the position of secretary was established, reporting to the finance manager. On its seventy-fifth anniversary recently, the company published an organization chart. The positions of controller, treasurer, and finance manager still exist side by side. The finance manager handles the pension plan and employee insurance, while the controller and the treasurer take care of the financial affairs of the business.

Most companies which have thought through the process of organization design emphasize the importance of this principle. American Enka Corporation, for example, ensures a uniform approach in the development of its organization by first determining the basic objectives and plans of the corporate enterprise and then developing an organization structure adequate to carry them out effectively.

The Electric Storage Battery Company designs its organization structure to conform to and facilitate the basic plans and objectives of the company. Electric Storage Battery arranges the structure so that it contributes to and is governed by the major functions and basic work processes of the business. An excellent example of the importance of developing objectives and plans as a basis for sound organization is found in the case of Lukens Steel Company.

Lukens Steel Company

Several years ago, Lukens Steel Company identified several weaknesses in its marketing and manufacturing operations and undertook a systematic planning approach to provide for additional kinds of work to strengthen and reinforce the basic organization structure.

Lukens is a relatively small enterprise as steel companies go. It is too small to compete on an equal footing with the giants of the industry. Size is one disadvantage; there are also other handicaps. For one thing, Lukens is not fully integrated. It does not mine its own ore or make its own pig iron. Therefore, it must buy pig iron and scrap on the open market to charge its furnaces. This adds measurably to its basic material costs.

Add to this the fact that the bulk of Lukens sales are specialty steel products, which are sold largely to capital goods producers in the electrical, machinery, and construction industries. These two factors tie Lukens costs to the market price for pig iron and scrap and its sales to the wide fluctuations of the capital goods market.

Determined to level out these ups and downs, Lukens in 1954 spelled out objectives for improving its position. To set its course, the company first established corporate and functional objectives. Its over-all company objectives are:

First, to promote reasonable and improving corporate earnings through productive effort applied primarily but not limited to the manufacture of steel plate, steel plate specialties, fabricated parts and partially or fully assembled units.

Second, to conduct the business in a manner that earns recognition as a constructive and honorable corporate citizen in its relations, designed to be mutually profitable, with stockholders, employees, customers, suppliers, community and government.

The company established objectives in other areas of the business. Those with respect to sales and marketing were designed to help improve earnings and acceptance of its products. They are:

1. To search out and develop satisfactory markets for products and services with special attention to more lucrative and stable markets than are traditional for the steel industry in general and for Lukens in particular.

2. To sell company products and services at prices which will yield a reasonable and improving return over costs.

3. To assist customers to develop and service their own markets to the benefit of Lukens.

What did this mean in terms of additional work to be done within the organization? The company decided first that it could stabilize its marketing cycle best by going after new sources of income outside the capital goods field. Helpful leads to these new markets would come from the existing field sales force and engineering and service people who are in constant touch with customers and potential customers. However, Lukens decided that it would be best assured of accomplishing its purpose if it made provision for a special type of work. To this end, it established a commercial research unit within the Market Development organization. This group is made up of an economist and a group of market analysts. They search out and investigate, on a systematic basis, possible new markets for Lukens products outside the conventional steel markets. They evaluate the prospects of stability and profit for each new lead and help to integrate this with the over-all market development activities of the company.

To further implement these objectives, Lukens also arranged for more comprehensive sales standards and controls, to help minimize sales costs. Since the company is not primarily an end-use producer, it made provision to reach end-use customers in an effort to have them specify use of Lukens steel. The company believes that it can assist customers to develop and service their own markets to the benefit of Lukens by encouraging customers and potential customers to see Lukens's production facilities at first hand. Accordingly, the company organized a Plant Visitations Unit within the Market Development Department which, among other activities, offers free plant service to customers who wish to visit the plant.

Other Examples

The need for organizing in terms of objectives and plans is illustrated in two other company examples. Consider first a large steel fabricating house that sells primarily through jobbers in the Middle West and East. It conceives of its marketing job primarily as that of calling on its customers and taking orders for whatever catalogue or special items they need. In this case, the primary marketing emphasis is on field sales, and we find sales identified as the primary subfunction.

Contrast to this an aluminum fabricator that sees its marketing objectives somewhat differently. This company sets as the objective of its marketing department that of finding customers who need its type of products, determining the dimensions of their needs, and persuading them to buy aluminum products designed to fill those specifications. It also expects its marketing function to service the product after it is sold to ensure customer satisfaction.

In this latter case, we find a much more elaborate marketing organization. Field sales are backed by market research, advertising, customer service, and sales training functions. There are product managers for extrusions, architectural, and consumer products.

ANALYZE THE EXISTING ORGANIZATION

Once the company has decided upon its objectives, analysis of the existing organization should be undertaken. This process of organization inventory encompasses study and cataloguing of the work that is being performed, the authority that is delegated, and the relationships that have been established. Since it is a faithful picture of the existing organization, it helps to identify existing strengths and weaknesses. Comparison of the existing structure with an ideal plan will indicate the changes that must be made to implement the organization the company has decided to adopt.

Organization analysis is an indispensable prerequisite to planned and orderly organization change. Whether or not change is indicated, however, organization analysis serves to define and clarify the existing organization. It can stand by itself as a means of eliminating overlap and duplication, minimizing friction and confusion resulting from faulty organizational relationships, improving administrative procedures, and for other values.

Information Required

As a first step in organization analysis, information must be collected and analyzed and basic decisions made concerning the nature of the organization structure. This includes the following:

1. What primary work must be performed to accomplish the objectives established?

2. How can the functions comprising this work best be grouped to provide an organization structure that will anticipate the long-term needs of the enterprise? A decision must be made at this point as to the type of basic structure best suited to the long-term needs of the company. Should it be functional? product division? geographic division? or a combination? Once the over-all structure is determined, the best pattern of grouping can be derived.

3. What work can best be broken out and grouped as staff to provide for specialization and to make services available to several units at lowest cost and with greatest effectiveness?

4. What management positions must be created to provide for effective planning, organizing, coordination, motivation, and control?

Interview Approach

The information required for organization analysis is available within the company by interview of the people doing the work. Through interview of key managers, it is possible to secure basic data covering the major functional areas. If complete coverage is required, personal interview of each position incumbent is indicated.

The usual procedure in organization interview is to start at the top and work down. The theory here is that if we follow the pattern of delegation and redelegation of responsibility and authority from one level to the next, we will in the process identify the important work areas. This is only partly true. The primary activities of the company take place only at the level where the end results of the enterprise are accomplished. This is at the point of contact with the customer or the level at which the product is designed or manufactured or serviced. Consequently, to identify accurately the work being done in the organization, it is necessary to interview each level independently, from the bottom up as well as from the top down, and then to reconcile the data we secure, one level with another.

If we interview only the manager of each unit, which is often done, we find that he will tend to rationalize the extent and importance of his job. In particular, he will tend to affirm that he does management work, which he *knows* he should perform, but which in actuality he does not.

The data the manager offers can best be substantiated in terms of the evidence offered and the work performed by those he supervises.

RESPONSIBILITY ANALYSIS

The first step in organization analysis is to identify accurately and concisely the work that is being done in each position. If we are to build a pattern of management work for each job, we should analyze it in terms of management activities. If the analysis is undertaken properly, we can, at one time, identify the management work which is being performed and also *that which is not*. Identification of omissions can be an important means of building each position to the full scope of management responsibility and of ensuring that each manager is concerning himself primarily with management work.

Combination Questionnaire and Interview

Responsibility analysis is best undertaken by use of a combination of questionnaire and interview. Preceding the survey, orientation conferences should be scheduled with all who will participate and the purpose and nature of the survey should be outlined. The questionnaire form should be explained and detailed instructions and examples presented for its completion.

A questionnaire with key items such as those outlined below is recommended to require managers to think through their work and to help shorten the interview process itself.

ORGANIZATION QUESTIONNAIRE

This form is designed to provide information to help clarify the work you do. Please complete each question in accordance with instructions received during the orientation session you attended.

1. What is the purpose of your job?
2. What contribution does your work make to the over-all success and profit of the company?
3. What *planning* work do you do in the areas indicated below?
   a. What work do you do in determining objectives and goals for the company or your unit?
   b. To what extent do you develop or contribute to the development of policies?
   c. What programs and schedules do you prepare?
   d. What procedures do you develop? To whom do they apply?
   e. To what extent do you prepare or participate in the preparation of budgets?

   f. What work do you perform in explaining, interpreting, and educating your subordinates in the meaning and use of objectives, policies, programs and schedules, procedures, and budgets?

4. What *organizing* work do you perform in the areas indicated?
   a. To what extent do you design and maintain the organization structure of your unit?
   b. What work do you perform in preparing and maintaining organization charts and position guides for your unit?
   c. To what extent do you define the responsibility, authority, and accountability of your subordinates?
   d. What do you do in defining and explaining relationships between yourself and subordinates, staff and line, and between people working on the same level?
   e. What work do you do in explaining the organization of your unit and the company and in educating your subordinates in application of sound organization principles?

5. What *coordinating* work do you do?
   a. With what other positions or units do you coordinate your work or that of your unit?
   b. What particularly difficult or unusual coordinating work do you form?
   c. With what other work do you have to time, unify, or integrate the work you do?

6. What *motivating* work do you do?
   a. To what extent do you select and place the people who report to you?
   b. What work do you do in appraising the performance of the people who report to you?
   c. What do you do in counseling and coaching your subordinates?
   d. To what extent do you determine the compensation of the people who report to you?
   e. What do you do in providing for participation of your people in the decisions and problems that affect them directly?
   f. What provision do you make for communication of information to your subordinates and to enable them to communicate with you?
   g. To what extent do you personally direct the people who report to you?
   h. What work do you do with respect to the dismissal, discharge, and termination of your subordinates?

7. What *controlling* work do you do?
   a. What standards do you set for performance of work done under your direction or management?
   b. What work do you do in recording the progress of work performed under your direction?
   c. What reports do you complete and forward? What is included in these reports? To whom are they sent?
   d. What provision do you make for evaluation of the work done

under your direction by comparison of actual performance against
the standards established for the work?

    e. What work do you do in taking corrective action to correct un-
satisfactory conditions?

8. What *operating* work do you do?

    a. What work do you perform other than indicated above which you
feel is a necessary and important part of your job?

9. Draw, in outline form, an organization chart showing those to whom
you report and the positions reporting to you.

As the analyst proceeds, he attempts to discover whether the work
being done is necessary to accomplishment of the objectives of the organization unit and of the company as a whole. He can do this effectively only if he knows these objectives and their implications.

In many cases, the person holding a job has a much different idea of
the relative importance of his various responsibilities than does his boss.
To the extent that these differences exist, there will be a difference in
emphasis and, consequently, effectiveness. One means of determining
the relative importance of position responsibilities, as between the position incumbent and his immediate superior, is by use of card ranking.
This device calls for writing each major job responsibility separately on
a 3- by 5-inch card. The position incumbent is asked to select the card
listing the most important and the least important responsibility. He
continues picking most and least important responsibilities from the re-
mainders until he has ranked all his responsibilities. These are recorded.
The process is then repeated with the immediate superior, who is asked
to rank the same responsibilities. Comparison of the two rankings will
usually reveal significant differences as to the necessity of various duties.
This ranking can also be used to good effect in the process of reconciliation.

AUTHORITY ANALYSIS

The authority vested in each position should be determined, preferably concurrently with responsibility analysis. In analyzing authority,
we are concerned primarily with limits, not gradations within those
limits. We want to know how far a manager can go in exercising his
rights and powers, not what he might do for each of several specific cases.

Authority analysis should be consistent with the over-all concept of
management and organization that we have established and should help
round out the picture of each management position. Authority should
be analyzed with relation to each item of work the manager performs.
Showing this relationship will at once establish the manager's accountability for that work, because we can hold him accountable only to the

extent that we give him authority to perform. It will also help to identify omissions in delegation of authority from his superior.

Linear Charting

The most effective means of authority analysis is by use of the linear chart. This requires that first we identify the significant authority limits and code them by numbers. The following is recommended:

1. *Final Authority.* Power or right to make final decisions.

2. *Must Be Consulted.* Final decision may be made after consultation. Disagreement must be carried to higher authority before final decision can be made.

3. *Advisory Authority.* Authority to advise, suggest, recommend, counsel, consult.

4. *Service Authority.* Authority to carry out for manager having final authority by specific and restricted delegation.

5. *Must Be Informed.* Must be notified of action taken. Applies only to notification outside normal channels.

Final authority indicates that the manager can make final decision, with obligation only to report what he has done within normal reporting channels. If this final authority is limited, in terms of dollars or other units, by budget, policy, or specific restriction, the limit is noted by means of an asterisk. The concepts of line and staff already presented govern the normal limitations of final, advisory, and service authority. It should be recalled that a subordinate reporting to a superior is in a staff (advisory and service) relationship to his superior. The superior is normally in a line relationship to his subordinate.

The number code outlined above is used to plot authorities for specific responsibilities against all positions involved. The linear chart is prepared as illustrated in Figure 13–1, page 290.

When completed, the linear chart provides an excellent means of identifying overlap and duplication in authority and responsibility. It will quickly show to what level specific work and authority have been delegated. It provides a ready index to the degree of decentralization and shows clearly when managers are performing nonmanagement work that could be delegated.

After organization data have been accumulated, they should be classified and analyzed. This is done by preparation of organization charts and position guides.

ORGANIZATION CHARTING

The organization chart is a graphic means of showing organization data. Organization charts are snapshots; they show only the formal or-

	Board of Directors	President	Vice President, Finance	Treasurer	Manager, Fiscal	Manager, Credit	Controller	Chief Accountant	Manager, Budgets	Mgr., Internal Audits	Vice President, Marketing	Mgr., Marketing Administration	Mgr., Market Development	Mgr., Advertising & Promotion
				Treasury			Controller				Finance Department	Marketing Department		
Company Marketing Objectives														
Division Marketing Objectives														
Pricing Policies														
Credit Policies														
Establish Prices														
Approve Credit														
Establish Finance Budgets														
Establish Marketing Budgets														

Figure 13–1. Linear Charting

ganization and depict it for only a given moment in time; an outdated chart is as useful as yesterday's newspaper. Charts are a valuable adjunct to organization analysis. They show overlap and duplication, dual reporting relationships, multitudinous levels, excessive spans of supervision, and other deficiencies.

Mechanics of Charting

In preparing the chart book, or organization manual, the management structure, including departments and divisions, should be shown first on an over-all company chart. Each department and division should then be broken down on succeeding chart pages.

Titling

The name of the company and of the component charted is indicated in the title, which is placed in the upper right-hand corner of the chart page, as shown in Figure 13–2. This placement simplifies identification as the pages are turned. A title box, placed in the lower right-hand corner, contains the date the chart is issued, the date of issue of the chart it replaces, and the name of the manager authorizing its issue, as shown also in Figure 13–2.

	Date Issued	Date Chart Replaced	No.
Whitestone Manufacturing Co.	1/8/5P	6/4/55	12-6
FINANCE DEPARTMENT Budget Section	Authorized By:	S. J. White Section Manager	

Figure 13–2. Title and Title Box

Chart Lining

Consistency should also be maintained in lining the chart. Vertical, horizontal, and side-arm lining may be used to fit the chart to the space allotted to it. However, the lining combinations used should be standardized for ease of reading and for good layout. Horizontal and vertical lining are preferred when space is not at a premium. If many boxes are to be shown in limited space, side-arm and vertical combinations are usually best. Figure 13–3 shows various types of chart lining.

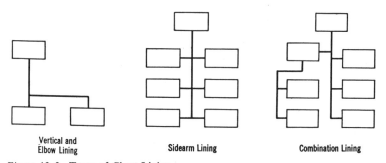

Vertical and Elbow Lining   Sidearm Lining   Combination Lining

Figure 13–3. Types of Chart Lining

Chart Boxes

Several standard sizes for chart boxes should be selected and consistency established in their use. Usually a rectangular box will best accommodate the printed material. The box itself should contain, on the first line, the name of the function, and on the second, the name of the position. Names of position incumbents, if included, tend to date the chart with each personnel change. They are best listed in a personnel index or roster, keyed as explained below.

Numbering

Charts should be numbered by a decimal system. Each function should be assigned a whole number and its subdivisions decimals of the whole number. For example, Finance might be assigned the whole number 12. The decimal numbering system would then be as shown in the following table:

Finance Manager	12–1
Controller	12–2
General Accountant	12–2.1
Manager Budgetary Control	12–2.2
Manager Internal Auditing	12–2.3 etc.

The whole numbers can be used as page numbers. To identify chart boxes, the appropriate decimal notation can be placed within the box. A separate personnel index can then be maintained for names of position incumbents and the name easily located in the index by use of the code number in the chart box.

PREPARATION OF POSITION GUIDES

A position guide is a means of defining responsibility, authority, and relationships for each position. It enables the organization analyst to classify and formalize the data he has already secured. Position guides should be prepared in draft from the questionnaire and interview data secured during organization analysis and reconciled before final statements are prepared.

Opposing Viewpoints

Two distinct schools of thought should be noted as to the desirability of written definitions of responsibility. One holds that writing out a manager's responsibility puts him in a strait jacket. By strictly limiting him to one area of work, the written definition stunts his management growth and makes it impossible for him to be other than a narrow specialist. Furthermore, definition is said to hamper teamwork and group action because it precludes one person coming to the aid of another or helping to fill in for him when he is overburdened. Definition of responsibility is also supposed to put too much emphasis on accountability. By making managers overly conscious of what they may be held for, it encourages buck passing and reluctance to take on work unless it is specifically written into the responsibility definition.

The general conclusion of this line of thought is that managers should be given general areas of work and authority. They should be permitted to take over additional work and exercise authority as they show capacity for it. As time goes on, the argument proceeds, everybody will find his best place, differences will be recognized, and a team will be developed that is tailored to the special strengths and skills of its members.

This argument has some validity. So long as the enterprise grows and develops its people from within so that they can adjust and gradually fit to the pattern, so long as expansion and diversification do not require the introduction of large numbers of new employees, so long as job requirements remain relatively static, lack of definition may not work undue hardship. However, it has serious disadvantages when applied to the rapidly growing and diversifying business in which this stabilized situation does not prevail. When this is the case, the strong and aggressive tend to take over the work that they like best, or that which gives them greatest recognition. There is haphazard and unequal distribution of work. The same activities may be performed in two or three different places, or some management work may not get done at all because nobody wants to do it.

When properly undertaken, written definition of responsibility and authority is of enduring benefit to the company. In practice, the responsibility specification does not limit a manager to specific actions but, rather, puts up fences beyond which he cannot pass without encroaching on another. Within the area of work allotted to him, the individual can use his imagination, ingenuity, and initiative to the utmost. In doing so, he is assured, however, that he will not overlap or arouse resentment in a fellow-manager.

Since he is confined to the performance of specific work, the manager can be appraised on the manner in which he does that work and trained to do it better. If he is being developed for a bigger job, the responsibility specification for that position enables him to anticipate and prepare for the duties that he will be required to assume.

Clear-cut, written definition is the best basis for delegation. It enables a manager to determine what part of his work to reserve and what to delegate. Written definition is also a basis for executive control. It is difficult to hold people to account for mistakes or omissions unless there is clear understanding as to who is to do what work.

As we have noted, definition of responsibility and authority may occur by informal means. When people work together over a long period, when groups are small and there is frequent interaction, each member of the group assumes his own role and plays it out consistently as part of the team effort. The difficulty lies in maintaining this condition in the growing, changing enterprise. When people are brought in, rotated, or transferred, the pattern of teamwork changes. It is at this point that written position guides can help ease the transition and facilitate the development of a smoothly functioning informal organization within the framework of the formal structure.

Defining Responsibility

Work should be defined in general terms. The aim is to define *what* is to be done, not *how* it is to be done. Compare, for example, two statements used to describe work done by credit managers in two different companies in the same industry.

Company A

1. Place rubber stamp on export orders for all divisions and plant orders indicating "credit approved" or other payment terms and scan those orders for objectionable terms and conditions.

2. Compile card record files for credit purposes and set credit limits for individual companies within which orders may be approved.

Company B

1. Study and develop the procedures, forms, and methods to be used by operating divisions in investigating and granting credit to customers. Recommend efficient methods for these functions to the Treasurer and, with his approval, to operating divisions.

2. Supervise application of approved methods for credit work to the operating function performed for centrally located operating divisions.

The first example obviously holds a manager to narrowly restricted activities. It goes so far as to specify that he is to use a rubber stamp and card files. This restriction bears out the worst fears of the opponents of definition. In the case of Company *B,* we have an example of good definition. Here the manager is held to certain work, but he is given great leeway in deciding how he will do it.

These examples illustrate that major duties only should be specified in the position guide. Routine and detail generally apply to the "how" of performing and should be filled in by the position incumbent to fit the informal structure he develops for his job.

Use of Management Categories

The job of the manager can be analyzed most conveniently if the work performed is broken out in terms of management categories; that is, planning, organizing, motivating, coordinating, and controlling. This arrangement has several advantages. It enables us to determine whether we have built into the job all important aspects of management responsibility. If the incumbent does not have the responsibility for developing his subordinates, he cannot be held to account for performing that work.

This approach also lends itself to development of *management* performance standards. Since the job is broken down in terms of management items, the yardstick used to measure it can most easily be developed in terms of management. Again, by identifying the *operating* work for which the manager is responsible, we can determine whether he has reserved work which might be delegated. A breakdown of the position of president in terms of management categories is shown below.

PRESIDENT

PURPOSE

As chief executive officer, to plan, organize, motivate, coordinate, and control the company as a whole to meet objectives established by the Board of Directors.

RESPONSIBILITIES

A. *Planning*

1. Maintains continuing study of the requirements of the business with respect to the development, manufacture, and marketing of its products and services and its relationships to employees, stockholders, and the public.
2. Recommends to the Board of Directors, and advises and assists in the development of over-all objectives, policies, programs, and budgets for the conduct of the company's business.
3. Interprets and explains the purposes and plans of the Board to managers and employees of the company, and the public at large, as appropriate.
4. Establishes and approves objectives for subordinate elements and provides for development of implementing plans in all units of the company.

B. *Organizing*

1. Develops and recommends to the Board of Directors a company plan of organization designed to facilitate growth and continuity in consonance with approved objectives and plans.
2. Provides for implementation, accomplishment, and control of the plan of organization in all units of the company.
3. Provides for continuing review and analysis of the plan of organization to achieve improved efficiency in management and operation.
4. Defines responsibility and authority of subordinate positions and establishes standards of accountability.
5. Establishes harmonious working relationships among all components of the organization.

C. *Coordinating*

1. Coordinates the activities of all elements of the company so as to maintain satisfactory progress toward approved objectives.
2. Ensures that operating units of the company receive adequate specialized advice and service from staff units and promotes cooperative effort between line and staff at all levels.

3. Coordinates the affairs and interests of the company with the demands of stockholders, employees, and the public, so as to provide for appropriate contribution to the interests of each while maintaining the integrity and momentum of the company's activities in all its aspects.

D. *Motivating*
1. Establishes and maintains a climate which stimulates and encourages maximum productivity on the part of all employees and managers of the company.
2. Provides for appropriate means of selecting, placing, compensating, and developing employees and managers and protecting their interests as individuals.
3. Establishes sound channels of communication among all levels and groups of employees and between the company, its shareholders, and the public.
4. Provides for participation in the affairs of the company by all levels and groups to the maximum extent practicable.
5. Appraises, counsels, and coaches immediate subordinates and provides for adequate succession to management positions.

E. *Controlling*
1. Establishes standards for evaluating the progress of the company and each of its components toward approved objectives.
2. Provides for continuing and accurate recording and reporting of the progress of the company toward its objectives.
3. Appraises and evaluates the operating results of the business and directs corrective action where required.
4. Reports the progress of the company to the Board of Directors, as required.

F. *Operating*
1. Directs the operations of the business so as to attain objectives within the scope of established policies.
2. Represents the company, when appropriate, and promotes good relations with customers, employees, stockholders, governmental agencies, suppliers, and the general public.
3. Signs, executes, and delivers in the name of the corporation such bonds, mortgages, deeds, contracts, and other instruments authorized in accordance with the bylaws of the company.

G. *Relationships*
1. Reports to: Board of Directors
2. Supervises: Chief Operating Officer
General Manager, Metals Division
General Manager, Wood Division
General Manager, Plastics Division
Director, Finance
Director, Personnel
Director, Manufacturing
Director, Marketing

THE ORGANIZATION MANUAL

The organizational manual is a repository for organization data commonly used by company managers. It has many values as an administrative tool to help the manager do his job more effectively. It enables him to visualize the company organization as a whole and to see his own responsibilities as part of the total picture. The position guides, which form the heart of the manual, spell out his responsibilities and the results for which he is held accountable. They also define the relationships which will guide him in developing teamwork and in working with other managers.

The organization manual should be made up as a permanent, hardcover, loose-leaf volume. Individual position guides and organization charts may be prepared by accountable managers, using a format prescribed by company procedures, or by the organization planning function *for* accountable managers. The manual itself should be maintained by the organization planning function.

Distribution

Each manager should be given the general material which is part of the manual, together with copies of the organization charts and position guides which relate to the organization component of which he is a part or for which he has accountability. Top managers and central specialized staff should have copies of the complete manual. The division top manager should have a copy of the complete company manual but his staff and functional heads should have only the divisional charts and position guides. The complete manual should be available for inspection within each department and division. Restriction of distribution in this manner minimizes the labor and expense of distributing changes and of keeping the manual up to date.

Contents of Manual

It is particularly important to include all pertinent material related directly to the company organization in the manual, so that managers at all levels can use it as a convenient source of reference. The manual should contain the following data:

1. *Statement of Company Objectives and Policies*

Major objectives and policies should be stated in the introductory section to the manual. Since the organization structure itself is predicated upon these statements, it is logical to place them before all managers accountable for developing and maintaining organization units.

Organization objectives and policies, in particular, should be spelled out. These state the company organization aims and specify those management decisions related to organization which are binding on all managers in the company.

Crown Zellerbach Corporation has stated the following company organization objectives:

1. To arrange functions so that personnel can perform their job most effectively.

2. To create an organization which will offer the greatest opportunity for individual development.

3. To organize each unit so that the corporation may take full advantage of growth and expansion opportunities.

Standard Oil Company of California states its company organization objective as follows: "To develop and maintain a sound and clear-cut plan of organization through which management can most easily and effectively direct and control the enterprise."

Organization policies which are to apply to all units of the organization are frequently stated as organization principles. An illustrative statement is that of the Atlantic Refining Company:

ORGANIZATION PRINCIPLES—ATLANTIC REFINING COMPANY

I. *Objectives*

The objectives of the enterprise must be defined.

A. Organization must distinguish between the principal and auxiliary objectives of administration in order to permit concentration of administrative efforts on the principal objective.

B. The organization should be built around the main functions of the business and not around an individual or group of individuals.

II. *Distribution of Functions*

The proper distribution of functions is a primary objective of organization planning.

A. Auxiliary functions which do not contribute directly to the main task and are performed mainly for one unit should be assigned to that unit. Assignment of such functions to another unit might result in ineffective performance since the unit primarily served would have no direct authority over the execution of the auxiliary functions.

B. Functions should be allocated so as to avoid duplicated or overlapping functions, the neglect of essential functions, and the overemphasis of subsidiary functions.

C. The organization structure should be kept as simple and economical as possible. Increasing the complexity of the organization structure

augments expense and makes effective coordination more difficult.
  D. The functions assigned to an organizational unit should be as
     homogeneous as practicable. Inherent nature of the work and simi-
     larity in technical knowledge or skills required are two of several
     criteria useful in determining homogeneity.
  E. Responsibilities are better performed by individuals than by groups.
     Individuals act while groups debate. Action depends upon decision,
     and decisions are made most expeditiously by individuals who rep-
     resent a single source of accountability.

III. *Responsibility and Authority*

Responsibilities and authorities must be defined and their interrelation-
ship established.
  A. Definitions of responsibility and authority should be clear and pre-
     cise. Failure to establish and implement such definitions leads to
     confusion, misunderstanding, and the warping of organization ac-
     cording to personalities.
  B. Authority and responsibility must correspond. To hold an individual
     accountable for activity of any kind without assigning to him the
     necessary authority to discharge the responsibility is unsatisfactory
     and inequitable.
  C. Authority to take or initiate action should be so placed as to per-
     mit the great bulk of routine decisions to be made at lower levels,
     with only exceptional matters to be decided by higher levels.

IV. *Delegation*

Delegation is an essential feature of sound organization.
  A. No organization can function effectively without delegation. Lack
     of courage to delegate properly and of knowledge of how to dele-
     gate is one of the most general causes of failure in organization.
  B. Organization must distinguish between planning, doing, and con-
     trolling as phases of administration and, of these three, doing is the
     most adaptable to delegation.
  C. Less important duties should be delegated and those of greater im-
     portance reserved.
  D. The chain of delegation should be as short as practicable. The
     longer the chain, the more time is consumed in reaching decisions
     and the greater the cost in reduced effectiveness and unproductively
     employed manpower.
  E. Means should be provided for furnishing qualified replacements for
     all positions. Delegation of authority and responsibility is an effec-
     tive means of training and testing personnel for higher levels of
     supervision.

V. *Supervision*

There are limitations on the supervisor.
  A. An executive should not have reporting to him, directly, more than

five (or at the most six) subordinate executives whose duties overlap or are interrelated.

B. Supervision of an individual should be exercised only by one immediate superior.

VI. *Control*

Increased delegation necessitates increased control.

A. Provision must be made for adequate control. Since an executive does not relinquish accountability upon delegation, means must be provided for keeping him informed concerning the manner of performance of the responsibilities he has delegated.

2. *Glossary of Terms*

To establish a common nomenclature for administrative terms used in the manual, it is advisable to establish a glossary of management terms. The following listing defines words most commonly used, consistent with the concepts and principles outlined in this volume.

GLOSSARY OF TERMS USED IN EXECUTIVE RESPONSIBILITY STATEMENTS

Accountability. The obligation to carry out responsibility and exercise authority in conformance with designated standards.

Administration. The total activity of the manager. It includes the work of planning, organizing, motivating, coordinating, controlling, and operating.

Analyze. To divide a complex whole into its constituents. Analysis involves study and examination of something complex and the separation of its more simple components.

Approve. To accept as satisfactory. Approval implies that the thing approved has the endorsement of the approving agency; however, approval may still require confirmation by somebody else. A manager approves plans subject to authorization by the accountable executive.

Assist. To help by providing advice and service. Assistance involves providing aid without exercise of command authority. For example, the personnel manager assists the president.

Assistant. Personal staff position.

Authority. Powers or rights delegated to or assumed by a person for the purpose of performing work.

Authorize. To give final approval. This implies final endorsement, such that no further approval is necessary. Thus, the president approves, the Board of Directors authorizes, over-all company objectives.

Budget. An estimate for use. A budget is an estimate of the number of units of money, time, materials, and so forth that will be required to accomplish specified plans.

Chief executive. The *individual* position that has accountability for the over-all management and operation of the enterprise as a whole. The Board of Directors, which is a committee, is superior in position to the chief executive.

Collaborate. To work together. Collaboration involves two or more people cooperating to produce a joint end product. It implies that no member of the group exercises command over the others. Collaboration implies equality in relationship. For example, the production control manager and the production superintendent collaborate to develop a production schedule.

Committee. A body of persons appointed or elected to meet on an organized basis for the consideration of matters brought before it. Since it must be an organized body, a committee must have objectives; it must have defined responsibility and authority and specified relationships with the individuals and groups with whom it deals.

Control. The evaluation of work after it is performed, in terms of predetermined standards. Control involves the establishment of performance standards, the measurement of work by recording and reporting, the evaluation of actual performance against the standard, and the institution of corrective action in terms of exceptions or variances.

Coordinate. To time, unify, and integrate work as it takes place. Coordination refers to the activities the manager undertakes to ensure that different kinds of work, or work performed by different people, proceed harmoniously and in balance toward the desired end result.

Decentralization. The systematic and consistent delegation of authority to the levels at which work is performed.

Delegate. To entrust to another the performance of responsibility or the exercise of authority.

Develop. To build by successive additions. Development refers to the process followed in creating plans and ideas by pooling the suggestions of many people, or in building by increments from a simple beginning.

Direct. To command. Direction implies giving orders that will require another person to do something. Direction implies authority, and, hence the power to invoke sanctions in case of disobedience. A manager directs that action be taken. This direction may be by letter, telephone, at firsthand, or farther removed. *Supervision* denotes one kind of direction, that is, personal direction.

Enterprise. Organized endeavor.

Executive. A manager in the higher levels of the organization. The specific level is a matter for arbitrary determination. The term "manager" is to be preferred.

Function. The total of positions encompassing one kind of work grouped to form an administrative unit.

Initiate. To begin something. Initiation refers to the first act that gets a series or sequence of events under way. For example, a manager initiates plans by putting a subordinate to work developing a program or budget.

Interpret. To explain the meaning of. Interpretation involves telling people what something means in terms of their interest and needs. A policy is interpreted when its meaning is clarified and applied to the situation or condition prevailing in a specific unit.

Leadership. Guidance and direction of the work of others.

Line. A relationship involving command authority with respect to end results. The "line" elements of the organization are those which have responsibility and authority for accomplishments of the primary objectives, or end results, of the organization.

Maintain. To keep in effective condition. Maintenance refers to the work necessary to keep something in a satisfactory condition. An organization is maintained by being kept in sound operating condition.

Manager. One who plans, organizes, motivates, coordinates, and controls the work of other people.

Motivate. To inspire, impel, and encourage action. Motivation encompasses all the actions undertaken by a leader to encourage highest productivity in those he leads. It includes selection, placement, compensation, communication, participation, and development.

Objective. Goal or purpose toward which work is directed.

Organization. The process of identifying and grouping the work to be done, defining and delegating responsibility and authority, and establishing relationships to accomplish objectives.

Perform. To carry out work. Performance refers to the process of accomplishing work to the point at which it is ready for measurement or evaluation. Performance implies continuing activity or observation until a designated end point is reached. A manager performs a function by working at it constantly. Performance can be accomplished in part by delegation.

Plan. A proposal designed to guide and direct work to be performed. Plans consist of five major elements: objectives, policies, programs, schedules, and budgets.

Policy. A standing decision to guide repetitive action. Policies are binding upon all parts of the organization to which they apply.

Position. Work grouped for performance by one individual.

Prepare. To make ready for use. The process of getting something ready for presentation or final use. For example, a policy is developed, then prepared in written form to present to management.

Prescribe. To direct specified action. This implies that action must be carried out in a specified fashion. A manager may prescribe on his own authority or through derived authority from a superior. When authority is derived, the source should be stated.

Procedure. A prescribed way of performing specified work.

Program. A sequence of action designed to accomplish a specific objective.

Recommend. To offer or suggest for use. Recommendation describes the presentation of plans, ideas, or things to others for adoption.

Reserved responsibility. That portion of a manager's work that he performs himself and does not delegate.

Responsibility. The work assigned to a position.

Review. To examine critically. Review implies close scrutiny of something to determine its suitability or accuracy. For instance, a program is reviewed preparatory to approval or authorization.

Schedule. A time sequence for the accomplishment of specified work.

Span of supervision. The number of people supervised by a manager.

Staff. A relationship which involves one position or element of the organization providing advice and service to another position or element. "Staff" elements of the organization have a predominantly advisory and service role.

Staff, personal. Positions created for the purpose of providing advice and service to one principal.

Staff, specialized. Positions or organizational elements created for the purpose of providing advice and service in one functional area, such as finance or personnel, to all appropriate management positions.

Supervise. To direct personally. A supervisor exercises leadership by overseeing the activities of others in person. Supervision implies that the people supervised report directly to the person doing the supervision.

Work. Physical and mental effort.

3. *Organization Procedures*

What standard methods will the company require of all managers in organization matters? What organization work must be done the same in all units so that it will fit the pattern of over-all company organization activity? Organization procedures prescribe such uniformity. They may be prepared to include such matters as reporting organization changes and similar matters.

Reporting Organization Changes. If effective organization control is to be maintained, there should be clear channels for reporting organization changes. In most cases, changes should be approved by the accountable manager but cleared through the organization planning specialized staff or other staff unit to ensure coordination and distribution of change notices. The procedure maintained by Koppers Company, Inc., outlines such an approach.

KOPPERS COMPANY, INC.

REVISIONS TO COMPANY ORGANIZATION MANUAL

GENERAL:

The company Organization Manual deals with the company's organizational structure and key positions in each of the major units of the organization. The following points relating to each of these key positions are covered:

1. Basic Function
2. Scope
3. Duties and Responsibilities
4. Method of Measurement
5. Relationships with Other Units of Organization
6. Limits of Authority

In order to be of maximum value, it is necessary that the Organization Manual reflect the current status at all times. To this end all general managers and managers are expected to comply with the procedure outlined below.

PROCEDURE:

1. Continuous review should be made by the general manager concerned, by the unit's Control Section, or by an individual assigned this duty,

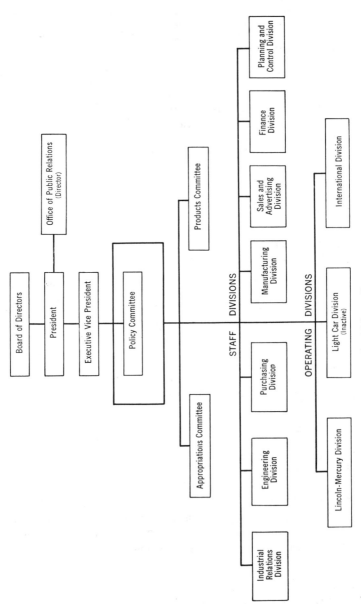

Figure 13–4. Organization Structure, August, 1946, Ford Motor Company

to determine where current organization practice varies from that described in the manual. In addition, the entire organization unit should be reviewed at least quarterly to assure complete coverage.

2. Where such review indicates the necessity of revision to reflect current status or whenever changes being made will result in the organization structure, limits of authority, or personnel differing from those portrayed in the manual, the following steps should be taken, as applicable:

   a. Prepare a job specification for new key positions not covered by the manual, following the form used for other positions.

   b. Prepare revised job specifications for existing positions affected. Such material should refer to the original job specification number. It is not necessary to rewrite paragraphs or sections which are not to be revised.

   c. New or revised job specifications should be approved by all intermediate supervisors and managers, and by the general manager or manager concerned.

   d. Prepare revised organization chart.

   e. Prepare revised limits of authority for all new or revised jobs.

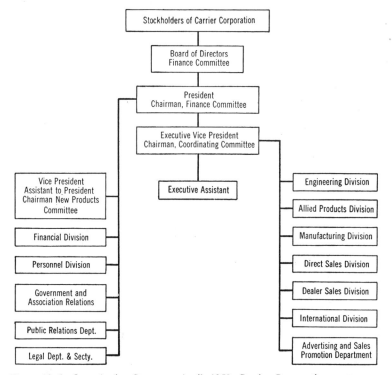

Figure 13–5. Organization Structure, April, 1952, Carrier Corporation

f. Prepare current index listing names of the personnel in each position covered in the manual.

3. All such material should be forwarded to the Central Staff Control Section for review and editing. All changes will be returned to the originating organization for approval before publication of new or revised sheets to the manual.

4. When new or revised sheets are received, they should be distributed to all employees holding the manual, who should place them in the manual, removing and destroying obsolete sheets.

ORGANIZATION ANALYSIS AS BASIS FOR CHANGE

When the data secured by organization analysis are collected and analyzed, they present a graphic picture of the current status of the organization. This becomes the basis for determining the need for change. Illustrative is the organization chart showing the status of Ford Motor Company after organization analysis in August, 1946 (Figure 13–4, page 304).

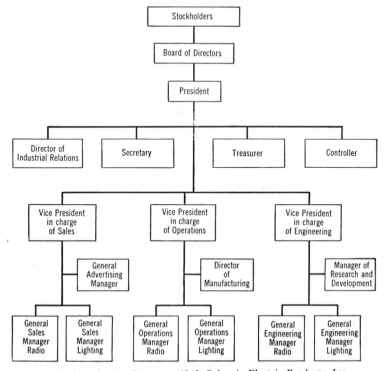

Figure 13–6. Organization Structure, 1943, Sylvania Electric Products, Inc.

Illustrative also is the chart for Carrier Corporation (Figure 13–5, page 305) showing its organization in April, 1952, after organization analysis.

A simplified organization chart for Sylvania Electric Products, Inc. (Figure 13–6), shows the organization after analysis in 1943, before divisionalization and decentralization were undertaken.

SUMMARY

Objectives are first developed in the process of organization change, then the existing organization is portrayed and inventoried by means of organization analysis. This involves first securing basic data about the organization by means of an interview technique involving responsibility and authority analysis. Organization charts, position guides, and an organization manual are then prepared to formalize and codify the data collected.

CHAPTER 14 *Dynamics of Change*

With the objectives prepared and the analysis of the existing organization completed, the company is in position to prepare an ideal plan. Then need for change is determined. Once the general dimensions of the required change are known, a systematic procedure can be undertaken to implement it. This involves, whenever possible, first trying out the change in a pilot run. Then phase plans are prepared which will carry the organization toward the desired end result, but which will, at the same time, make full provision for overcoming the resistance that is certain to develop on the part of the people involved.

PREPARE AN IDEAL PLAN

Before reorganization is undertaken, management should establish what kind of organization it will need to reach the administrative goals it has set for itself. What type of structure is best suited to the requirements of the business? What kinds of work must be performed? These questions can best be answered by preparation of the ideal or master organization plan

The ideal plan has several valuable purposes in organization planning. Representing, as it does, the structure toward which the company will work over a period of perhaps five or more years, the plan serves as a guide for all organization changes. When temporary deviations are necessary because of unforeseen contingencies, personality difficulties, or other factors, the long-range ideal plan provides an objective, carefully formulated constant to which such changes can be related. United Air Lines reflects the best current thinking when it says, "The purpose of the long-range plan is to establish the ideal organization to fit conditions expected at some future date. It is generally recognized that this ideal organization will probably never actually be effected, but it does help establish policies and philosophies which will serve as guides in making of short-term studies."

There is an increasing awareness of the need for preparation of an ideal plan before reorganization proceeds. Where this is not done, the company tends to extemporize its organization. New functions are added, old ones are changed, new products and even companies are added to the organization with consideration only of the immediate profit objectives. This results in a haphazard organization. Where growth occurs successfully, careful thought is first given to the development of an ideal structure adapted to the long-term changes envisaged. Then the new products, operations, markets, and people can be fitted into one consistent pattern and will not be successive grafts onto a questionable basic structure.

Organization changes in components and subordinate departments of the company should also be planned with reference to the ideal plan. The Atlantic Refining Company finds that the ideal plan provides a reliable guide to subordinate elements that might otherwise be required to check with the central office each time a minor change is made. The master plan provides both the pattern for such changes and a yardstick as to their effectiveness.

Advantages of Ideal Plan

Preparation of a master plan facilitates the administration of change. It enables the company to anticipate the breakup of social groups and to provide for participation and communication of the people who will be affected by each move. Because moves are *planned* and not haphazard, it is possible to commit capital funds better and to keep administrative expense at a minimum. One company with a large functional, centralized organization, for example, built a new headquarters building to house the top management group and all the centralized departments. Within five years the company grew so large that it found it necessary to decentralize on a product division basis. As the company attempted to decentralize to its divisions, it became necessary to separate the company and division headquarters groups from the plants and operating units. After trying many makeshift alternatives, it finally set up the headquarters units in a city 15 miles distant and leased the plant-site office facilities to another company.

Coordination of organization changes with related administrative activities is facilitated by use of an ideal plan. Two departments making complementary changes can coordinate their efforts best if both are proceeding according to the same master plan. For instance, one New Jersey company manufacturing household utensils added several new product lines which involved a good deal of door-to-door selling. This called for retraining of the existing sales force. Since the usual "apprentice" system followed in the company was too time-consuming, it decided to form a sales training unit. For almost three months the sales department tried to find a sales training manager. ⁻Finally, the sales manager, on a visit to one of the company's plants, discovered that the plant and division training functions had been combined and a highly qualified training man was about to be let go. The problem was solved, but with proper use of an ideal plan it need never have arisen.

The ideal organization plan is indispensable to long-term development of managers. Only if we know what positions will exist at a future period can we determine how many and what kind of managers we will need to fill them. By anticipating the programed growth of the business, the ideal organization plan makes possible systematic rotation and planned advancement of managers to positions of increasing difficulty and importance.

When personnel changes can be planned systematically, it is possible to identify those jobs for which understudies should be provided so that outsiders will not have to be brought in to fill the vacancies. Manpower planning such as this helps to maintain high quality of personnel and to minimize the expense involved in training. It also promotes morale by providing for promotion from within.

A West Coast aircraft company divisionalized on a geographic basis. The move called for the creation of four new divisional jobs for industrial engineers and the elimination of three tool engineers from the functional manufacturing department. Over a year's time, two of the three tool engineers were able to prepare themselves for positions as division industrial engineers by attendance at night sessions at a nearby university and by taking correspondence courses.

The perennial problems of building pools of specialized skills within the company and of hiring new college graduates are also greatly simplified if a master organization plan is employed. One large product-division company, for example, developed a master organization plan calling for a 10 per cent increase in the total number of management positions to be filled in five years. Instead of waiting and haphazardly trying to fill each position from within or paying premium wages for outside talent, the company calculated a reasonable turnover and mortality figure and increased its college graduate quota by approximately 5 per cent for each of four years. As each new position was created, the company promoted from within and took up the slack all down the line with smoothness and dispatch.

Possible Hazards

The ideal plan approach to organization change is by no means foolproof. Inherent in it are all the potential disadvantages of any type of prognostication. In actuality, the ideal plan is a form of organizational long-range planning. To the extent that the future is unpredictable, the master plan may be subjected to unusual influences which make it inadequate. A large airplane company, for example, predicated a 20 per cent expansion on a government contract for piston engine aircraft. It established a master plan calling for geographic divisionalization and segmentation of its large and unwieldy engineering force. Introduction of a new type of jet by a competitor resulted in drastic modification of the company's plans. The ideal plan was vitiated by a decision to hold the entire engineering force together on a functional basis so that the company could develop its own jet design.

There is a tendency also for a definite, written plan to discourage flexibility and initiative. Since money and effort are already committed to the master plan, the interests vested in it will resist modification. This is natural and to be expected. However, the potential disadvantages of the master plan approach are far less than the danger of undertaking organization change without a course charted and with no clear goal in sight.

Objectivity in Preparation

Perhaps the most difficult aspect of preparing the ideal organization plan is that of examining the long-term goals and needs of the company with perspective and objectivity. The tendency is to project into the future the personalities and problems that now beset the organization. This inevitably colors the master organization plan, carrying bodily over to it some of the deficiencies the company currently suffers.

The master organization plan can be objective only if certain precautions are observed in the steps of preparation. Most important is the need to ignore existing individuals and personalities now holding positions in the organization. The master organization plan must be designed for normal individuals with customary aggregations of personality traits and skills. However, it should not be patterned around individual personalities now on the roster. Will planning then not become an academic exercise? How can impracticality be avoided? The phase plans later described will make full provision for accommodating individual personalities.

To as great an extent as possible, the existing organization—its peculiarities and deficiencies—should also be ignored. The fact that a functional organization is working exceedingly well today should not be permitted to color the requirements of the business five years hence. Because a project type engineering organization is impractical today is no reason why it might not be most appropriate with different or expanded engineering, manufacturing, and marketing objectives and policies or other suitable modification of its structure.

Ideal Organization Chart

The ideal organization structure is formalized and recorded by preparation of organization charts. The master chart may be only a rough sketch kept locked in the president's safe. Or it may be a fully detailed document spelling out the organization of the company as a whole and each of its major functions and divisions. The method of choice will depend upon circumstances. If the company is firmly committed to change and has budgeted or spent capital funds for plant and equipment and has programed intermediate moves, a detailed master plan is a necessity. As a general rule, the more deeply the company is committed to the move and the closer it comes to implementation, the more specific the master plan should become.

Ford Motor Company. A classical example of long-term master planning is that of the Ford Motor Company. By 1946, Ford had completely outgrown its functional organization and its method of management. It was highly centralized; practically all decisions were made by a small group in the central office under Henry Ford. This group was both staff and line. It did the planning and ran the plants. There were no budgetary controls of any kind; in fact, it was impossible to tell which operations were losing money and which were profitable. At that time Ford had assets of around $800 million. The company was rapidly going bankrupt, but it had the distinction of being larger than any other company that had so far outgrown its organization.

When Henry Ford II took over the company in 1946, he brought in Ernest R. Breech. With organization and staffing the first plank in their program, they undertook divisionalization and decentralization as well as improvement of every phase of the company's administration. The net result is the most magnificent comeback recorded in business history.

Ford was forced to make organization changes and to make them fast. The key problem was to outline the company's organization requirements. What were the over-all objectives the company was trying to accomplish? What principles should be followed? What work should be done? Ford developed an over-all master plan to guide its reorganization. It knew that immediate changes would not approach the ultimate, but it wanted to be sure that each organization change would help carry it that much closer to the idea. A close approximation of the ideal plan for Ford's divisionalization is shown in Figure 14–1.[1] Here a clean break is made between line and staff. The operating divisions

---

[1] The grouping of the car and truck divisions shown is a later modification and has since been further changed. The Lincoln and Continental Divisions were combined, and an Edsel Division created. A later regrouping left the Ford Division separate, but combined all other cars in a second major product division.

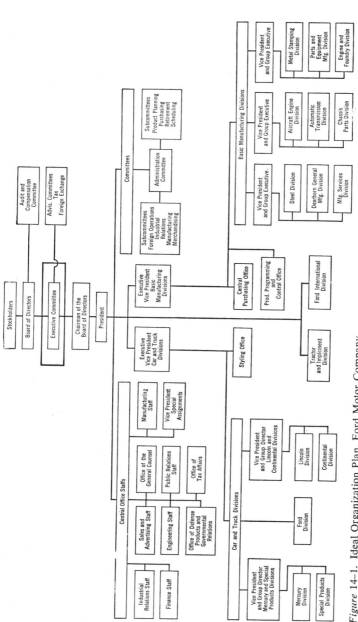

Figure 14-1. Ideal Organization Plan, Ford Motor Company

are broken out. Each is grouped for most efficient administration. A well-integrated committee structure is provided and the chief executive function is divided into manageable proportions.

Carrier Corporation. The planning which led to development of the long-term ideal organization plan for Carrier Corporation has already been described. The ideal plan developed for the company's divisionalization and decentralization in 1952 (Figure 14–2) shows the company's ultimate intention of providing for well-balanced, integrated operations in the product divisions, division of the total burden of administration among three top executive positions, and appropriate supporting staff for each major component of the company.

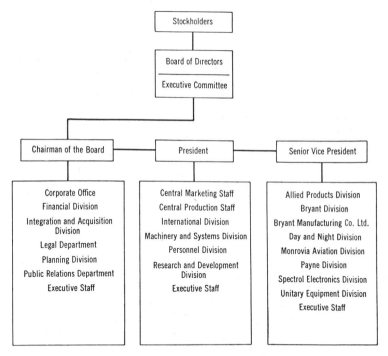

Figure 14–2. Ideal Organization Plan, Carrier Corporation

Sylvania Electric Products, Inc. The process followed by Sylvania Electric in deciding to reorganize has already been described. Sylvania's long-range plan is shown in Figure 14–3. Here we see a clear-cut divisionalization implemented on a product basis. Each division was designed to operate on a highly decentralized basis right down to the plant level. In fact, every plant manager was placed in competition with every other plant manager on productivity and cost, as measured in

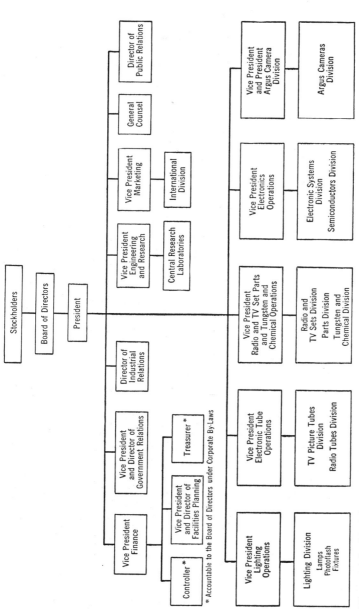

Figure 14-3. Ideal Organization Plan, Sylvania Electric Products, Inc.

terms of standard costs, relation of cost to selling price, and return on investment.

The product divisions, in turn, were established as profit centers within the limits of over-all objectives and policies. A central headquarters group of staff specialists was created to work with the line divisions, providing advice, service, coordination, and control.

TRY OUT THE PLAN

Should the company commit itself irretrievably to a major organization change before it knows whether the plan will work successfully in practice? It is obviously wise to pretest the final plan before large commitments are made. A pilot run of the new organization can usually be made by implementing the change in just one unit of the organization. For example, if a functional organization is to be changed to product or geographic divisions, a single product or geographic division can first be established and its operation carefully observed. Difficulties in administration of the change and deficiencies in the resulting structure can be identified and corrected before the over-all change is attempted.

Carrier Corporation, anticipating a move to product divisionalization, first established the Allied Products Division as an experimental operation in 1950. The engineering, manufacture, and sale of two product lines were turned over to this division, and it was held accountable for profit and loss. Profiting from this experience, Carrier was able to plan a major reorganization in 1953 with success.

Nationwide Insurance was faced with the need to reorganize because of its mushrooming growth during the postwar period. A planning committee directed by one of the senior executives reached a tentative decision that geographical divisionalization and accompanying decentralization were indicated. Before committing the company as a whole to this long-range pattern, a pilot study was made to determine its feasibility. Two pilot regional groups were established and their operation carefully studied. Once the company had learned how to organize these experimental groups, it proceeded with the establishment of the fifteen divisions.

PREPARE PHASE PLANS

After the potential pitfalls have been identified through a pilot operation, the company can install the over-all changes with assurance. We now must bridge the gap between the existing organization and the ideal organization we have set up as a goal. This transition is accomplished by the use of phase plans. These are intermediate organization steps, designed to implement the organization objectives as quickly and effectively as possible.

Consider Personalities

The phase plans should take into full account the individual personalities now in organization positions. They should be designed in terms of people. The goal now is to make fullest possible use of human assets by training, developing, upgrading, and promoting. If the phasing of the organization is to be successful, it is imperative that it proceed in terms of an over-all plan of management appraisal and development. To leave this aspect to chance or to neglect to provide for the maximum utilization of people who have already given faithful service to the organization is shortsighted.

Phase plans may require temporary deviations from the master plan to accommodate individuals with special combinations of skills or who have a special place in the organization. However, every such digression should be temporary. It should lead inevitably to the over-all pattern established by the ideal organization plan.

Phase plans can most effectively be integrated with personnel changes. When people are transferred, promoted, retired, or terminated, this should be made the occasion for organization changes.

As a general rule, reorganization should not result in loss of pay to individuals affected; nor, so far as possible, in demotion or loss of position. In some cases individuals cannot be accommodated within the confines of the phase plans and special provision has to be made for them. One large multiplant company which reorganized found that the functional manufacturing and engineering heads were too highly specialized to be entrusted with the general management of the newly formed divisions. Since both men were highly proficient technically, phase plans were developed to include two special consultant positions, both reporting to the chief executive. Both men held these positions for several years, until they retired. During this interval, both were able to make valuable contributions to the company because of their contacts and the special skills and experience they possessed. When they retired, the positions were abolished, without disturbing the structure.

Phase plans undertaken by Ford Motor Company, Carrier Corporation, and Sylvania Electric Products, Inc., illustrate the planned move from a carefully inventoried base toward a long-range ideal organization plan.

Ford Motor Company Phase Plan. One of the first phases of the Ford reorganization is shown in Figure 14–4, page 318. Before the reorganization in Ford, the huge Rouge River plant had been operated as one

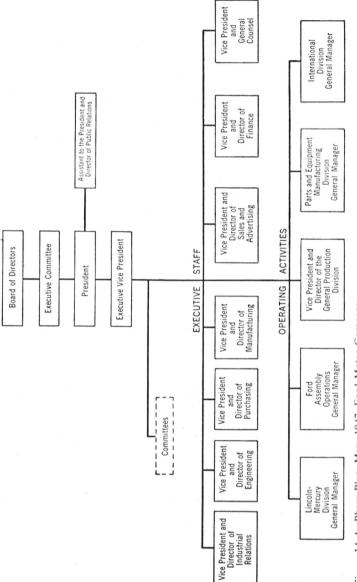

Figure 14-4. Phase Plan, May, 1947 Ford Motor Company

plant by the central office manufacturing staff. In the phase plan shown, the manufacturing operations were broken out as line activities with the formation of the General Production Division, the Parts and Equipment Division, and Ford Assembly Operations.

Phase by phase, the General Production Division was broken down into Rouge Automotive Manufacturing Operations. Then the General Production Division was separated into the Rouge Division and the General Manufacturing Division, bringing the Motor Plant under the management of Automotive Manufacturing Operations as part of the Rouge Division. As each division was set up, it was provided with the management tools it needed. Staff activities were organized for production programing and control, industrial relations, and finance.

Phasing in again, the manufacturing activities were further broken down into manufacturing groups. Each group was made up of a number of closely related product divisions.

Other changes were also phased in. The Policy Committee, which had been overwhelmed with the task of initial review of every major

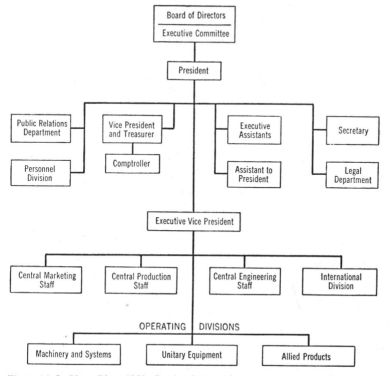

Figure 14–5. Phase Plan, 1953, Carrier Corporation

problem submitted to top management, was broken up. Appropriations and Product Committees were first established; later, the integrated committee system shown on the final Ford chart.

Carrier Phase Plan. In Figure 14–5, page 319, we see one of the phase plans which enabled Carrier Corporation to accomplish its divisionalization successfully. Here we have three primary divisional groups broken out. The Allied Products Division, which had been divisionalized on a pilot basis in 1950, was joined by the Machinery and Systems and Unitary Equipment Divisions. The three divisions are each accountable for their share of the total business. They handle their own development and design, factory engineering, purchasing, manufacturing, quality con-

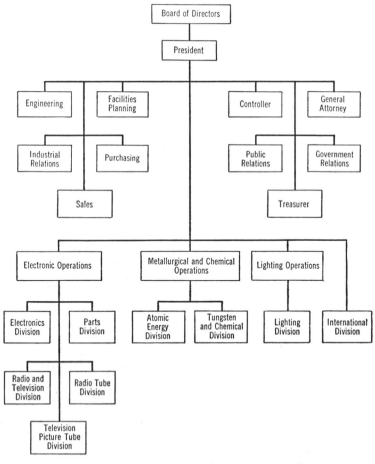

Figure 14–6. Phase Plan, May, 1953, Sylvania Electric Products, Inc.

trol, accounting, and distribution. Three staff divisions, in production, marketing, and engineering, report to the executive vice president. The burden on the chief executive has been lightened by having the head of each operating group report to the executive vice president, who becomes chief operating officer. This leaves the president, as chief executive, free for over-all planning and control in the key aspects of the company's business.

Sylvania Electric Products, Inc., Phase Plan. In carrying out its divisionalization, Sylvania provided one phase step involving formation of three major product groups: Electronics, Metallurgical and Chemical, and Lighting Operations (Figure 14–6). Corporate specialized staff groups were organized to provide advice and service in the establishment of over-all policy to guide the operations of the product groups and divisions.

ESTABLISH UNIFORM NOMENCLATURE

A consistent and systematic system of nomenclature should be developed for naming positions and elements within the organization. Haphazard title structures are the rule, rather than the exception; as a result, many a company has "supervisors" at the head of a sales crew in one district, "managers" and even "directors" in others. When localized and restricted, this probably does little harm. However, as soon as these inconsistencies come into opposition, either by reason of salary, status, transfers, or organizational level, friction is certain to ensue.

To illustrate: In one national service firm, every person having contact with the public is called an "Executive Manager." Some are paid $7,500 annually. Others go as high as $25,000. Although these designations are supposed to give prestige to the individuals and encourage public confidence, they have almost the opposite effect. Some Executive Managers are highly specialized experts; others are amateurs. Although the firm's clients may be taken in by an inexperienced Executive Manager title the first time, they are not likely to make the mistake twice. Inside the firm, there is great resentment among the higher salaried specialists because the method of designation belittles and cheapens their status.

In another firm, which has grown to a leading position in its industry, there is a haphazard method of titling that also causes much confusion. On the same specialized staff level is a manager of personnel, a director of purchases, and a supervisor of traffic. The operating divisions of the company are headed by a Division General Manager, a Divisional Vice President, and a President. Although there are logical personal and historical reasons for these titles, the confusion they cause gives little justification for their continuance.

Titles are among the least expensive and most effective means of affording personal recognition and establishing some degree of consistency among levels of the organization. From an organizational point of view, if consistent titles are used and if definite relationships are established among titles, the company will benefit in many ways: A title can be made to indicate the kinds of work a person does, his approximate level and degree of authority, and the organization component to which he belongs. The title "director," for example, can be reserved for staff positions; that of "manager" for line. If a proper sequence is established, a "foreman" will always be at a lower organizational level than a "superintendent."

Dangers

The system of nomenclature adopted must not be too rigid or it will create difficulties. When the organization grows and new levels or kinds of positions are to be added these become apparent. In one company, for example, a system was adopted that called for all management positions in salary levels from $10,000 to $14,000 to be called "managers"; those at $6,000 to $10,000, "administrators"; and those up to $6,000, "supervisors." Several years after the scheme was put into effect, the company found itself paying $11,000 for graduate engineers who had once been available for $4,000. In some cases the equivalent existing management positions were still being paid at the rate of $7,500 to $8,500. The first attempt to have a newly hired "manager" report to one of the established "administrator" positions led to abandonment of the system.

Various Types of Titles

Effective use of a system of nomenclature requires recognition of the difference between external or "public relations" titles, organizational titles, official titles, and job evaluation titles.

Public Titles. Special titles often are developed for the express purpose of stimulating or creating public recognition and respect for employees who deal outside the company. A potential customer prefers to be referred to an "assistant vice president" rather than to a "supervisor" or a "claims specialist." Public titles, when used in addition to an established organizational system of nomenclature, may be extremely confusing. The best alternative is to design the organizational system so that the titles used have sufficient dignity and status to serve both externally and internally. Certainly there is little point in "dressing up" an employee for the public if his title in the company is not comparable.

Organizational Titles. These are the names used on the organization chart, in company communications, and in position guides. This set of titles should be sufficiently flexible to serve the ordinary needs of the business. They should differentiate organizational levels and major relationships.

Job Evaluation Titles. A system of occupational titles is sometimes developed for use in classifying people for pay purposes. Usually this antedates organizational nomenclature and, as a result, is sometimes forcibly adapted to organizational use. This is rarely desirable. The better alternative is to use for compensation a nomenclature based on grades or classes of functions and not attempt to relate this directly to organizational nomenclature; for example, Class 1, Production, Class 2, Production, and so forth; or Grade 6, Finance, Grade 7, Finance. If there is need to relate an organizational title to a job classification, ·this can easily be done by combining the two titles as required; for example, Grade 6, Finance (Supervisor, Budget Section).

Official Titles. Officers of the corporation may carry official titles because they have responsibility or authority for corporate duties over and above the work assigned to them in their organizational positions. A vice president may have corporate obligations or liabilities which are assigned to him because he is a vice president and not because he is controller or production manager. Official titles should not be used *in place of* organizational titles unless it is certain that the incumbent of a position will always bear the official as well as the organizational title. To illustrate: The bylaws may require that the finance manager always be a vice president. In this case, the title Vice President, Finance would be appropriate and meaningful. If this were not true, it would be better to call the finance head Director of Finance and, if he was also a vice president, Vice President and Director of Finance. Thus, consistent titling would be possible.

A suggested title structure follows. This differentiates among levels by incorporating the name of the component in the title. Director, Corporate Finance is obviously higher in the organization than Manager, Division Finance. Differences as to function are recognized by use of the appropriate functional or specialty title; for example, Division Purchasing Agent, Plant Purchasing Agent.

DEVELOP COROLLARY PERSONNEL PROGRAMS

As we have seen, organization is part of the total administrative task of the manager. To be effective, reorganization must anticipate and provide for such corollary personnel activities as staffing and salary administration. As organization changes are effected, people must be

Title Structure   *Divisionalized Organization*

Position title	Component title	Function
Board Director	Board of Directors	Member of Board of Directors
President	Chief Executive Office	Chief executive officer of company
Executive Vice President–Operations	Chief Executive Office	Chief operating officer
Executive Vice President–Staff	Chief Executive Office	Chief staff officer
Director Corporate Finance (or other staff) Department (or as appropriate)	Finance (or other staff) Department	Head of corporate specialized staff department
Vice President and Director, Corporate Finance Department (or use specialty titles)		
Corporate Controller	Finance Department	Controller
Corporate Treasurer	Finance Department	Treasurer
Group General Manager	Operating Group	Head of two or more operating divisions grouped for administrative purposes
Division General Manager	Operating Division	Head of a production or geographic division
Manager, Division Finance (or other staff) Department	Division Finance (or other staff) Department	Head of divisional specialized staff department
Works Manager	Works	Head of two or more plants grouped together for administrative purposes
Plant Manager	Plant	Head of a plant
Manager, Plant Personnel (or other staff) Department	Plant Personnel (or other staff) Department	Head of plant personnel (or other staff) Department
Manager, Plant Production (or other line) Department	Plant Production (or other line) Department	Head of department

found to fill the positions created and to assume new responsibilities and authorities. As we have noted, this requires the initiation of a comprehensive program of appraisal, counseling, coaching, and training to ensure that managers are developed to perform with greatest efficiency in their existing positions and to be prepared for promotion.

A sound program of personnel selection should accompany that for development. Unless people with proper basic qualifications as to training, experience, and personality are brought into the company, it will be difficult and expensive to develop the manpower resources required. Special attention should be paid to selecting people with specialized skills for staff positions. One of the predominant needs after reorganization is likely to be for highly skilled people who can act as internal consultants, helping to upgrade existing skills and to provide the advanced thinking needed for the improvement of performance and profit potential.

Provision should also be made for development of a comprehensive system of salary administration. The newly established organization provides a logical basis for institution of such a system. Analysis of positions, balancing of work assignments, and elimination of overlap and duplication by organizational means will provide an excellent base for institution of a sound job evaluation and salary administration program.

OVERCOME RESISTANCE TO CHANGE

"There is nothing more difficult of success, nor more dangerous to handle, than to initiate a new order of things," said Machiavelli some five hundred years ago.[2] The truth of this is forcibly brought home to the manager attempting to put into effect an organization change. Planning an effective strategy for reorganization involves recognition that there are two phases to the process. First is the design of the structure itself; second is the movement and rearrangement of the people involved. When both phases are properly integrated and effectively implemented. reorganization can have many far-reaching benefits for the enterprise. If one or both are improperly handled, however, the repercussions are likely to be immediate and troublesome. The greatest difficulty and danger lie in overcoming resistance of the people who will be affected by the organization change.

Reorganization can be a highly disruptive force. Need for change may be recognized only at the height of crisis. Sweeping reforms may be initiated, new methods introduced, and many new managers hired. People are torn from their long-established social groupings. Fre-

[2] Niccolo Machiavelli, *The Prince*, New American Library, New York, 1952, p. 55.

quently demotions and discharges take place. The net result is fear, insecurity, discontent, and diminished efficiency.

A large Eastern manufacturing company undertook an organization survey in an attempt to identify the reason for a slackening of sales and profit. Over a period of several months a crew of analysts visited the plants and offices of the company, studying operations, questioning managers, and investigating reports and records. It was obvious to everybody that a major study was under way and that it was being directed from top management. The grapevine was soon loaded with rumors: a merger was in the offing, a large stockholder was trying to wrest control from the incumbent management, a major economy drive was under way. Uneasiness spread. A gradual increase in turnover of younger managers occurred; absence and tardiness became more noticeable.

The survey findings pointed to need for change from a functional to a divisionalized form of organization, with many far-reaching administrative modifications. The change-over was completed, physically, within a few months. Over one hundred people, including many managers, were given two weeks' notice because their talents and personalities were not right for the new organization. Mechanically, the change was well planned. It went off smoothly, with no stoppage in production. Psychologically, however, it almost wrecked the company. Turnover in all ranks went up sharply as people began to look for more secure berths; the union became recalcitrant; efficiency dropped. Instead of improving, as the technical excellence of the reorganization plan promised, production and profits continued to deteriorate. The climax saw two of the top officers of the company joining the job seekers, while a new chief executive was brought in. It took him almost five years to bring the company back, motivationally as well as organizationally.

Fitting people to the organization plan and motivating them to work at high productivity within its confines is probably the most difficult administrative problem confronting company management. Resistance arises to organization change because it is a threat, direct or implied, to the position, status, and opportunities of every person in the company. Of primary concern to the organization planner is how to anticipate and overcome this resistance, how to get people to accept a change and even to welcome it with some enthusiasm. The factors that will ease the transition are those basic to all sound motivation—participation, communication, and education.

Participation

People who have an opportunity to participate in planning for organization changes will have some feeling of commanding their own destiny and not of being pushed around like so many pawns on a chess-board. Participation helps give the people involved in the organization change a feeling of importance. It makes it obvious that the company needs and wants their opinions and ideas and is unwilling to go ahead without taking them into account. This is highly reassuring and facilitates the transition from one order of things to another.

As a general rule, those people who will be directly concerned and affected by a certain organization change should be given opportunity to participate in that change before the final decision is reached. Top officers participate in the design of the over-all structure, subordinates in organizing their departments and sections. The procedure followed by Carrier Corporation, discussed earlier, is a highly effective approach. If committees are not to be used to effect the planning, coordination and participation can be centered in an organization planning staff group or an outside consultant. Specific delegation can then be made to accountable managers to secure participation from their subordinates in planning the changes.

A skillful consultant always insists on maximum participation by employees and managers in arriving at his recommendations. The objective of the professional is to secure understanding and acceptance of the change before it is undertaken. He does this by ensuring that the new plan, as it emerges, directly reflects the needs and aspirations of managers at all levels. If he reaches an impasse, he does not commit it to paper and leave it behind as an irreconcilable dilemma; rather, he helps the managers involved to reach a solution that will work for them, even though it may be circuitous and not quite in keeping with the theoretical principles he would like to see put into effect.

Communication

Every effort should be made to let people know about organization changes. This involves not only people within the company but also dealers, stockholders, and the public. The best practice is to tell as much as possible as soon as possible. In some cases, specific details may have to be omitted for competitive or other reasons. However, simple announcement that the company or division or plant is undertaking an organization study to plan for its long-term growth, to improve efficiency, or for other reasons will answer many questions and can have little repercussion.

Communication to Employees. Internal announcements are best made through the medium of conferences and meetings, the employee newspaper, and bulletins. Some companies schedule a series of conferences to announce and discuss the changes to be made. These usually start with the chief executive and his key officer group. Each executive then carries the information to his own group, and so on down the line until the lowest company level is encompassed. When Ford Motor Company undertook its major reorganization in 1947, it started the process of communication in a series of management meetings in which the chief executive and his key officers followed the process outlined above and continued it through the foreman levels.

West Penn Power Company started with a company-wide series of meetings when it announced its reorganization in 1954. The president first outlined and explained the over-all plan. Department heads then described the new organization of their own functions. Visual aids were used in outlining the organization and the changes involved. Following announcement to the top management group, the message was carried to plants, stations, and offices of the company by accountable managers.

The company or plant newspaper can be an excellent medium for conveying information about organization changes. General Foods, for example, announces major organization changes, shifting of personnel, closing of plants, and other matters related to organization as far in advance as possible. It gives the reasons for the change in detail, tells how employees will be affected, and emphasizes the advantages that will accrue to the company as a whole and to individual employees.

General Motors also fully publicizes organization changes before the event, whenever possible. Plants and operating divisions of the company usually carry full spreads in their employee paper, showing organization charts, pictures of the managers involved, and explaining in full how the change will affect the operation and its people.

Communication about reorganization can be handled systematically by use of a series of letters or bulletins to all managers. These should include as much detail as can be released. Accountable managers, in turn, should pass on the information to their immediate subordinates. Feedback should be encouraged. Employees should be given opportunity to ask questions, particularly with reference to their own status under the proposed changes. If the supervisor cannot answer these questions satisfactorily, he should be able to refer them to his own superior or to a staff group that will get the information or answer for him.

Communication to the Public. Information to the public is conveyed through press releases and both formal and informal talks by company management. Care should be exercised that people within the company are notified before outside news agencies carry the story. General stories concerning organization changes are usually carried in the local paper, for plants located in smaller towns, and in metropolitan dailies. In multiplant companies with metropolitan headquarters, appropriate releases naming local people involved in the change should be sent to suburban daily and weekly newspapers.

Stockholders are notified by special reports addressed directly to them, or in the regular company quarterly or annual report. Since stockholders are particularly interested in the implications of the change with respect to their investment, they should be told of unusual capital or administrative expenses and the possible effect on the long-term growth prospects for their holdings, dividend appreciation, and so forth.

Communication to Dealers. Dealers are often a forgotten category in communicating organization changes. The dealer has special questions of his own with respect to company reorganization and he will want to have these answered as fully and promptly as possible. This is especially true when changes involve the sales function and the field sales operation of the company. Carrier Corporation, when it carried out its reorganization in 1953, published a special number of its dealer magazine, *Inside Carrier,* devoted to announcement of its divisionalization and decentralization. This carried complete text, organization charts, details as to how the change affected the internal operations of the company, and a special section "What Does the New Setup at Carrier Mean to Dealers?" This anticipated and answered such questions as changes in the working arrangements between Carrier distributors and Carrier field offices, additional assistance that would be available to dealers because of the new organization, implications for the company's franchise policy, and so forth.

Education

A large part of the task of reorganization is education. People must be indoctrinated in new relationships, taught new skills, helped to change attitudes, given the information they need to understand where they fit into the picture and how they will be expected to operate.

The educational process can be aided by training classes, meetings, and conferences. However, to be successful, education must become part of the manager's everyday activity on the job. Creating understanding of new assignments, educating people to the implications of new roles and relationships, can be accomplished only if each manager first establishes an example in his own attitudes and behavior. He must observe his subordinates in their methods of delegating new responsibilities, their organization of their own work, and the manner in which they apply company policies and principles of organization.

Some companies maintain formal training programs in organization which involves all managers. Humble Oil & Refining, for example, has sessions devoted to recognition of general principles of organization and application to the job situation. Armstrong Cork Company schedules regular training conferences in organization planning for all supervisors and managers. Here the basic fundamentals of organization are presented, case studies are analyzed, and general discussion encouraged.

Esso Standard Oil Company maintains a comprehensive program for training employees and managers in the company organization and organization planning. Minneapolis Honeywell trains all supervisors and managers in the fundamentals of organization planning as part of the over-all company management development program. McKesson & Robbins, in its management development program, also provides for training of all supervisors and managers in the principles and application of sound organization.

THE FUTURE OF ORGANIZATION CHANGE

Our study of management and organization has established a pattern of growth and development that is common to all commercial enterprises. As the embryologist is wont to say, "Ontogeny recapitulates phylogeny." That is, the life history or development of an individual organism tends to retrace the history of the race. So, also, we have found that the individual business enterprise tends to retrace in its growth the development of all businesses.

We find that it is normal and necessary for the business to operate under personal, centralized leadership during its early years. The danger is not in the existence of personal leadership as such; rather, it lies in continuance of this form of leadership past its term of greatest usefulness. Inevitably, the form of organization which tends to encourage strong and dynamic individualism gives way to forms which foster teamwork and cooperative effort.

Reorganization must be a constant accompaniment of these changes. Preferably, organization change will anticipate the growth stages of the company and facilitate rather than hinder them. However, whether it comes early or late, whether it is done efficiently and economically or haphazardly and wastefully, organization change must occur.

Eventually, the successful company develops an organizational arrangement that enables it to adapt to its current needs. Once an eminently successful adaptation is reached, a very real danger presents itself. Now the urge to change and improve is diminished. Successful, profitable management tends to relax and contemplate its laurels. At this point, the factors that made the company successful tend to become institutionalized. They are passed from one management generation to another, intact and unquestioned, as part of the culture of the company.

This reverence for the successful stereotype engenders a deep and prevalent fear of changing the *status quo,* of leaving the certainty of the tried and proved for the experimental and, hence, dangerous innovation. Just as the pattern of success becomes a way of life, so with reluctance to change. In this pattern lie the seeds of disaster. In a competitive economy, small, aggressive organizations abound, instantly alert to the need for change and instantly capable of accomplishing the modification required. In this threat lies the constant spur to progress and, at the same time, the key to the vitality of our economy.

SUMMARY

After the ideal plan is prepared, as an over-all guide, change should be accomplished by first trying out the proposal on a trial basis, to identify potential trouble spots and over-all feasibility. Next, phase plans should be prepared, designed to make full use of the human assets of the company and to carry the organization forward step by step in a transition to the ideal plan established.

People can be conditioned and reconciled to change by ensuring maximum participation on the part of all those who will be affected, providing for communication of as much information about the changes as soon as possible, and by providing for the education of people to understanding and acceptance of their new roles and mastery of the work assigned to them.

Bibliography

HISTORICAL AND DEVELOPMENTAL BACKGROUND

Childe, V. Gordon, *Man Makes Himself,* New American Library of World Literature, Inc., New York, 1951.

Crum, William Leonard, *The Age Structure of the Corporate System,* University of California Press, Berkeley, Calif., 1953.

Dubin, Robert (ed.), *Human Relations in Administration,* Prentice-Hall, Inc., Englewood Cliffs, N.J., 1951.

Gras, N. S. B., Ph.D., *An Introduction to Economic History,* Harper & Brothers, New York, 1922.

Gray, Henry, F. R. S., *Anatomy of the Human Body,* Lea & Febiger, Philadelphia, 1942.

Greenberg, Benjamin C., and N. Eldred Bingham, *Biology and Man,* Ginn & Company, Boston, 1944.

Haskins, Caryl P., *Of Societies and Men,* W. W. Norton & Company, Inc., New York, 1951.

Lin Yu-táng (ed.), *The Wisdom of Lao-tzū,* Modern Library, Inc., New York, 1948.

Ranson, Stephen Walter, M.D., Ph.D., *The Anatomy of the Nervous System,* W. B. Saunders Company, Philadelphia, 1943.

Ritchie, John W., *Biology and Human Affairs,* World Book Company, Yonkers, N.Y., 1948.

Toutain, Jules, *The Economic Life of the Ancient World,* Routledge and Kegan Paul, Ltd., London, 1930.

BASIC CONCEPTS OF MANAGEMENT

Appley, Lawrence A., *Management in Action,* American Management Association, New York, 1956.

Barnard, Chester I., *The Functions of the Executive,* Harvard University Press, Cambridge, Mass., 1956.

Bethel, Lawrence L., Franklin S. Atwater, George H. E. Smith, and Harvey A. Stackman, Jr., *Industrial Organization and Management,* McGraw-Hill Book Company, Inc., New York, 1951.

Brech, E. F. L., *Management, Its Nature and Significance,* Sir Isaac Pitman & Sons, Ltd., London, 1948.

Cordiner, Ralph J., *New Frontiers for Professional Managers,* McGraw-Hill Book Company, Inc., New York, 1956.

Davis, R. C., *The Fundamentals of Top Management,* Harper & Brothers, New York, 1951.

333

334	*Bibliography*

Dooher, Joseph M., and Vivienne Marquis, *The Development of Executive Talent*, American Management Association, New York, 1952.

Drucker, Peter F., *The Practice of Management*, Harper & Brothers, New York, 1954.

Ethe, Solomon, *Forecasting in Industry*, National Industrial Conference Board, Inc., New York, 1956.

Fayol, Henri, *General and Industrial Management*, Sir Isaac Pitman & Sons, Ltd., London, 1949.

Gulick, Luther, and L. Urwick (eds.), *Papers on the Science of Administration*, Institute of Public Administration, New York, 1937.

Haire, Mason, *Psychology in Management*, McGraw-Hill Book Company, Inc., New York, 1956.

Koontz, Harold, and Cyril O'Donnell, *Principles of Management*, McGraw-Hill Book Company, Inc., New York, 1955.

Lansbrugh, Richard H., and William R. Spriegel, *Industrial Management*, 5th ed., John Wiley & Sons, Inc., New York, 1955.

Learned, Edmund P., David N. Ulrich, and Donald R. Booz, *Executive Action*, Graduate School of Business Administration, Harvard University, Division of Research, Cambridge, Mass., 1951.

Lepawsky, Albert, *Adminsitration: The Art and Science of Organization and Management*, Alfred A. Knopf, Inc., New York, 1952.

Likert, Rensis, *Developing Patterns of Management*, American Management Association, General Management Series, no. 182, New York, 1956.

Metcalf, Henry C., and L. Urwick (eds.), *Dynamic Administration: The Collected Papers of Mary Parker Follett*, Management Publications Trust, London, 1949.

Moore, Wilbert E., *Industrial Relations and the Social Order*, The Macmillan Company, New York, 1946.

Newman, William H., *Administrative Action*, Prentice-Hall, Inc., Englewood Cliffs, N.J., 1951.

Owens, Richard N., *Management of Industrial Enterprises*, 3d ed., Richard D. Irwin, Inc., Homewood, Ill., 1957.

Prentis, H. W., Jr., *The Principles of Business Management*, Armstrong Cork Company, Lancaster, Pa., 1955.

Riegel, John W., *Executive Development*, University of Michigan Press, Ann Arbor, Mich., 1952.

Simon, Herbert A., *Administrative Behavior*, The Macmillan Company, New York, 1947.

Taylor, Frederick Winslow, *Shop Management*, Harper & Brothers, New York, 1911.

———, *The Principles of Scientific Management*, Harper & Brothers, New York, 1942.

Tead, Ordway, *The Art of Administration*, McGraw-Hill Book Company, Inc., New York, 1951.

Urwick, L., *The Elements of Administration*, Harper & Brothers, New York, 1943.

Villers, Raymond, *The Dynamics of Industrial Management*, Funk & Wagnalls Company, New York, 1954.

Whyte, William H., Jr., *The Organization Man*, Simon and Schuster, Inc., New York, 1956.

ORGANIZATION PLANNING

Allen, Louis A., "Organization Planning: A Tool for Better Management," *The Management Record*, October, 1954.

Baake, E. Wight, *Bonds of Organization*, Harper & Brothers, New York, 1950.

Brown, Alvin, *Organization, a Formulation of Principle*, Hibbert Printing Company, New York, 1946.

Dale, Ernest, *Planning and Developing the Company Organization Structure*, American Management Association, New York, 1952.

Dennison, H., *Organization Engineering*, McGraw-Hill Book Company, Inc., New York, 1931.

Gillmor, R. E., *A Practical Manual of Organization*, Funk & Wagnalls Company, New York, 1948.

Holden, Paul E., Lounsbury S. Fish, and Hubert L. Smith, *Top-Management Organization and Control*, McGraw-Hill Book Company, Inc., New York, 1951.

Kimball, Dexter S., and Dexter S. Kimball, Jr., *Principles of Industrial Organization*, McGraw-Hill Book Company, Inc., New York, 1947.

Milward, G. E. (ed.), *Large Scale Organization*, MacDonald & Evans, London, 1950.

Mooney, James D., and Alan C. Reiley, *The Principles of Organization*, Harper & Brothers, New York, 1939.

Porter, Robert W., *Design for Industrial Co-ordination*, Harper & Brothers, New York, 1941.

Wrapp, Edward H., "Organization for Long Range Planning," *Harvard Business Review*, January–February, 1957.

DESIGN OF THE STRUCTURE

Allen, Louis A., *The Organization of Staff Functions*, National Industrial Conference Board, Inc., New York, 1958.

Davis, Ralph C., *The Influence of the Unit of Supervision and Span of Executive Control on the Economy of Line Organization Structure*, Ohio State University, Bureau of Business Research, Columbus, Ohio, 1941.

Dewing, Arthur S., *The Financial Policy of Corporations*, The Ronald Press Company, New York, 1953.

Finley, James A., and Malcolm C. Neuhoff, *The Duties of Financial Executives*, National Industrial Conference Board, Inc., New York, 1952. (1st edition.)

Foulke, Roy A., *Diversification in Business Activity*, Dun & Bradstreet, Inc., New York, 1956.

Healey, James H., *Executive Coordination and Control*, Ohio State University, Bureau of Business Research, Columbus, Ohio, 1956.

Murphy, Robert W., "Corporate Divisions vs. Subsidiaries," *Harvard Business Review*, November–December, 1956.

Seybold, Geneva, *Company Organization Charts*, National Industrial Conference Board, Inc., New York, 1953.

DELEGATION

Allen, Louis A., "The Art of Delegation," *The Management Record*, March, 1955.
———, "The Doctrine of Completed Work," *The Management Record*, December, 1954.
Argyris, Chris, "Human Problems with Budgets," *Harvard Business Review*, January–February, 1953.
Cartwright, Dorwin, and Alvin Zander (eds.), *Group Dynamics: Research and Theory*, Row, Peterson & Company, Evanston, Ill., 1953.
Kahn, Robert L., and Daniel Katz, *Leadership Practices in Relation to Productivity and Morale*, University of Michigan, Institute for Social Research, Ann Arbor, Mich., December, 1952.
Lieberman, Seymour, *The Relationship between Attitudes and Role: A Natural Field Experiment*, University of Michigan, Survey Research Center, Ann Arbor, Mich., 1954.
Pelz, Donald C., "Leadership within a Hierarchical Organization," *The Journal of Social Issues*, vol. 7, no. 3, 1951.
Pfiffner, John M., "How to Delegate Authority," *Public Management*, December, 1943.
Raymond, John, *Problems of Delegation of Authority*, College of Technology, Industrial Administration Group, Birmingham, England, January, 1954.
Redfield, Charles E., *Communication in Management*, University of Chicago Press, Chicago, 1953.

DECENTRALIZATION

Allen, Louis A., "The Urge to Decentralize," *Dun's Review and Modern Industry*, December, 1957.
Baker, Helen, and Robert R. France, *Centralization and Decentralization in Industrial Relations*, Princeton University, Industrial Relations Section, 1954.
Dale, Ernest, "Centralization versus Decentralization," *Advanced Management*, June, 1955.
Gibson, Edwin T., *Policies and Principles of Decentralized Management*, American Management Association, General Management Series, no. 144, New York, 1949.
Mitchell, Don G., *Big Business in Small Plants*, American Management Association, General Management Series, no. 154, New York, 1952.
Simon, H. A., G. Kozmetsky, and G. Tyndall, *Centralization vs. Decentralization in Organizing the Controller's Department*, Controllership Foundation, Inc., New York, 1954.

STAFF AND LINE

Allen, Louis A., "Can You Eliminate Assistants?" *Dun's Review and Modern Industry*, December, 1956.
———, *Improving Staff and Line Relationships*, National Industrial Conference Board, Inc., New York, 1956.

Bryson, Lyman, "Notes on a Theory of Advice," *Political Science Quarterly*, vol. 66, pp. 321–339, September, 1951.

Sampson, Robert C., *The Staff Role in Management*, Harper & Brothers, New York, 1955.

TOP MANAGEMENT ORGANIZATION

Baker, John Calhoun, *Directors and Their Functions*, Graduate School of Business Administration, Harvard University, Division of Research, Cambridge, Mass., 1945.

Mylander, William H., "Management by Executive Committee," *Harvard Business Review*, May–June, 1955.

Read, Alfred, *The Company Director, His Functions, Powers and Duties*, Jordan & Sons, Ltd., London, 1953.

DYNAMICS OF ORGANIZATION CHANGE

Allen, Louis A., *Charting the Company Organization Structure*, National Industrial Conference Board, Inc., New York, 1958.

———, *Preparing the Company Organization Manual*, National Industrial Conference Board, Inc., New York, 1957.

Benn, A. E., *The Management Dictionary*, Exposition Press, New York, 1952.

Habbe, Stephen, *The Appraisal of Job Performance*, National Industrial Conference Board, Inc., New York, 1951.

Hall, George Lawrence, *The Management Guide*, Standard Oil Company of California, San Francisco, 1948.

Jacques, Eliot, *The Changing Culture of a Factory*, Tavistock Publications, London, 1951.

Keller, A. G., and Paul R. Lawrence, *Societal Evolution*, Yale University Press, New Haven, Conn., 1931.

Ogburn, William Fielding, *Social Change*, The Viking Press, Inc., New York, 1952.

Ponken, Harriet O., and Paul R. Lawrence, *Administering Changes*, Harvard University Graduate School of Business Administration, Cambridge, Mass., 1952.

COMPANY GROWTH AND DEVELOPMENT

Ackerman, Carl W., *George Eastman*, Houghton Mifflin Company, Boston, 1930.

Allen, Hugh, *The House of Goodyear*, The Goodyear Tire and Rubber Company, Akron, Ohio, 1949.

Beaton, Kendall, *Enterprise in Oil: A History of Shell in the United States*, Appleton-Century-Crofts, Inc., New York, 1957.

Broderick, John T., *Forty Years with General Electric*, Fort Orange Press, Albany, N.Y., 1929.

Campbell, Murray, and Harrison Hatton, *Herbert H. Dow*, Appleton-Century-Crofts, Inc., New York, 1951.

du Pont, B. G., *E. I. du Pont de Nemours and Company: A History*, Houghton Mifflin Company, Boston, 1920.

Dutton, William S., *Du Pont, One Hundred and Forty Years*, Charles Scribner's Sons, New York, 1942.

Ewing, John S., and Nancy P. Morton, *Broadlooms and Businessmen*, Harvard University Press, Cambridge, Mass., 1955.

Garbedian, H. Gordon, *George Westinghouse: Fabulous Inventor*, Dodd, Mead & Company, Inc., New York, 1946.

Gray, James, *Business without Boundary: The Story of General Mills*, University of Minnesota Press, Minneapolis, 1954.

James, Marquis, *The Metropolitan Life*, The Viking Press, Inc., New York, 1947.

Knowlton, Evelyn H., *Pepperell's Progress*, Harvard University Press, Cambridge, Mass., 1948.

Lief, Alfred, *The Firestone ,Story*, McGraw-Hill Book Company, Inc., New York, 1951.

May, Earl Chapin, and Will Ousler, *The Prudential*, Doubleday & Company, Inc., New York, 1950.

Nevins, Allan, *Ford: The Times, the Man, the Company*, Charles Scribner's Sons, New York, 1954.

————, *John D. Rockefeller*, Charles Scribner's Sons, New York, 1940.

Passer, Harold C., *The Electrical Manufacturers, 1875–1900*, Harvard University Press, Cambridge, Mass., 1953.

Pound, Arthur, *The Turning Wheel*, Doubleday & Company, Inc., New York, 1934.

Tarbell, Ida M., *The History of the Standard Oil Company*, McClure, Phillips & Co., New York, 1904.

Wilson, Charles, *The History of Unilever: A Study in Economic Growth and Change*, Cassell & Co., Ltd., London, 1954.

Name Index

ACF–Brill Motors Company, 30
ACF–Wrigley Stores Inc., 30
Aeroquip Corporation, 85
Alan Wood Steel Company, 212
Allis-Chalmers Manufacturing Co., 168
Aluminum Company of America, 84, 137, 144
American Air Lines, 138, 145
American Enka, 117, 130, 146, 230, 277, 282
American Management Association, 213
American Radiator and Standard Sanitary Corp., 97
AMI, Incorporated, 12, 20, 138
Ansul Chemical Co., 130
Armco Steel Corporation, 209, 229
Armstrong Cork Company, 40–41, 191, 218, 329
Arnold, Paul D., 159
Atlantic Refining Company, 12, 28, 79, 115, 184, 298

Barnard, Chester I., 207
Bemis Bros. Bag Company, 117
Bethlehem Steel Company, 138
Bigelow-Sanford Carpet Co., 258
Blaw-Knox Company, 234
Boeing Airplane Company, 85, 218
Borg-Warner Corporation, 105, 200, 273
Breech, Ernest, 175
Brown, Alvin, 117
Bryson, Lyman, 244
Burroughs Corporation, 162

Carborundum Company, 36–37
Celanese Corporation of America, 277
Carrier Corporation, 96, 262, 279, 306, 314, 316, 320–321, 327, 329
Chance Vought Aircraft, Inc., 177, 146, 147, 181, 186, 213
Chrysler, Walter P., 176
Chrysler Corporation, 87, 165, 176, 277
Cleveland Electric Illuminating, 27, 128

Cluett, Peabody & Co., 279
Columbia-Geneva Steel Division, U.S. Steel Corporation, 183, 235
Continental Can Company, 123, 162, 218
Continental Oil Company, 63, 104
Creole Petroleum Corporation, 127, 212, 277
Crown Zellerbach Corporation, 132, 298

Davis, Arthur Vining, 84
Detroit Edison Company, 150
Dow Chemical Company, 26–27
Dresser Industries, 115
Dryden, John F., 84
Du Pont, General Henry, 15
Du Pont de Nemours, E. I., and Company, 11, 15–16, 93–96, 105, 189, 191, 212, 228–229, 265–268
Durant, W. C., 173
Duryea, Charles, 173

Eastman Kodak Company, 6
Electric Storage Battery Co., 282
Esso Standard Oil Company, 143, 330

Fayol, Henri, 11, 158
Feldman, Maurice, 214
Firestone Tire and Rubber Company, 6
Fish, Lounsbury S., 32, 62, 115
Flanagan, John A., 152
Food Machinery and Chemical Corp., 105, 132, 184, 185, 191
Ford, Henry, 139
Ford, Henry, II, 175
Ford Motor Company, 6, 65, 87, 105, 117, 129, 165, 175, 180, 182, 191, 193, 229, 262, 276–277, 312–314, 317–320, 328

Galvin, Paul V., 160
General Electric Company, 12, 105, 167, 219, 220

Subject Index

Participation, 43, 68, 142, 215, 326–327
by line subordinates, 215
in motivation, 142
in organization change, 326–327
People, influence of organization on, 58, 68
Performance appraisal, 47
Performance standards, 45, 47, 122–123, 150–151
to evaluate delegation, 151
for profit-center accounting, 195
staff aid in developing, 236
for supervisors, 137
Personal leadership, 5, 6, 15, 159–173
in Dow Chemical Company, 6
in Du Pont, 15
in Eastman Kodak Company, 6
evaluation of, 6
in Firestone Tire and Rubber Co., 6
in Ford Motor Company, 6
in General Motors, 173
in Motorola, Inc., 160
in O. A. Sutton Corp., 159
weaknesses of, 6–7
Personal staff (*see* Staff, personal)
Personnel administration policy in General Foods, 188
Personnel changes, planning for, 310
Personnel department, duties in motivation, 236
Personnel function and organization planning, 277
Personnel programs, 35–37
in organization change, 323–325
Phase planning in reorganization, 316–321
Pilot reorganization, 316
in Carrier Corporation, 316
in Nationwide Insurance, 316
Planning, 25–41, 286
in AMI, Incorporated, 20
analysis of work of, 286
in centralized company, 166
concepts of, in Du Pont, 16
in Continental Oil Company, 63
definition of, 25
by General Foods, 25
by International Harvester Co., 25
by Pullman Standard Car Mfg. Co., 25
elements of, 24–41
in General Foods, 19
influenced by organization, 63
in Lever Brothers Company, 18
in Radio Corporation of America, 19
reciprocal nature of, 46
reserved responsibility for, 126, 127

Planning, separation from doing, 201
specialized staff aid in, 231–234
use of staff in, 201
Plant staff departments, role of, 238–242
Policies, 32–34, 145–188, 231–298
centralization of, 162
and communication, 145
in decentralized companies, 182
divisional, 182
in Green Giant Company, 33–34
in McKesson & Robbins, Inc., 32–33
personnel, 188
staff aid in developing, 231–232
staff interpretation of, 232
stated as organization principles, 298
Position guides, 292–296
philosophy in preparing, 292–293
responsibility definitions, 292–296
method of preparing, 294
use of management categories in, 294–295
President, duties of, 208–209
need for staff assistance of, 200
(*See also* Chief executive)
Principles of organization design, 71
Problem solving, sequence of, 245
use of staff in, 246
Procedures, 37–39, 303–306
defined, 37
in Koppers Company, Inc., 38–39
organization, 303–306
staff preparation of, 233
Product divisionalization (*see* Divisionalization, product)
Production planning, duties of, 235
Profit centers, 172–195
and centralization, 178
controls for, 195
in decentralization, 172
in Du Pont, 176
in Ford Motor Company, 175
in General Foods, 177
in General Motors, 174
as motivational factor, 172
in Sylvania Electric Products, 316
Programs, 34–37, 180, 232–233
authority for annual operating, 180
in Carborundum Company, 36
defined, 34
personnel, 35–37, 323–325
staff preparation of, 232–233
Public relations, staff role in, 214
Purchasing, centralized, 161
as line function, 212